Always a Rebel
and Never Without
A Cause

Georgette Vikingstad Valle

Always a Rebel and Never Without a Cause

Managing Editor and Book Design: Jan Foster, Blue Sea Publishing
Cover Design: Jan Foster, Blue Sea Publishing
Original drawings by Odd Valle: Norwegian Spoon, Fisherman, and Viking
Original drawing by Georgette Valle: Chickens
Maps from MapQuest.com

Library of Congress Control Number: 2007924366
ISBN 0-9741741-7-3

10 9 8 7 6 5 4 3 2 1
1st printing March 2007

Printed in USA

Blue Sea Publishing
P. O. Box 2371
Oak Harbor, WA 98277

Profits from this book are donated to three nonprofit organizations: Washington State–Environmental Science Center, Minnesota–The University of Minnesota, School of Occupational Therapy, and Arizona–The Educational Enrichment Foundation.

Dedication to
My Wonderful Family

To My Husband Odd, for being so understanding of my passion for the world of politics. He turned his lack of patience into political signs that were constructed perfectly, meticulously erected in a perfect spot that visually showcased the RALLY TO VALLE sign for the voters as they passed. Even as we drive through our district today he remembers where each sign was placed.

And for keeping the fires burning at home while I have been away.

To My Children, Peter and Christine, who continue to support my political desires and direction of my zealous pursuit of far off goals of today and the future of my passions.

To My Grandchildren, Alicia, Erica, Bryan and George, whose future is speedily coming faster and more quickly than we all could have imagined. I continue to hope our love may influence their future education, profession and their lives. 🔥

ACKNOWLEDGMENTS

I acknowledge my cousin, Carol Sue Johnson Broyles, who has kept me on target, corrected my punctuation, asked pertinent questions intermittently, and encouraged me in the writing of this book. It has been a long ordeal, and I am grateful for her splendid help. She has helped me to do what was difficult become much easier to do. She deserves my eternal thanks!

My Arizona Scribblers Class has been of tremendous support in assisting me while I have read to them the chapters of the book by critically evaluating the story line, bringing out some flaws in my thought process, and subjecting me to what a critical audience wants. Those people are Meg Altstaetter, Eleanor Berg, Ed Blake, Babs Campbell, Nancy Dorian, Mary Ewing, Don Gatzke, Don Karaisko, Harold "Rip" Ripley, Paul Ziegler, and Marilyn Wilson. Each of these writers are extremely competent scribes in their own right. Thanks to each for being so honest with their criticisms.

Georgette Vikingstad Valle and cousin Carol Sue Johnson Broyles, July 1991

Dean Foster, former Clerk of the House and Senate, has helped me to be accurate with names and dates. It has been a joy to talk to him. When I was in trouble in my campaign, his advice was to "get out of town." He, perhaps, saw some of the "rebel" in me. I rarely took his wise words to heart, but I appreciated the advice!

Georgie Kunkel

To Georgie Kunkel, I say thank you, over and over again. She was the driving force on the team in the final edit to downsize this book for publication. Her contribution as a longtime colleague and political ally has been invaluable. Also, as I perused the old clippings and started writing this book, I realized what a vast amount of writing Georgie had done for me. When I saw all my press releases that were printed verbatim in the local papers, I knew she had performed a great service for me and my campaign. She was always accurate in reporting my actions or inactions. I understood how valuable it was to have an accomplished writer assist me in developing my ideas in the local papers. In the hurly, burly of a campaign, as a candidate, you barely have time to eat your meals, let alone scan an article for its impact on the voters. Georgie's honest review of the issues, their fiscal impact on the state, and adopting and presenting these facts for the voters in the 31st and the 34th Districts really helped me win in the race for State Representative! She may have helped my many "causes" without my realizing what an impact her articles had on the voters. Thank you again!

To my son Peter and daughter Christine, thank you for your questions, corrections, and insights from your perspectives. To have the maturity of your own children reflect in what is written is invaluable.

To the doctors, nurses, and physical therapists that have helped me develop a healthy lifestyle, I say thank you. Dr. Van Bodegom has been a constant medical physician and giver of medical advice that has benefited my body and spirit. Rarely do nurses have time to stop long enough for you as a patient so that you can read their names, but a bouquet of thanks must go to them also.

The Highline Hospital Emergency Room got a little exasperated seeing me in with my left hip out of the socket four times. The medical personnel knew who to call, and Dr. Susie O'Brien came in and put my hip back in the socket three times. "Thanks" is insufficient as a word to say to anyone, when you are so relieved that the hip is put where it should be. Finally I went to Providence Hospital where

Dr. Ray Robinson screwed the hip onto my hip socket. He later did my left knee, so now I am a bionic writer with two knees replaced and two hips replaced twice. The airport security really goes wild when I go through the gates!

The North Highline Firefighters are heroes too, having to carry me out on a stretcher with my hip out of joint three times from Evergreen Swimming Pool and once at home. I am sure that I know every pothole on the road to the Highline Hospital Emergency Room. I was later told that the appliance that had been put in my hip socket was too small and, therefore, kept coming out of the socket!

All and all I have been very fortunate to have had kind and considerate people come to my assistance for many years in the Highline Community, now the city of Burien. After a car ran a red light into my vehicle, I fainted at the scene. As I fainted, my neighbor Dick Burrows pointed out to the bystanders that I was their State Representative. Police Officer Wing Woo very nicely helped me, insisting that I needed to go to the Highline Hospital Emergency Room. This has been the story of my life! People helping me!

CONTENTS

Contents (continued)

Contents (continued)

INTRODUCTION

Norwegians haunted by hardships at home.
Dreaming of another land to the west—
Sailed the waters as in days the Vikings roamed.
To live a life of religion with freedom was best . . . .
So families, with heads held high, gathered daughters and sons
And with tears and sadness left Norway and their loved ones.

They sailed forth to an unknown world so new
Fishermen, farmers, writers, nurses, teachers, and theologians.
They were fathers, mothers, unborn babies, and children too.
To be explorers in an American history of proud Norwegians.
To United States of America and to Canada they came—
To love and live a new and better life not asking for fame.

No one certain aim was evident in their desires—
Only to love and to work and to help one another each day—
In word, in deed, and in song, their hearts set on fire . . .
To practice their American freedom with thoughts of Norway.
Their independence, their pride expressed in letters sent
To mothers and fathers, sisters and brothers with messages well meant.

Not always was life in the new land easy
With tuberculosis and cholera the young died of disease
But life's challenge was to be better or even best.
The promise of the future was bright with young and old—they sowed the seeds
Building houses, barns, churches, school buildings with Norsk zest
Norwegians learned to be unafraid, to follow, and to lead.

ALWAYS A REBEL AND NEVER WITHOUT A CAUSE

THE TENOLD FAMILY

They seemed to come suddenly upon happiness as if they had surprised a butterfly in the winter woods.

Edith Wharton

Tenold Migration from Norway to Iowa

As I pondered the many reasons for my relatives leaving Norway for another world, two butterflies flew past me with sudden swift movements, darting here and there as if flirting knowingly with each other. This act of nature was so simple yet so straightforward. I knew my relatives would have enjoyed this sight. Later the rising golden moon lit up the whole mountainous scene of the suburb of Green Valley. This same moon was probably shared in some of the conversations of my relatives as their words reflected on living in a better world. Not only would another world be possible, perhaps this land would offer freedoms not yet granted in Norway.

There is nothing more exciting than to discover a book about your relatives and engross yourself while reading it on a cold, winter night in Arizona. *The Land Beyond*, written by Vern Tenold, a cousin of my maternal grandfather, Peter Tenold, was given to me by my cousin, Carol Sue Johnson Broyles. While reading the book I was transported to Norway, with vivid images of the many difficulties encountered during ocean voyages in the 1880s. When I read about my relatives, I thought about hard winters and little food in Norway compared to their better lives in the Midwest of the United States.

In stark contrast to those times, my husband, Odd, and I traveled from Odda, Norway, to Vik in northern Norway in the 1980s. We rented a vehicle at a cost of $300 for a three-day journey while Odd and I were trying to locate my Tenold relatives. We were fairly successful in locating the right people who assured us that the Tenolds as a family were originally from Vik.

During our excursion, a comedy of errors occurred. We learned that Enid Hanson, who supposedly had all the Tenold information, was at her cabin located about half an hour from Vik, so we decided to stay overnight in Vik. We arose early the next morning to contact her at her cabin only to find that she, too, had arisen early that morning and had already driven back to Vik. Later, via mail, Enid wrote informing us that an Ole Tenold, my great-great-great grandfather, was a member of the Tenold homestead in Vik. The family later moved south to Lerdahl, Norway. We had confirmed that the Tenolds had indeed lived in the Lerdahl area before their ocean voyage to the United States.

> Joy seems to me a step beyond happiness—happiness is a sort of atmosphere you can live in sometimes when you are lucky. Joy is a bright light that fills you with hope and faith and love.
>
> Adela Rogers St. John

Peter and Christina Tenold and Family

Peter and Christina Peterson Tenold, my maternal grandparents, began their married life in the town of Frost, Minnesota. Both were energetic, good looking, religious Scandinavians. Peter owned a dry goods store and boasted on a small postcard advertisement with his picture that he had the "best flour" in Frost, Minnesota. Perhaps it was the very best in town simply because there was no other grocery store in town. Christina baked at least four to six loaves of bread every other day and also made his favorite dough-nuts with that wonderful flour.

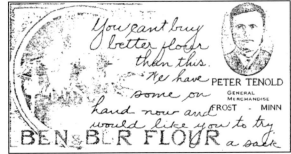

You can't buy better flour then this. We have some on hand now and would like you to try a sack

PETER TENOLD
GENERAL MERCHANDISE
FROST - MINN

BEN BUR FLOUR

Luella Tenold Monsen (my mother's sister), of Eau Claire, Wisconsin, contacted Vern Tenold, author of *The Land Beyond*, informing him that her great-great grandfather may have been Ole O. Tenold (1790-1840). His son, Ole P.

Tenold (1816-1876), immigrated to America. Vern Tenold confirmed the accuracy of this Tenold relative information.

Luella Monsen writes about her family memories. In 1853 Grandfather Anders Tenold married her Grandmother Anna "Tenold," (born 1828). Vern Tenold quotes her in *The Land Beyond:*

> My dad (Peder) was born just south of Blue Earth in Pilot Grove Township, Minnesota, on August 16, 1861, in a sod hut. They moved to Dell by 1868, because in 1868 his mother [Anna] was buried in the Dell cemetery. They had a one-room log cabin there. After that my grandfather stayed with us. I have only a vague remembrance of him. Then we moved to Frost, Minnesota, where my father ran a General Merchandise store. My father's sister, Andrina, and family then lived on the farm. Grandpa stayed with them because he didn't like the "city." Grandpa passed away in 1905, but we continued to look for him in his little bedroom. (Luella was only five years old.)

> I have several pictures of my father as a young man—sideburns and all. He never walked slowly, but moved quickly. He had an unusual sense of humor.

> My father took great pride in his horses, and beautiful surrey . . . It really did have a fringe on the top too . . . . He was not a large man but wiry, and I don't remember him ever being ill until he had a heart attack in 1930 . . . . From then on he did no farming, but was around driving his car. Peder Tenold, my father, died at home in Dell in May of 1936.

> The original 80 acres that my grandfather started with is still owned by my sister Emily. The buildings, not used for many years, are not usable.

Peter A. Tenold (left) was a handsome man with a nicely tailored mustache, very high cheekbones, and a finely shaped nose that fit his ruddy complexion. He was a mild mannered man, about average height, which complemented his slender build. He loved the yellow lemon hard candy that he carried in his pocket to distribute to his children and grandchildren. Occasionally, it was mixed in with some chewing tobacco.

Christina (right) was a "no nonsense" grandmother who was busy baking bread and frying doughnuts for the family's sustenance. She would sometimes whip her wide, big apron if she did not want to be bothered with grandchildren's questions!

Her sister, whom I knew as Auntie Grauie (below), also lived in Dell and was an exceptionally talented

seamstress. The secret to success in that day was being able to dress your girls in fine frocks and tailor your boys in handsome suits to attend the Norwegian Lutheran Sunday School. Grandmother Tenold appreciated the fact that her husband owned a dry goods store, so she could have fabrics readily available for her sister to sew.

The Tenolds were thrifty people, but they were always generous with their grandchildren. I never really heard Grandma Tenold speak English very much, as Norwegian was her first language. My mother, Emily, spoke Norwegian to her, so they always understood each other.

Peter and Christina Tenold had nine children, and Grandma Tenold became alarmed at the prospect of raising four boys and five girls in the big town of Frost, Minnesota: Anna (1887-1964), Clara Amanda (1889-1904); Nordahl (1891-1953), Emily (1895-1983); Clarence (1897-1949); Gullick (1893-1975); Luella (1899-1988); Rudolph (1903-1945); and Clara Priscilla (1905-1995). Peter took his wife's advice and purchased 120 acres in Dell, Minnesota. He made sure that the property was close to a good Norwegian Lutheran church.

The Tenold family first lived in a house west of the church. A school and the small Chilson store were also located nearby. The two-story house was probably more comfortable than the house in Frost. For Peter, however, the house was not exactly what he had envisioned when he moved from Frost. Subsequently, he built his bride and family a new, attractive two-story square house with five bedrooms on the second floor which provided the family with adequate sleeping quarters.

Walnut floors were installed throughout the house, and the sturdy, wooden doors were encased with beautiful cut glass. The downstairs was comprised of a large kitchen, a dining room and parlor, and a downstairs bedroom and indoor toilet. The entry to the house had a spacious porch that was screened in for mosquito protection during the hot Minnesota summer nights. As a child I slept there with the sound of cottonwood leaves swishing in the wind, lullabying me to sleep. I used to dream of Norway as I slept with visions of Northern Norway, Vik, and Lerdahl in my far-off dreams.

The Tenold Family in 1916. *Left to Right:* Clara Pricilla (11), Emily (22), Luella (16), Anna (29), Nordahl (27), Gullick (25), and Rudolph (13). *Front row:* Christina and Peter (Clarence is missing.)

The Tenold family prospered on the land where there was plenty of room for the nine children to roam. Christina would prepare their favorite jellies and jams from the fruit of the trees throughout the property.

There was always a cookie in the cookie jar or a doughnut for Grandpa Tenold's enjoyment. Those were his favorite goodies to indulge in, along with a cup of good, strong Norwegian coffee.

Peter Tenold felt strongly that all of his children needed a post-secondary education even though not all Norwegian families believed in females gaining

Tenold girls
From left: Emily, Anna, Clara Amanda
(who died in 1904 at age 12),
and baby Luella

advanced education. However, only the boys were instructed in driving by their father who did not heed their sisters' protests that they, too, wanted to drive. The Tenold children were venturing out into the world.

The Tenold boys were serious men, all business. Clarence Tenold served in World War I. The other boys in the family also served in the military. One of the younger sons, Gullick, fibbed about his age and was able to serve for several months until he was discovered by Navy officials and consequently sent home to Dell, Minnesota. Nordahl was given an exemption from the war because he was in charge of the farm.

Emily, Luella, and Clara all attended Waldorf Lutheran College in Forest City, Iowa. After graduating, Emily completed teacher's training. All four surviving Tenold daughters (Anna, Emily, Luella, and Clara Pricilla) married, moved away, had children, and did what was expected of young women to do in that era. All of the traditional roles for women were evident in my family, but I also had role models that influenced my future career in politics.

The eldest daughter, Anna Tenold, married Ed Mondale, uncle of Walter F. "Fritz" Mondale of Elmore, Minnesota. After they were married, the couple boarded a train to Montana to begin their newly-married life. It was a very sad day, and there was not a dry eye to be seen at the train station that day, as no one thought they would ever see Anna again. All the handkerchiefs were full of tears as the entire family waved goodbye to the newlyweds.

Tenold Family Gathering. *Lower left:* Oceil, Mabel, Nordahl Tenold, Roseline Tenold, Angeline and Rudolph Tenold, Peter and Christina Tenold, George Vikingstad, Anna Mondale, and Luella Monsen. *In front:* Merle Tenold, and Georgette Vikingstad. *Picture taken by Emily Vikingstad.*

Cousins Oceil Tenold and Georgette Vikingstad by haystack

Uncle Stanley and Aunt Clara Johnson and Georgette

9

In later life, Peter's favorite pastime with his grandchildren was to let them ride on his back feeling the bumps on his head. There were shrieks of laughter erupting on Sunday afternoons as we examined this phenomenon called "wens" on his head. We certainly thought that we had the best grandpa with "bumps on his head."

Grandma Tenold was very ill at Christmastime in 1935. I was a happy eleven-year-old rejoicing in a favorite Christmas present from my Uncle Harold. He gave me a gold carved bracelet with a chain and clasp to keep it secure on my wrist. My mother, being concerned about her sick mother, scolded me for my Christmas joy!

Grandmother Tenold must have sensed her impending death in early 1936 at age seventy-six, as she wrote a tender farewell letter to her husband and children in Norwegian, which her daughter, Clara, translated as follows:

> To my dear children,
>
> It is lonesome today. Nordahl and Emily and their families have gone home. I feel as though I will leave, too, and so I must write and say goodbye to you all. You are all very dear to me. Oh, that we could meet in heaven with God. I can't think of anyone being lost. I have been a poor mother, but I saw that too late, but the Lord Jesus has paid for all my sins when he shed his blood on the cross of Calvary. God so loved the world that He gave His only begotten son that whosoever believeth in Him should not perish but have Everlasting Life. This is Everlasting Life that you know the one True God and His Son, Jesus Christ.
>
> Dear children, seek Jesus Christ while you are young and well and love one another. Do not disagree, but love one another.
>
> Be kind to Rudolph, who left home when he was so young, and I may not see again in this world.
>
> Sorrow not over me, bury me as cheaply as you can. Tell the preacher not to praise me. He could so easily say something that wouldn't be true and that would not be becoming for a preacher.
>
> Dear children, be kind of Papa. Don't let him stay alone. I wish he would live a clean life with our Lord.

Goodbye dear Papa. Do what you can for our dear children. How I wish one of our children would stay with you all the time. Goodbye, goodbye. I thank God because I have been permitted to live so long with you. It has been a great blessing.

May God bless you all until the end.

Goodbye, goodbye to Papa and Children,

From Mother Tenold

Grandmother Tenold was a very loving and giving person. Even though she was raising nine children of her own, she would often invite people who had no food to the Tenold home for a delicious home-cooked meal.

After her death, her husband, Peter, declared that he had no desire to live. He died in May 1936.

Recently I met Oceil's daughter, Carol Marie Tenold Flynn and Larry Flynn who are snowbirds in Mesa, Arizona, from Minnesota!

Cousin Audrey Monsen in her high school days

Below: Three cousins gather in July 1946: Astrid Vikingstad, Audrey Monsen, and Georgette Vikingstad

Cousins: Merle and Leslie Tenold in back and Georgette and Oceil Tenold in front

Four Tenolds: Luella Monsen, Nordahl Tenold, Anna Mondale, and Emily Vikingstad

Cousin Richard Johnson came to visit Representative Georgette Valle in Olympia in February 1982.

Aunt Clara Johnson, Georgette, and Aunt Luella Monsen at her home in Eau Claire, Wisconsin

THE VIKINGSTADS

You may be disappointed if you fail, but
you are doomed if you don't try.
                                        Beverly Sills

The Vikingstads in Norway and in America

A baby boy named Nils (Nels) J. Vikingstad, my paternal grandfather, was born on December 27, 1860, in the bedroom of a log cabin. The cabin was on the windswept island of Karmøy in a little settlement in southwestern Norway called Vikingstad. As was the custom, the family took the surname of Vikingstad because my father's grandmother Vikingstad was the wealthiest person in the family. She inherited land and, therefore, had more property than her husband. The paternal name of the family was Nelson, and some of the children later took the Nelson name when they came to America. Employees at the U.S. Immigration Office thought the Nelson name would be easier to spell and pronounce than the Vikingstad name.

By the year 1951 I had been a Vikingstad for twenty-six years, being very proud of the name which means "Place of the Vikings" in Norwegian.

Odd and I found our Vikingstad relatives on the Island of Kamøy in the settlement also called Vikingstad. This was the island where the Vikings had built their boats and sailed for all parts of the New World. I wondered if any of the "Viking" philosophy of exploration of new lands and causes was affecting my life, because at this very moment I was far from Elmore and Blue Earth, Minnesota.

Our taxicab driver had found the "right" relatives—Konstanse, Josephine, and Knut Vikingstad. They were all cousins of my grandfather, Nels J. Vikingstad. My father, George Vikingstad, had been corresponding with them for years, so they knew who we were.

13

At this point, I relied on my husband, Odd, to interpret. He was fluent in Norwegian, since he was born and raised in Norway. It was exciting to enter this Vikingstad house in Norway and walk into the living room and see my grandfather's picture in his *prestekrage* (priest's collar) on the living room wall!

We were offered a cup of coffee and some *lefsa* (a salty Norwegian tortilla). I was worried about the taxi meter that was running outside, so I shook my head no.

Konstanse said in Norwegian, "They come all the way from America, and they don't have time for a cup of coffee!"

I understood her remark and rethought my answer to the offer and said, "Yes!" We told them we would like to come back the following day to take some pictures after spending the night at the small town of Kopervik.

Georgette Valle is seen in 1951 near the log cabin by the sea where N. J. Vikingstad was born on December 27, 1860, on Vikingstad farm on Karmøy Island.

On the following day, Odd and I took a bus out to a road that had a Vikingstad sign on the crossroad. We walked more than four miles to the Vikingstad settlement, stopping at houses by the roadside to make sure that we were on the right road. After a lot more walking, we finally located our relatives.

It must have been difficult for the Vikingstads to eek out a living in the 1860s. We were shown the church where the Vikingstad family were baptized and confirmed. The church was said to be over one thousand years old.

In the 1750s to 1850s, life in Norway was extremely difficult. Here on the island most of the people fished for a living. Others delved into carpentry, small farming, teaching, and theology. Karmøy's landscape was very desolate with barely any trees on the island due to the strong winds and little vegetation.

The Vikingstads departed for the New World in late 1880. Nels J. Vikingstad, a graduate of Kopervik Teachers Training College (1878-80), was the eldest child of Endre Nilson (Nelson) and Oline Margrete Vikingstad, with Ed Nelson, Lydia Vikingstad, and Ben Nelson following. The family settled in Story City, Iowa, where Nels attended and graduated from Augsburg Lutheran Seminary in Minneapolis, Minnesota (1884-91). He was a very bright student and graduated with honors.

Ed Nelson, his brother, became a teacher and a farmer. He was a favorite uncle of my father, George. He enlivened many conversations about religion, politics, and family life in his hometown of Lake Mills, Iowa. He was also very bright and entertained my father with his tales of Norway.

Lydia Vikingstad married Ed Stenberg and settled in Lacota, Iowa. As a child, I remember visiting them in their new home with the beautiful oak floors, doors with shining glass, and the indoor toilet!

Ben Nelson remained in Story City, Iowa, where he lived until his death.

The Vikingstad/Nelson families remained in the upper Midwest close enough for them to visit each other's families and to retain much of their Norwegian/European heritage and culture. Sundays were usually the days that were saved for family outings and trips to each other's farms. Reading, debating, and discussion of the Scandinavian novels, articles, and speeches was a Sunday afternoon special event. I used to creep into the living room to listen to each of the men's comments on the latest radio speaker's remarks. I remember listening to everyone expressing themselves in opposition to the radio speaker without animosity to each other. 🚣

Life is easier than you'd think; all that is necessary is to accept the impossible, do without the indispensable, and bear the intolerable.

Kathleen Norris

Norway's T. H. Wald Family Embark for the New World

My paternal grandmother, Julia Wald, was born during the Civil War. The Wald family departed from the eastern part of Norway in 1866 on a ship bound for a new continent and a new life. The vessel stopped in Ireland, and one of the passengers who boarded the ship there had contracted cholera. Tragically, the cholera swept through the ship, taking the life of young Julia, the Wald's only child. She was buried at sea. My grandmother was conceived during that same ocean voyage, and it was decided that if the new baby was a girl, she would be named Julia.

Reverend T. H. and Anlen Wald entered the New World equipped with the skills and education acquired in their homeland of Norway. They disembarked the ship with high hopes of establishing a home in one of the Midwestern states. Baby Julia was born January 29, 1867, in Illinois. My grandmother told me about her family life in Oshkosh, Wisconsin. As the wife of a minister, Anlen Wald's life was a "life on the move." Hilda, their second child, was born in 1870, with Constance following in 1872. Emma, the youngest daughter, was born in 1876. All three girls were born in Michigan where the Walds had relocated.

My grandmother told tales about of her mother, Anlen, who danced for the delight of my grandmother and her sisters and brother. George Wald, the youngest child born in 1879, especially enjoyed this rather secret activity. Father T. H. Wald was a soldier, a teacher, and a preacher and might not have been aware of this form of entertainment that was rather frowned upon in the Lutheran Church congregations in those days.

Julia and two of her sisters married. Julia married Reverend Nels J. Vikingstad in 1892.

In about 1901, the Vikingstad's home at Spring Grove was the scene of the marriage of Constance Wald, who became the bride of Dr. T. A. Lid. Reverend Vikingstad officiated at the ceremony. Both Julia's brother, George Wald, age twenty-two, and her son, Endre Wilhem George Vikingstad, age seven, watched the wedding festivities that summer day from the side of the Vikingstad parsonage.

Julia's sister, Hilda, married Andrew Mathison and settled in Menominee, Michigan. Her sister, Emma Wald, a librarian, never married. Julia's brother, George Wald, never married and was not in good health but able to be an itinerant minister.

> Life, for all its agonies of despair and loss and
> guilt, is exciting and beautiful, amusing and
> artful and endearing, full of liking and love, at
> times a poem and a high adventure, at times very
> gay; and whatever (if anything) is to come after
> it—we shall not have this life again.
>
> Rose Macaulay

Nels and Julia Vikingstad Family

Reverend Nels J. Vikingstad served in several parishes before he accepted a position in a Marinette, Wisconsin, church from 1891-1896. It was there that he met Julia Wald, eldest daughter of Reverend T. H. Wald. After courting for some time, Julia Wald and Reverend Nels J. Vikingstad were married in 1892 in Marinette by her father. Julia's bridesmaids included her sisters Hilda, Constance, and Emma.

Julia, a bright girl with a great deal of optimism, was said to be very much in love and happy in her marriage to Nels J. (N. J.) Vikingstad. Julia had completed a teacher's course, so she was now prepared to use that knowledge to assist Reverend Vikingstad in teaching Sunday school.

On June 3, 1894, my father Endre Wilhelm George Vikingstad was born in Marinette, Wisconsin. He was a large baby, around eleven pounds. Julia's three sisters (Hilda, Constance, and Emma) were happy to take care of their baby nephew.

Three months after the birth of his son, N. J. announced to Julia and her family that he was having health problems from severe insomnia. He decided to return to stay with his relatives in Norway to determine if his health problems could be resolved. He set sail for Norway, leaving behind Julia and their three-month-old son, Endre.

With her confidence and sense of adventure, she applied for a teacher's position in 1894 and subsequently became the Principal of the Marinette Elementary School.

Reverend Nels Vikingstad stayed in Karmøy, Norway, with his Vikingstad cousins for a year, delivering stimulating sermons at the local parish. He also added some beautiful wallpaper to the Vikingstad house in Norway. After sleeping his way back to good health, he returned to his family and to his Marinette congregation.

You never heard a whisper of any unhappiness N. J. may have caused my grandmother. Julia was happily disposed wherever she lived. The family grew. Constance was born in 1899. Frichuf or Fred (1902) and Harold (1907) were born in the beautiful, large parsonage in Spring Grove, Minnesota, which provided a bedroom for each child.

Many Scandinavians traveled to the Midwest, as did the Walds and Vikingstads. Ministers of the Lutheran faith were eager to find their parishioners wherever they could. Both Lutheran ministers, the Reverends T. H. Wald and Nels J. Vikingstad were thought-provoking men. In 1894 Reverend Vikingstad discussed the possibility of there being no hell in a sermon at the Waterloo Ridge congregation. That was a departure from the religion of old.

While in a tavern in Marinette, Wisconsin, Nels J. Vikingstad encountered an eighteen-year-old lad playing an organ exceptionally well. F. Melius Christiansen was that young lad. With my grandfather's encouragement, Christiansen became one of the world's greatest arrangers and composers of sacred Lutheran music. He went on to become part of the music staff at St. Olaf College in Northfield, Minnesota, and became the founder and director of the world-famous St. Olaf

Lutheran Choir. Reverend Vikingstad was then serving as pastor near Spring Grove, Minnesota.

N. J. ruled his family with an iron hand. My father once stopped him from giving Harold, the youngest son, a beating. Julia, always the loving wife, was never critical of her husband. When the Vikingstads arrived to visit us on the farm, she was the one who carried the water up the stairs to the second floor bedroom so her husband could take a bath.

Who's Who Among Pastors in Norwegian Lutheran Synods of America

1913

From *Who's Who Among Pastors in the Norwegian Lutheran Synods of America,* 1843-1927, 7th edition, 1928.

Vikingstad, Nils Johannes
Ord. 1891. U.S., 1891-14

Born Dec. 27, 1860, at Haugesund, Norway, of Endre Nilsen and Oline Margrete (Vikingstad). Attended Kopervik Teachers' Training School, 1878-80. Immigrated 1881. Attended Augsburg Sem., 1884-91 (A. B., C. T.). Pastor, Marinette, Wis., 1891-96; Waterloo Ridge Cong., etc., near Spring Grove, Minn., 1896-09; Cooperstown, N.D., 1909-14; lived in Elmore, Minn., 1914-21; Minneapolis, Minn., 1921—Teacher, Augsburg Sem. 1889-90. *Julia Anette Wald, 1892. Died 7-22-36.

Make-believe colors the past with innocent distortion, and it swirls ahead of us in a thousand ways—in science, in politics, in every bold intention. It is part of our collectives lives, entwining our past and future . . . . a particularly rewarding aspect of life itself.

Shirley Temple Black

Vikingstad Aunts and Uncles

It was exciting to visit my Uncles Fred and Harold and Aunt Constance in Minnesota. He married Marjorie Henderson in the first airplane marriage in Minnesota in 1927. This was news that made the *Minneapolis Star.* Marjorie was divorced and had a personable young daughter named Jeanne. It was so exciting to have a cousin close to my age who lived in Minneapolis. As we grew to be six or seven years old, she taught me how to tap dance, sing a bit, and giggle. What fun! Eventually, alcoholism took its toll on Fred and Margie's marriage. After Grandmother Julia died, they divorced. Fred later met Kathleen, and they lived in Richland, Washington, where Odd and I were able to visit.

Uncle Fred and little
Georgette Vikingstad

Harold, my youngest uncle, who attended the University of Minnesota, married Mary (below left). She called him Vik with a long "I." They had

Mary Vikingstad, Georgette Valle, Astrid Alexander, and
Harold Vikingstad in September 1983

one son, Frank, whom I played with as a child.

We recently renewed our acquaintance as cousins with several long distance telephone calls. During the Minnesota winters, Frank and his wife Mitzi live in Florida. He sent this nice picture of their children, their spouses, and the grandchildren.

Mitzi and Frank Vikingstad in Australia

Cousin Frank and Mitzi Vikingstad's family on Christmas Day 2005

Back row: Daughter-in-law Katie and son Eric Vikingstad, son Brian Vikingstad and grandson Trevor Vikingstad

Middle row: Grandson Colton, daughter Kristin and her husband, Greg Liehr

Front: Granddaughter Katelyn

Constance Vikingstad married Karl Palmer Sr., a Swedish man in the insurance business, from St Cloud, Minnesota. Karl never let us forget the differences between Swedes and Norwegians. Every year our family usually drove to St. Cloud from Elmore for Easter Sunday dinner, where we had many a good laugh around the dinner table. Their son, Karl Jr., called Bud or Buddy, practiced many years as a physician in Minnesota. I considered him a friend.

Karl, Connie, and Buddy Palmer in their St. Cloud home in Minnesota

The mere sense of living is joy enough.

Emily Dickerson

Vikingstads and Tenolds

Since I was the eldest grandchild on the Vikingstad side, I had an opportunity to get acquainted with Grandmother Julia over a long span of time. There was a great contrast between the Grandmothers Tenold and Vikingstad. Grandmother Christina Tenold was quiet and reserved, while Grandmother Julia Vikingstad had a humorous outlook on life and was always open to conversation. Grandmother Julia was a continual optimist, and in my own mind I called her Grandmother "Pollyanna."

Grandmother Tenold spoke Norwegian and understood English, but spoke English infrequently. Grandmother Vikingstad spoke both languages fluently and used both often. I can still hear her say, "Please give me the crust of the bread. That's my favorite!" and "If you please, I'd like the neck of the chicken! But, no sugar on the strawberries!" In spite of the personality differences the "grand" ladies enjoyed each other's company and remained great friends.

Julia Vikingstad and Christina
Tenold at the Vikingstad farm on
September 10, 1934

Wisconsin is a land of vacation lakes where Julia swam, feeling refreshed in the cold water. She was an avid swimmer while living in Marinette on Lake Michigan and still enjoyed swimming after she was blind, but her sister, Emma, would watch her while she was in the water.

Reverend N. J. Vikingstad and
Peter Tenold share the afternoon
newspaper, the *Minneapolis
Tribune*, at the Vikingstad farm on
September 10, 1934.

The N. J. Vikingstads visited the George Vikingstads at least once a year in the summer. This "vacation time" at the farm for Julia and Nels became a hardship for my mother. Water had to be carried into the 1890 farmhouse and heated for use. We did have rainwater in the cistern that was pumped into the house by a hand pump and heated for washing. I had to carry the water which we used for drinking and cooking from a deep well outside in the pump house. I still think that Minnesota well water is the best tasting in the nation and remember the taste of it from the old "community dipper!"

Needless to say, today's Minnesota farms have running water, electricity, and indoor plumbing. My father, George, worked with the Cooperative of the Federal Electric Association, established in 1934 under Franklin Delano Roosevelt.

The elder Vikingstads' summer vacations were a frugal way to see their relatives and enjoy their grandchildren. Nels had lent his brother, Ben Nelson, $10,000 before the 1929 stock market crash, mortgaging the Vikingstad farm without his wife's knowledge. That equity in the farm was their retirement fund. Ben did not pay the $10,000 back to Nels, so the Vikingstads lost their 320-acre farm.

Grandma Julia Vikngstad, baby Georgette, and Aunt Constance Vikingstad in Minneapolis, Minnesota

The Nels Vikingstads lived in poverty. In those days there were no pensions for retired ministers and no Social Security for either Julia or Nels. Harold and Fred Vikingstad owned a small grocery store in south Minneapolis and delivered lots of bags of fresh food to their parents. Karl and Connie Vikingstad Palmer, who lived near St. Cloud, probably helped when they could. Fortunately, we lived on the farm and always had plenty of food available.

Because there was a lack of money, Julia did not go to the doctor for an eye examination nor relate any of her eyesight difficulties to anyone. She knew that there might be a possibility of blindness because her father had been blind for thirteen years. By the time she discovered she had glaucoma, it was too late for help. Julia lost one eye and suffered blindness in the other eye for eleven years.

There was a Wisconsin pension for the blind, but Julia was much too proud to accept it. So a monthly check of $30 arrived from George every month after the death of Nels Vikingstad at the age of seventy-six in 1936. Julia died at the age of ninety-four in 1961.

Blindness, as tragic as it was, brought laughter to Julia as she recalled how one dark night she found her way to what she thought was the bathroom. She gradually realized that she was in a closet. She had to pound on the door for some time before she awakened her sister, Emma, to let her out. Julia lived with Emma, a retired librarian, for the majority of the twenty-eight years after Nels Vikingstad's death.

I penned this birthday greeting to celebrate my grandmother's ninety-second birthday.

Happy Birthday Grandma Julia

Grandma Julia Vikngstad crochets
with sight in only one eye.

A birthday of my Grandmother who is 92—
Has just passed and belatedly I send my best
wishes too.
One should pay tribute to someone so
young at heart,
To live so long and always have a happy
word for all is indeed an art.

There are times when a grandchild named
Georgette
Married, two children she did beget,
Did ask of herself, "What did my
Grandmother V. give me?"
A rush of visual memories move swiftly for
her eyes to see—

Those pots and pans did please that first
grandchild—
Billy Goat Gruff and Grandma's broken hip
made my imagination go wild!
To surprise Grandmother at the 1800 1st
Ave. South apartment door was a
          Christmas delight.
Drilling that grandchild on her multiplication tables was quite a site.

Most of all I remember Grandma's thoughts for others—
Her words and deeds a golden rule to follow for all grandmothers!

A rhyming gesture this is indeed,
A book of prose is Grandma's life for all to read.
Darkness now prevails over Grandma's eyes.
Yes, this burst of memories brings forth a tear and a few sighs.

To some you are Sister Julia, others Aunt Julia, and to four just plain "Ma."
There's just one conclusion I can draw Grandma dear,
May good health be yours in your 92nd year!
To me you'll always just be dear "Grandma."

Georgette

> It's easy to be independent when you've got money. But to be independent when you haven't got a thing—
>
> Mahalia Jackson

George Vikingstad and Emily Tenold

George Vikingstad

George blossomed into a sturdy and handsome young lad. He was expected to work to help his parents on the farm and was absent from school during the fall harvest season. He spent many hours studying to catch up and still managed to graduate with his school classmates as Valedictorian from Cooperstown High School, North Dakota, in 1913. The theme for his speech was "How Labor Unions Will Affect Our Country." N. J. Vikingstad was pastor at Cooperstown from 1909 to 1914.

Although he attended the University of Minnesota for only six months, his life was a scholarly one—with many books and magazines surrounding him. There were a series of small jobs, which my father considered to be something that would tide him over until he actually was able to attend college, but it was not enough.

Being the eldest son carried with it many responsibilities. The country was drafting soldiers for World War I. George decided to enlist with the thought of being able to choose his position in the Army. After six weeks of Army training, to the wartime tune of *Over There, Over There*, he was deployed to France. Army life certainly was not as glamorous as the movies portrayed. War made a deep impression on my father. He would spend the rest of his life opposing war and the ravages of war reflected in our economy.

My father did enlighten us with stories about life behind Army lines. His mother, Julia Vikingstad, sent him a fruitcake for Christmas, which he generously divided into fifty-four pieces in order to share it with the other soldiers. Since the Army wasn't always able to feed the soldiers well, it was no surprise when a hot pie, cooling outside a French home, suddenly disappeared.

One U.S. Army General made impossible demands upon his troops. After a difficult night of fighting the Germans, some ambitious U.S. soldier dug out the bullets around a tree where the General had been standing. When the bullets were counted, it was found there were more U.S. bullets than German bullets. My father said from then on, the General was considerably more reasonable with his battle requests.

George arrived safely back in the United States on April 28, 1918. While George had not met Emily, this was to be his future wife's birthday. As the eldest son, I'm sure that the Vikingstad family would have liked him to seek a career in the ministry. However, George had a great many questions about the church and the world in general. He respected the call of the ministry and living in a minister's house. As long as he lived with his father and mother, he did not cater to playing cards, drinking liquor, or dancing. There certainly was no money available for college. World War I was nearly over and the country was in debt. Depression was settling upon the U.S. and the world. Prices for produce gave the farmers little for their labor.

George had aspirations to become a railroad engineer. He made arrangements to train for this occupation. When he arrived at the train depot in Elmore, a call came from his mother imploring him to please come home and manage the farm. Nels J. Vikingstad was not a farmer, even after retiring from the Lutheran ministry. My father reluctantly left his ambitions behind to return to the farm.

The Vikingstads attended a Norwegian Lutheran Church in Dell, Minnesota. It was a long ride to the church, almost thirteen miles by horse and buggy or in a horse-drawn sleigh down a snow-plowed road. This weekly trip to the new church introduced them to many new friends and eventually resulted in the marriage of two young people from the Tenold and the Vikingstad families.

Emily Tenold

Emily (Agnetta) Tenold in 1916 beginning her teaching career, which lasted eight years.

Emily (Agnetta) Tenold had her own ideas about how her life would be lived. She had attended Waldorf Lutheran College and was ready to complete her teacher's training so she could teach country school. This was a demanding job, as in those times a teacher also served as the janitor, the bell ringer, and the disciplinarian for all eight grades totaling up to thirty-eight children in a one-room schoolhouse.

Emily, who had already gone to court and paid eighty dollars to change her name from Agnetta to Emily, was not particularly pleased when she received no response after asking her brothers to teach her how to drive the automobile. There was always the usual banter that transpired between sisters and brothers.

One Sunday morning, when Emily saw the keys in the car, she turned the key on, got out and cranked it in the front, jumped back in the car, and off she went to church. It was only a short distance, approximately a fourth of a mile to reach Dell Lutheran Church. Surely, she could arrive at the church with no problems. She had been watching as her brothers drove, so she knew about the "clutch" business. Everything was clear as she turned left to drive on the gravel road over the bridge, past the school, and into the church driveway. Everything was going fine until, all of a sudden, she forgot how to stop! What should a driver do to stop this automobile? In desperation, she drove towards a buggy and hit the buggy's wagon wheel with a thump and a screech from the automobile's wheels.

This was all very embarrassing for this new school teacher. She discovered the buggy she hit was the Vikingstad buggy. Her Uncle, Nels Henjem, came to her aid and took the wheel to Frost, Minnesota, to have the buggy repaired. That was how Emily Tenold and George Vikingstad first met. It was truly an "accidental" meeting.

My father knew Emily Tenold was the girl for him the moment they met. I think my mother thought it was a very interesting moment when she met my father because she was not that enamored with the local young men in Dell or Frost. Since my father desired a higher education beyond his Cooperstown High School diploma, my mother must have been pleased.

George and Emily in the fall of 1920, probably just engaged to be married in December 1920

Engagement and the Wedding

This is a nice picture of my mother and father walking arm in arm in the cool, crisp Midwestern autumn of 1920. They had just become engaged. George could not wait until the evening hours to present Emily with her engagement ring. The ring was a diamond in a beautiful, ornate white gold setting. He proudly drove his first car, a 1918 black Ford four-door sedan, thirteen miles from Elmore to Dell, Minnesota, to the schoolhouse where Emily was teaching, arriving during the school noon hour to make the presentation in the enclosed hallway. All the students remembered peeking through the keyhole to view the special event.

Both my parents were attractive, hard-working people. Before her marriage, my mother visited sick families during the flu epidemic when those who were dying received little help. Some nurses and doctors died during their attempts to save patients' lives. There were many words of thanks and appreciation for Emily's generous assistance.

Emily Tenold in her georgette over white satin wedding dress with beaded trimmings on December 29, 1920

Endre Wilhelm George Vikingstad on his wedding day, December 29, 1920

Emily taught school for four years before she was married. She even taught her sister, Clara, who was eight years younger. Emily was a little apprehensive about the fact that she would not be able to discipline her sister, but Clara was very reliable and took the responsibility of coaching other students seriously. Mother was concerned about the older boys who were not passing their exams to qualify them for graduation. It was common to keep less able students in school much longer. Since there was no special education, these students became restless toward the end of each school year. Even later in her life, many of her former students remembered Mother fondly with flowers and cards.

The Vikingstad farm shows Elm trees surrounding the farm. The white house (lower left) was built in the 1890s. The Van Buren white school house sits in the upper right area.

George was an industrious farmer. There were always advantages in assuming farming as a profession as you were self-employed, plenty of food was provided for the table, and the responsibility for managing finances fell on the farmers' shoulders. Most of the farms surrounding our farm were bequeathed to sons or daughters by wealthy farmers. When Nels Vikingstad lost the farm, the Federal Land Bank owned the farm. Nels then rented the farm from the Federal Land Bank. In the next chapter there is the story of my parents purchasing the farm.

In preparation for their wedding day, George purchased his wedding suit from Luthold Barnes in Blue Earth, Minnesota. George and Emily's wedding day was a great day! He drove with his parents to the Tenold home to dress for the ceremony, but discovered that there was just one thing missing —the trousers to his wedding suit. He then drove thirteen miles back to Blue Earth in a horse-drawn sleigh in the snow to recover the missing part to his suit!

Aunt Grauie, Grandma Tenold's sister, sewed mother's wedding dress. It was a simple georgette organdy dress with short sleeves. Mother was known as the girl with the most beautiful slender arms and trim ankles. (Occasionally, mother would unwrap the beautiful, slightly yellowed dress for me and my sister to see. The short bridal veil was still intact with pearls sewed in the crown.) Reverend Mosby, minister of the Dell Lutheran Church, officiated at the church ceremony. Afterwards, the Tenolds provided George and Emily with a festive dinner reception at their home. The weather, as well as Emily's responsibilities as a teacher, prevented the bride and groom from celebrating with a long honeymoon.

> Idealists . . . foolish enough to throw
> caution to the winds . . . have advanced
> mankind and have enriched the world.
>
> Erma Goldman

Life on the Farm
The George Vikingstads

Newly-married life is often thought to be virtually trouble free, but by the end of 1921, the George and Emily Vikingstad family found themselves $5,000 in debt. That amount translates to approximately $120,000 in 2006 money! The debt was a shock to my parents. My mother was thankful she still had her teaching career. In the early 1900s married women teachers were generally not allowed to teach school, but teachers were in short supply, therefore the school board made the decision that even if mother were married, she would be allowed to teach. She had to drive to Bricelyn, Minnesota, in all kinds of inclement weather. Turning over her eighty-dollar monthly check to the family bank was a hard pill for her to swallow.

George was soft hearted as far as the family bank account was concerned. His brothers, Fred and Harold, were launching a new grocery business in Minneapolis. They visited George at the farm with some regularity and asked to borrow $500. It was difficult, if not impossible, to obtain a bank loan in Minneapolis at this time. It was a pretty attractive arrangement considering George charged no interest on the loan, set no due date for repayment, or even whether repayment was expected. Emily was not always happy about the generous terms extended to the Vikingstad brothers when she was in need of so many items for her family. Replacing the worn rug, the tattered furniture, and the need of a washing machine were family priorities in her mind, but George was head of the family and made such decisions unilaterally in those days.

Because of the loss of the farm by the N. J. Vikingstads, the Federal Land Bank became the new owner of the farm. George had learned that being an articulate spokesman was an advantage when dealing with bank loan officers. He had to pay rent to the Federal Land Bank and financial transactions took place in the privacy of an office in the bank.

Eventually, George and Emily Vikingstad bought the 320-acre farm for $240,000, which amounted to $75 per acre. That figure does not include interest paid on the loan. Both George and Emily knew that some of their neighbors were also attempting to purchase the land, but apparently those neighbors did not offer sufficient money for the transaction. My father maintained the confidence of the Federal Land Bank executives, proving his ability to keep up regularly with his payments. What was particularly upsetting was that for many years, my parents did not have a deed to the property. The day did arrive when my father obtained the deed, and I know my mother and father celebrated that day quietly.

There was a great deal of back-breaking labor with little, if any, monetary return at year's end. With the deepening depression, farm prices fell to the point where the farmers actually wondered if it was worthwhile to take the product to market. Occasionally there were bright spots in the farm market as pig prices rose.

We traveled to Minneapolis to visit our family for a brief weekend, and upon our return home, we discovered our pigs had been stolen. This catastrophe for us was the talk of the neighborhood. Eventually we learned the culprits included the son of the richest family in the area, the Henry Geshe family, and the son of our close neighbor, the Jake Taylor family.

The fathers of both boys arrived to ask my father to testify for leniency in court for the boys. After some time had elapsed, George did testify for both of the boys in court. The boys were both sentenced to prison. Harvey Taylor, one of the accused, made my mother a beautiful, black, beaded purse while he was incarcerated at the Stillwater, Minnesota, prison. He remained in contact with my parents, sending them Christmas cards and words of thanks for the kindness extended to him during his confinement. Harvey went on to become a successful family and business man in the San Francisco area.

A more entertaining and amusing part of our life on the farm were memories of the hired men who worked there. Many itinerant men were hired to work on the farm, and they enjoyed mother's delicious meals after spending long, difficult days working on the farm. They also benefited from a good, clean bed and fresh clothing for the next working day. One particular hired man named John was extremely tall and also very bald. Our potbelly stove had an angle pipe which was about the same height as John. Not only did he walk under this pipe, which was very hot, but he burned his bald head and ended up with several large blisters on the top of his head. This was unpleasant for him, but I thought it was funny at the time.

Ray, another of our hired men, was a former teacher, who had fallen from grace from his teaching position because of alcoholism. At that time there were no programs to assist him with his addiction. One night, after my mother had retired, she heard my father laughing when he arrived home from an evening meeting. He came into the kitchen to find an inebriated hired hand with his head and feet sticking out of the wood bin in a very rumpled fashion. While laughing, my father picked him up and carried him off to bed.

Ray was particularly interested in helping me with my declamation (dramatic presentation) piece that I was to recite to the assembly at Elmore High School.

After a bout of the chicken pox, I suffered some temporary hearing loss. Ray coached me on how to effectively speak while delivering my speech.

As I performed before the assembly, it seemed as if several teachers were yelling at me to speak louder. Everyone was giving me advice, which became very confusing to me. I was the only student to represent Elmore High School at another forum, gaining more experiences.

The hired hands who helped us pick the sugar beets were Mexican. I played with their children and learned some Spanish, but I could not understand why they did not go to school with me. The Mexican families were given separate housing on the farm, consisting of a small kitchen, dining room, and bedroom. They received one dozen eggs per week, a garden area to grow their vegetables, a portion of a pig, and an outdoor biffy just like ours. One day the head of one of the families came and asked if he could take the day off. When my father inquired as to his reason, he said, "I'd like to get married." My father gladly gave him the day off.

There were times when my parents made money on the farm, but this was because of World War II. My father was happy to make money, but not because of the war. His unhappiness with war after World War I continued with World War II, the Korean War, and the Vietnam War. Although he served in World War I, he later said that the world powers could have negotiated a peaceful settlement.

One day in 1948 we heard that Congress had passed the first Armed Military Treaty Agreement between the United States and the country of Turkey to the tune of $400 million. Mother told me to drive out to the field to tell my father. He was working the west portion of our farm. I drove the old truck, being careful not to shift incorrectly so I would not ruin the transmission. He was not surprised at the news. He had been very opposed to such an action, believing it would lead to wars—not prevent them. This treaty was the first of the military alliances that consisted of military hardware that eventually surrounded the Soviet Union in the Cold War.

A nation that destroys its soils destroys itself. Forests are the lungs of our land, purifying the air and giving fresh strength to our people.

Franklin D. Roosevelt

Birth of Daughters, Tornados, and Mother's Chickens

Georgette

My mother's teaching career in rural schools ended after my birth, which meant that her monthly income of eighty dollars stopped. Every school check she had brought home went for farm expenses, but she was determined to take her last check and purchase a sewing machine just for her, which she did. Emily, as a very busy "mother to be," sewed my baby clothes.

I was born on October 31, 1924, and that was a great event for both my father and mother. The *Faribault County Register* reported that after my birth, my father wore the biggest smile in Faribault County. As their firstborn, I was named Georgette Wald Vikingstad. Georgette, a French name, was given in honor of my dad's service in France during World War I. My middle name was given to me in honor of my paternal grandmother, Julia Wald Vikingstad.

There was a great deal of speculation about the date of my baptism. My parents wanted to wait until Christmastime so that my Grandfather Vikingstad could be present to baptize me. Some of my relatives were afraid that if I didn't live until Christmas, I would go to hell. My parents prevailed, and I was baptized in Minneapolis on Christmas Day in 1924.

It must have been during the mid-1920s, after I was born, that the farm income proved to be inadequate. A new source of revenue needed to be found. My mother agreed to the proposal of raising five

Georgette at age two displays her Little Red Riding Hood outfit.

hundred baby chickens. After all, raising tiny baby chickens did not appear to be a tremendous task.

Even though I observed my mother and father's participation in difficult, backbreaking labor, I thought life on the farm was pleasant. Mealtime always provided good conversation. My father initiated the topic of the day, which helped remind both Mother and me how important our work was to the success of the farm. The daily discussion of the events of the Vikingstad farm helped to alleviate the aches and pains resulting from the day's labor.

My father was an enthusiastic reader and retained most of what he read. After a long workday, he read from 8 p.m. to midnight, providing that the horses, cattle, or chickens did not escape. If that occurred, all of us had to rouse ourselves to retrieve them. How I hated to get up from a wonderful, sound sleep in a warm bed to go out and retrieve the animals after they somehow slipped through a broken fence. There was never any question whether we would help my father.

My father was harsh in his discipline, but he did not ever subject me to physical punishment. I always obeyed quickly to avoid any such action. That quality of his made me see his restraint and equity to other people. I experienced the benefit of his wisdom as I grew up in the family.

The 1929 stock market crash brought tough times. Fortunately, we had food on the table for the hungry workers. The need to raise additional revenue to supplement the farm rent, buy supplies for the family, and pay wages for harvest time workers certainly contributed to the need to expand the five hundred chickens my mother initially agreed to raise. One thousand more baby chickens were bought for my mother to raise for the "egg money."

As soon as I was old enough to help, I fed the chickens, hoping the chickens would not peck me to pieces. They were certainly hungry and thirsty. Five-gallon pails of water hung on either side of my shoulders and had to be carried to the chickens. My grandmother Vikingstad yelled at me, predicting that I would someday have a bad back.

Because I took after the Vikingstad side of the family, especially my father, I didn't think I would ever be a "raving beauty," but I was certain that I would possess a distinguished and interesting personality. My father was a likable fellow: well spoken, good looking, and could hold his own in any conversation. I thought if I could emulate him, I would be pretty happy with my lot in life.

For me, school days provided relief from the necessary work on the farm.

I learned to follow orders from my father who would say, "Hold the sack straight" or "Would you like to plow the northeast field this afternoon?" I was not very enthusiastic about field work. Earlier I had caught my foot in the evener that connected the plow to the horses. I stopped the horses and shed a few tears about my foot. Then I heard my father say, "Do you want to quit now?"

My thought was, "I think I quit!"

Astrid

On November 7, 1932, my sister Astrid Emily Vikingstad was born. It was an exciting time for me to experience the arrival of a baby sister after eight long years of being the only child. I arrived home from school to find my father holding my new baby sister in front of our black, potbelly wood stove. Only her cumberband surrounded the middle portion of her body. She was so tiny, but so beautiful. Also on that same day, Franklin Delano Roosevelt had been elected President. He swept the United States in victory, so we were all very happy.

Life on the farm in 1930s was difficult for my parents. Now we were a real family with two children. Even if we were poor, children do not notice poverty on a farm. Food abounded. Mother was a good cook. We were always hungry and appreciated the efforts she made in providing healthy meals.

Astrid's arrival at the Vikingstad farm in 1932 certainly made life much more interesting for me. I looked forward to coming home from school and welcomed babysitting or playing with my new sister. My free time was always interrupted with tasks that were much too mundane for the hired help, but just the perfect task for me to perform.

An elderly man who visited our home was fascinated with two-year-old Astrid, and he held her on his lap telling her interesting stories. One day he noticed that Astrid had some trouble breathing and told my mother she should take her to the doctor. Sure enough, the doctor discovered there were particles of congealed matter on her lung.

My father determined it should be Mother who was to go to the Minneapolis doctors to get results of what was to be done. Mother telephoned my father that an operation was recommended and would cost eighty dollars. With a series of mirrors and suction tubes, the particles were sucked out of her lung. They were unchewed popcorn!

As Astrid grew, she was very pretty and had a great personality. She was called the "Shirley Temple" of the Vikingstad family. Mother curled her hair, and on occasion we could afford one of the "Shirley Temple" dresses for her, and she certainly played the part. Astrid favored the Tenold side of the family and grew to be an attractive young lady like my mother.

I remember pictures being taken at the Blue Earth Photographers. Astrid wore her Shirley Temple dress and had her own picture taken at about age

Georgette and baby Astrid on the Vikingstad farm at Elmore, Minnesota, in early spring 1933

Astrid Emily Vikingstad's Shirley Temple photo

four. Her picture was placed in the window of the photo shop, and she was thrilled. Mother had enough money for one picture of the two us. When we saw how cute Astrid was in the picture, Mother knew she had to buy the picture of her too. I never knew how Mother managed with the "egg" money. You could not tell the hens to lay more eggs, but I was sorely tempted to "eggersize" the chickens. We all dreamed of the day when egg prices would increase.

Astrid had a spunky attitude and demonstrated a certain amount of independence. However, she sometimes had what we thought were temper tantrums. Mother and Father didn't exactly know how to deal with these events. There were times when she would slump to the floor and lie there, apparently not breathing. We were all paralyzed with fear. Dr. Summers said the best procedure was to pick her up and shake her upside down, so she would regain her breathing function again. This was done with a certain amount of trepidation as we weren't sure this procedure was appropriate.

Her temper tantrums grew less and less. She had a habit of biting others when things didn't please her. She bit me on several occasions, so I really felt like I was the victim. One day she bit me, and I simply bit her in return. After that I was never bit again.

Tornado Weather and Chickens

Radio reports about farm weather were always the last news item our father would listen to before he retired for the evening. He believed that farmers were the biggest gamblers in the world. The weather broadcasters reported that tornadoes had been sited in the area. The tornadoes came so quickly with their dark-blue funnel shapes that we always took off in a fast run for shelter. The cellar was the deepest and safest refuge. The cellar gave me a creepy feeling because it had a dirt floor. I was certain mice inhabited the cellar, so I was a little uncomfortable being there. Sometimes we stayed upstairs in the living room. On one occasion on a pitch black night, after the noisy tornado disappeared, we discovered the door to the cellar in the living room floor was an open hole. Darkness precluded my grandmother from seeing the opening. She miraculously walked around that open space many times with Astrid in her arms.

Mother used to say that raising fifteen hundred chickens every spring was like having a new baby every spring. After one severe storm and tornado had subsided, mother could not sleep not knowing how her baby chickens were faring. She sleepily awoke and dressed to walk down to the area where the chickens were. In the farmyard, every building looked pretty much intact, with some branches strewn around. As she approached the chicken houses, she sensed that something was very wrong. The big chicken house that held one thousand chickens was completely destroyed, with dead chickens and moaning injured ones strewn everywhere! The small chicken house had been picked up by the tornado and moved intact one hundred feet.

Mother fainted and fell to the ground after experiencing this deadly view. When she awakened, she struggled to her feet and went to check on the five hundred chickens in the small chicken house. Amazingly, those chickens in the small chicken house were alive and well, busy eating what was left of last night's feed. Mother did take some of the injured chickens into our warm house and kept them in the wood box.

Even with so many chickens and the big chicken house destroyed, we counted our blessings. We would just have less egg money in the year ahead. The big chicken house was rebuilt and once again filled with baby chicks. Never again did a tornado touch our chickens or our chicken houses!

> If truth is beauty, how come no one has
> their hair done at the library?
>
> Lily Tomlin

Beauty Within Our Family

Beauty is only skin deep—beauty is as beauty does. Some are preoccupied by the subject. I think it can be honestly said that I was too busy growing up and assisting my mother and father on the farm to realize what beauty really was. At the same time I must say that beauty surrounded me everywhere. I grew up to be a very tall girl. My mother was beauty in full bloom. She had all the features of a Miss America, but was not aware of how beautiful she was. Instead, she was totally immersed with her younger sisters and their beauty. Money was not always available for a marcel, a stylish process done by a hot curling iron that resulted in a wavy hairdo and curly

Georgette with her mother,
Emily Vikingstad

41

Beauty in the 1920s was in the Tenold family. Here are Luella, Clara, and Emily in the Tenold yard.

ends, but a good haircut was affordable and looked strikingly beautiful on my mother.

All three of my mother's sisters were attractive young women of the 1920s who did not realize their own potential, whether it was on the beauty scale or with their own potential professional skills. All did what was expected of young women to do in that era, to marry and have children. My favorite memory was a picture of my mother and her two younger sisters sitting on a round, cement flower container in the front yard of my grandmother's home in Dell, Minnesota. The Tenold good looks remind me of the natural Nordic beauty prevalent in the 1920s.

The least concerned about physical beauty were my grandmothers. Christina Peterson Tenold (left) was seventy-six when she died, and she had just a few gray hairs on her head. She wore her hair combed straight back into a very tight bun. Her features were delicate, of Nordic quality, and very pleasing to her husband.

My other grandmother, Julia Wald Vikingstad was known as the "Pollyanna" of the family. She could always find the bright side of any incident. After N. J. left her and baby Endre to return to Norway, she started teaching and then became the principal of Marinette Elementary School, which was a special accomplishment in those days for a woman. She scarcely had time to think about the virtues of beauty. Her hair turned white at the age of thirty, so she knew her life was not going to be a bed of roses.

Aunt Grauie had a perpetual smile on her face and as a seamstress always loved to attempt to get you to stand still as she was pinning the fabric in just the right position. She loved her sewing, and it reflected in her personality.

Youth has a way of subscribing early forecasts on their lives. Then I considered my little sister, Astrid, a picture of beauty. She favored the Tenold side of the family. I favored the Vikingstad side of the family and didn't think I would ever be a "raving beauty."

Beauty in the 1920s was to have visually pleasant features as a person—

Aunt Grauie, and Grandma Julia Vikingstad were very good friends.

but more than that a young woman was to have a "sterling silver" character. That meant your word was your bond, your heart was true to your emotions, and you delivered in word and deed. 🚢

Astrid, age 4

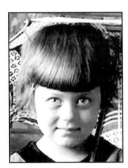

Georgette, age 5

Poverty often deprives a man of all
spirit and virtue; it is hard for an
empty bag to upright.
Benjamin Franklin

Summertime on the Farm

The seasons in Minnesota were marked with hot and humid summers and autumn, with colorful arrays of red-orange to gold-brown leaves falling around us as we gathered in the oats, barley, and corn. I was thankful that the harvest was secure, as the late fall weather turns to silent snow that blankets the earth that had been plowed.

Toward the end of winter on the farm, dreams of spring and summer were very near to all of us as we thought of warmer weather being right around the corner. But that does not always happen in Minnesota. Winter lasts a good six months with below zero winds whistling around your nose and freezing your toes. Of course, you won't realize that you have chilblains from frost until summertime. Chilblain is a painful swelling or sore caused by exposure to the cold, especially on the fingers, toes, or ears. It really seems that I had cold feet in Minnesota all the time until I tried other climates. Then I actually found I had warm feet.

It was great when the wind began to warm up and I could hear the meadowlarks singing as I walked that quarter of a mile to the Van Buren Country School. I knew spring was near when I walked home and that winter jacket was just too warm to wear. I remember my father was occupied with getting the soil ready for planting the corn, barley, and alfalfa. Mother was busy thinking about the strawberries and potatoes.

Sometimes I had to help my father by holding the flashlight while he was fixing the farm machinery. My father was diligent about keeping the farm machinery in good running order. Knowing the machinery was ready for use was a relief. When a piece of farm machinery was not working, he did not rush into town to get a new piece of equipment. He fixed the machinery, as we did not have any extra money to buy new equipment like our neighbors.

I marveled at my parents' work ethic. They arose early in the morning and toiled until seven-thirty or eight o'clock in the evening. Mother arose early to build the fire in the kitchen stove so we could have a hot breakfast. The cobs and wood were located right beside the stove in the kitchen. Filling that box was my task. The potbelly stove burned both coal and wood. It was always delightful to stand with one's back warmed by the heat produced by the stove. As the weather grew warmer, we could let the potbelly stove rest for the remainder of the spring and the summer.

While I normally slept soundly in my south bedroom, there were two things that would wake me. I experienced what I would call "growing pains." Other people doubted my reports of this discomfort, but I can still remember feeling the growing pains within my muscles. When I did not sleep well at night, my sister Astrid would wake me in the morning asking me if I would please get up and play with her. She did not have any playmates her age that lived near our farm. I think I should have had more compassion for her because she was a little lonely.

In the spring of 1937, after completing the confirmation series classes under Reverend Gjerde, I was ready to be confirmed. I really liked his teachings in our confirmation series and thought Reverend Gjerde was a better teacher than a preacher. I had not really expected to enjoy the "teaching" of the Bible and was not always supportive of the "preaching" of Reverend Gjerde's sermons. In the middle of his sermons, there were always unusual people, such as Eleanor Skjeldahl, popping up saying that ever since she had been "saved," ALL the cows gave more milk!

As we progressed to Confirmation Sunday, we were asked to answer in front of God and the congregation whether we would abstain from alcohol and dancing for the remainder of our lives. I thought this matter over carefully for a week. I said in front of God, my parents, and in front the congregation that no, I could not promise to abstain from alcohol and dancing. I was the lone member of the confirmation class that made that decision. Everyone else said yes, they would abstain. I was comfortable with that decision and did not think of myself as a "rebel" teenager.

At the age of thirteen, I encountered a series of infections: an earache, a stomachache, and soreness in my muscles. It seemed to be very serious, so

Dr. Sommers called in a specialist to see me. My parents must have thought it was quite serious also because they put me in their big bedroom. We did not go to the hospital. I don't think we could afford the expense of a room in the hospital with nurse's care. It remained my mother's responsibility to care for me.

Georgette, 13 years old, and Astrid, 5 years old, resting after Georgette's bout with rheumatic fever.

I was diagnosed with rheumatic fever and had hallucinations as my temperature rose to serious levels for several days. My swollen legs looked like I had elephantiasis. I don't think I would have survived this illness if it had not been for mother wrapping hot towels, steeped in wintergreen oil, around my legs. I remember seeing the ceiling rippling as if it were a gray ocean of watery waves. My sister was not allowed to be near me because of the threat of spreading an infectious disease. This was the first time we had been separated. Gradually, the fever subsided, and I slowly returned to good health.

Antibiotics became available on the market after I recovered from my illness. I was thankful for the return of my health, but I had a full year of recovery before me. Dr. Sommers ordered that I not be allowed to participate in physical education classes. Now, there was time to catch up with my studies. I was absent from Elmore High School for at least six weeks. There were other matters to be thankful for: no damage to my heart, no arthritis (yet), and no apparent damage to my muscular structure. But I was constantly told that I could not participate in any physical education activities.

Summer weather in Minnesota is muggy. There are lots of mosquitoes, but the majority of the days were good for growing corn, barley, and alfalfa. The strawberries and potatoes did well too. We all had to inspect the corn because it had to be "knee high by the fourth of July." We were very fortunate that our

46

crops were never hit by tornadoes. Occasionally, we had a crop drown out in a particular spot on the farm, but that was the extent of the damage. We had no money to buy hail insurance for crop damage, so we were very fortunate. Daddy said farmers were the biggest gamblers on this earth. When I'd hear our parents worry about the weather and the farm prices, I'd include these fears in my summer good night prayers. But there were times that praying didn't help.

The most important concern for our father was to be able to hire the thrashing crew when the grain was ripe and the weather was right. When it came to the weather, prayers were sent up asking for lots of good sun. Thrashers were the hired help who came to cut and bundle the grain into shocks for the farmers. Having enough food for the thrashers was a full two- or three-day task. Mother was very skilled at making tasty and delicious food. There were times when the thrashers were asked if they wished to have a second piece of pie. Mother served it quickly only to be told, "That was so good, I'd like a third piece!"

Occasionally we could leave the farm for a few hours. There were good speakers that arrived from Norway, Sweden, and the League of Nations. It was a chance to meet and greet our friends who were working just as hard as we were to acquire our farms debt-free. It was our chance to hear new thoughts, rethink old ideas, and reflect on whatever the future held for us.

Whether it was summer or winter when it came to farming, my father was an independent farmer. I heard him say many times that he did not want any county agent telling him what to do as far as farming was concerned. He knew the lay of the land, he knew he had rich black soil, and he knew where he needed drainage. Observing my parents' independent views, I was determined to pattern my existence with a similar kind of independence in my own life. Perhaps this is where a certain amount of rebelliousness developed in my early life. 🚢

Yesterday, December seventh, 1941, a date which will live in infamy, the United States of America was suddenly and deliberately attacked by naval and air forces of the Empire of Japan.

Franklin D. Roosevelt

More than an end to war, we want an end to the beginning of all wars—yes, an end to this brutal, inhuman, and thoroughly impractical method of settling differences between governments.

Franklin D. Roosevelt

Political Life of George Vikingstad

The lives of the George Vikingstad's family revolved around my father's political life. Political times were tough. Farmers worked through four seasons and frequently did not have any money at the end of the year for their own families. I remember my mother calling the Elmore Produce and asking them the price they were giving for a dozen eggs. I heard her say, "Five cents?" She began to cry and hung up the phone. A few moments later the phone rang and my mother answered. The Elmore Produce Company called back to ask if she was the one who had just called about the price of a dozen eggs. Mother said yes, and then they said only "for her" would they pay six cents a dozen.

Farm Holiday Association

Sunday was supposed to be a day of rest, but for my father it became a day of work. Farmers were being thrown out of their farm homes due to bank foreclosures. Farm product prices had fallen to a new low. Farm families had nowhere to go, received little or no pay for their products, and had no money to pay for the interest on their farm mortgages. George's help was welcomed in organizing the farmers to defend the farmers faced with foreclosure.

My father told of a foreclosure conducted by the local sheriff who was armed. My father, who was six feet tall, took off his mackinaw and whipped his sheepskin jacket over the sheriff, thereby immobilizing him. The farmers did not carry guns.

Many of the farmers were injured in these survival fights with the banks and the local sheriff and his officers. Some farmers gained some time in fighting their foreclosures. After some of these altercations, some farmers ended up in local hospitals with no money to pay for the hospital bill.

Gradually, the farmers who participated in these farm foreclosure fights organized into the Farm Holiday Association. Their plight was recognized by the politicians of the day—some who were sympathetic and some who sided with the banks and their partners. Meanwhile, as a family, we were always on the edge of never knowing if we had enough money for the Federal Land Bank loan.

Farm Labor Party and Trouble at School

The Farm Holiday Association, with a growing number of farmers, workers, and small business citizens formed what was known as the Farmer Labor Party. Minnesota was a state where third parties were formed, grew with the depression, and at times won elections. George was as active as his work as a farmer would allow. During the formation of the new party, he was most attracted to attorneys who were helpful to the cause. The new network spread throughout Southern Minnesota and into the Twin Cities area of Minneapolis and St. Paul.

Our immediate neighbors were financially secure because they had inherited their farms and thus had no mortgage debt. Some saw this as an avenue to purchase additional farms when another farmer would lose a farm due to foreclosure. This tension of the depression would occasionally erupt into school children's taunts. One Minnesota morning, at the Van Buren Country School, bullying shouts were heard about Farm Labor politics and George Vikingstad. I was a very quiet child with a tendency to cry easily, so I was an easy target for bullies. The noise of the school children grew very loud, and I finally said, "Is it any of your business?"

Everyone was surprised that I had any kind of a response. After all, I was the one who on another occasion was rolled around in the mud.

Suddenly Miss Carrie Bruvald, our Van Buren schoolteacher, rang the school bell at 8:45 a.m. That was fifteen minutes early. It is true I seemed to be the brunt of any bully in the school. It was difficult for me to understand. This was the first time anyone in the school had come to my rescue. How could I enjoy the "learning" part of our country school so much and be so unhappy with recess?

Sometimes it was a lonely feeling to be a Farmer Laborite who was poor among wealthy German farmers' sons and daughters. I comforted myself that the early school bell clanging was a signal to me that perhaps I did have one friend.

The Farmer Labor Party prospered as a popular political party with the candidacy of Floyd B. Olson for Minnesota Governor. He ran on a progressive platform which was supported by my father and citizens who had fought the banks, the railroads, and the landed aristocracies of the era. It was a great victory when he was elected Governor, with people immediately crying for him to run for President. My father was very pleased to meet and talk with the new Governor in the Minnesota Capital of St. Paul. The Gover-

Governor Floyd B. Olson of Minnesota

nor was an accomplished speaker and supported both state and national issues effecting farm issues. In the 1930s, legislation was passed by the Minnesota Legislature to stop the current farm foreclosure practices, and the bill was subsequently signed by a pleased Governor Olson. It was such a pleasant time to have such a popular political figure in Minnesota government. However, it was short lived because Governor Olson was stricken with deadly cancer. I remember Minnesota newspapers reported his funeral being attended by the greatest number of people in Minnesota history.

Saturday Nights in Minnesota

Saturday night was the greatest night of the week. Not only did I receive a nickel for an ice cream cone, but my mother and I went to the movies. There have been stories about how Hollywood cheered the hearts and minds of people in the great depression. That's right. I can attest to that. We saw Paulette Goddard in the *Perils of Pauline* triumph against poverty and war. It was a way for us to lose ourselves for a while in a double feature at a cost of only ten cents. Once when *Drums Along the Mohawk* was being shown, the theater was deathly silent. Before a painted Indian was about to strike Maureen O'Hara, I let out a terrorized scream to warn her, thus frightening the whole theater. Henry Fonda did save her in the end.

George in his Veteran of Foreign Wars (V.F.W.) hat

My mother and I would hurry to the car after the movies, so my father would not have to wait for us too long. He usually was talking with other men about politics or farms prices. We could not get him interested in going to the movies. If a movie were a historical saga, then he would go only to see if history was depicted accurately. We also had to endure thirteen miles of King Edward cigar smoke going to and from the movie theater. It was unbearable, and my mother and I complained. Eventually, George did quit smoking "cold turkey" when his father died of cancer.

George and Emily Vikingstad
Twenty-fifth Wedding Anniversary

I wrote this poem for my parents' twenty-fifth wedding anniversary on December 29, 1945:

Many are the tales of song and
    dance.

Many are the songs of myths of
    old and new,

But best of all are the tales of
    romance

That warm your heart through
    and through . . . .

I'll tell you a tale of a romance true,

That began some five and twenty
    years plus a month or a few—

Emily and George I'm sure you all
    know are the two

That eventually wound up saying
    "I do."

It was on hot summer's day that it
    all began

When Emily and that Model-T Ford into the Vikingstad buggy ran,

A garage bill of seven whole dollars by Emily was paid,

And with the meeting of George a better bargain by Emily was
    never made.

George was the brave young man on the farm who had just come
    back from the war,

While Emily was the school marm who sometimes found other
    lads a bore.

So she chanced a date to the Soldier's Homecoming at Blue Earth

And found to her delight this date full of sparkle and mirth.

Georgette Vikingstad Valle

Often in a horse and buggy, Emily and George went for a ride—
To talk of the birds and bees and maybe the countryside.
There was the time when George lost his hat in the slough,
But later lost his heart to Emily's eyes so blue.

A year of dates, letters, and romance brought marriage.
Four years later on Halloween came Georgette in a baby carriage.
George wore the biggest smile in Faribault County twas said,
Perhaps not realizing it was one more mouth to be fed.

Hard at work, morning noon, and night and after that machinery
    to fix.
Still George had time to dabble in politics,
Emily occupied herself with chickens not a few,
While Georgette cleaned many an egg and sighed, "Phew!"

It chanced that a newcomer came to the George and Emily
    domain.
Twas Georgette who searched for the stork in vain.
Grandma felt super that day and was filled with glee,
As she heard that both Roosevelt and Astrid were both in safely!

George promptly named the newcomer "Two Bits!"
But now that name anything but fits.
We all have to grow up and so—
Tis quite expected the years should go.

And now my story's quite up to date—
To recall a past like this is never too late—
There have been trails and tribulations
But conquered they have been with one or two alterations.
Twenty-five years of happy married life have come and gone,
More love and joy are at the dawn,
That burst forth into an endless span so free—
So may more happiness, love, and joy be yours for an eternity!

Emily Vikingstad exiting the *Oslofjord* in
Oslo, Norway. George, my father, would not
go to Norway until he had saved enough
money. They sold 120 acres of the farm to
travel to Norway and buy a winter retirement
house in Mesa, Arizona. They rented out the
rest of the farm and moved to Blue Earth,
Minnesota, in 1956.

Some things . . . arrive in their mysterious hour, on their own terms and not yours, to be seized or relinquished forever.

Gail Godwin

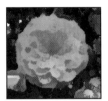

Sister Astrid, Daughters Stephanie and Camille, and In-Laws

Astrid and I were living separate lives. She was graduating from college at the University of Minnesota with a degree in education. She was also making her own friends in the Twin Cities area and beginning her kindergarten teaching life in Minneapolis. In Seattle and the Normandy Park area I was busy being a dentist's wife, mother of a growing child Peter, and starting my life as a community activist.

So it was truly exciting to hear that my sister was going to be married in the fall of 1954. When you are eight years older than your sister, you know it is time for her to be making her own decisions. Astrid asked me to be the matron of honor, so I raced into action. I had to make reservations for a baby sitter, and Odd would have to miss the wedding because he had too many patients scheduled for him to leave the office.

Astrid Emily Vikingstad's fiancé was a nice, easygoing Minnesotan, Colin "Cody" Connel, who lived in the Twin Cities area. She had grown into an attractive, young, cosmopolitan woman who was interested in the politics of the day, world affairs, and current events of the Twin Cities area. Her good looks stood her in pleasant company with several young male fans. Cody was an affable and interesting conversationalist, amusing, and had good sense of humor. His pleasant, ruddy complexion with a crown of rusty-red hair complemented Astrid's fair, Nordic skin and contrasting dark-brown curly hair.

The wedding was to be held in Cody's parents' home in the Twin Cities, which had many charms that enhanced the festive wedding. Astrid look regal and beautiful in her white satin gown with a short veil adorned with beading gathered as a crown on top of her brown curls. The Connel home held many of Astrid and Cody's friends who came together to celebrate and congratulate the young couple.

Guests rarely pay attention to the matron of honor, but people greeted me in my shiny, Kelly green, tight-bodied organza dress with matching green shoes as if I was the guest from the West. I was a guest, and so glad to return to Minnesota again and receive such a warm welcome. It was the first time I had left baby Peter, so I boarded the first plane back to Seattle as quickly as I could schedule a flight.

Cody and Astrid moved into a comfortable, older, three-story Minneapolis home on Minneapolis Avenue which had hardwood floors and ample space for a growing family. In late spring of 1955, Stephanie was born with Camille following in 1957. Astrid was busy teaching kindergarten in the Minneapolis Public School District. It was a busy life with Astrid working full time and mothering her two children. Cody worked for the Minneapolis Park system.

Stephanie and Camille Connel at the 1962 World's Fair in Seattle

Grandparents George and Emily came to the Twin Cities many times to baby sit and share in the endless housework that accumulates over time when there is a working mother and father.

Stephanie, whose Tenold looks very much mirrored her grandmother when she was young, grew and prospered with the love and attention given her by all her relatives. Her shyness was overcome by her companionship with Camille, who resembled her mother in blond curls and good looks. During the many Christmastime visits, the three cousins (Christine, Stephanie, and Camille) looked like triplets with cousin, Peter, the handsome escort in his black suit and bow tie. Uncle Cody played well with the cousins, with the children responding happily to his good nature.

As life progresses, not all lives go in the same direction. As such, Astrid and Cody went their separate ways. Single working mothers did not always have the help that they have today, but Cody kept his bargain as a father and shared his earnings to help his family.

Camille Connel smiles as she relaxes in the warm Minnesota summer in her late teens.

Retired teacher Astrid Alexander taught kindergarten during her teaching career in Minneapolis.

Astrid married a Minneapolis cardiologist with a ready-made family. She tried to embrace both families with love for all. With the greatest of these human recourses, in the end she found comfort and solace in her teaching career. Many families complimented her for her many years of devotion and attention to many kindergarten class students and parents.

Astrid is enjoying her granddaughter, Sarah, Camille and Don Ritter's daughter, who is the replica of Camille as a child. This is evident from the yearly Christmas photos that reveal her beauty and growing maturity.

Camille graduated from the University of Minnesota and has been employed in the housing industry. She has a smart and pleasant attitude towards the public. Don Ritter is a registered nurse and is employed in the Twin Cities area. They have a home in St. Louis Park, Minnesota.

Stephanie has led a life of varied occupations. As a teenager she traveled to San Francisco and worked as a nanny. Later she came to Olympia, Washington, and worked as a legislative clerk to the Social Welfare and Health Legislative Committee. Stephanie has held various other jobs in Minneapolis. She displays an

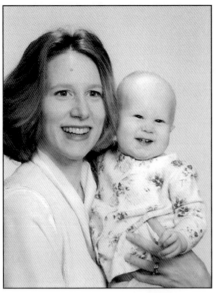

Camille Connel Ritter with baby
daughter Sarah Ritter
on October 2. 1996

Sarah Ritter contemplates
Christmas 2000 as she dreams in
this picture.

Stephanie Vikingstad Connel in
1994 while she was attending
the University of Minnesota

independent spirit, which she frequently asserts off and on the job. In the 1990s, she attended the University of Minnesota with special success in various writing courses. Stephanie fully participates as a meaningful member of Twin Cities society, including politics. 🚢

SCHOOL DAYS

My mother drew a distinction between achievement and success. She said that achievement is the knowledge that you have studied and worked hard and done the best that is in you. Success is being praised by others, and that's nice too, but not as important or as satisfying. Always aim for achievement and forget about success.

Helen Hayes

It's Only a Quarter of a Mile!

My father said, "It's only a quarter of a mile!" It was 20 degrees below zero, and he said it's only a quarter of mile! In 1934 I did what I always did on those cold Minnesota days. I walked to my country schoolhouse in Van Buren School District 66. The morning was clear and crisp with the air whistling up my nose. I had bundled up so I was warm and shouldn't have complained about Minnesota winters. I was thinking that maybe Pete Olson,

 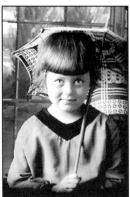 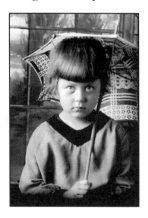

father of classmate Arden Olson, would bring his son to school and would stop and give me a ride along the way. I always thought it was an act of generosity to stop for me, even if I was halfway to school. There was no car in sight, so I comforted myself with the thought that my desk was in the back of the one-room schoolhouse next to the potbellied stove, where I would be toasty and warm. The school housed about thirteen students; it waivered between nine and thirteen. I thought about today's classwork and hoped I had written a correct report for my fourth-grade Minnesota history class.

I finally arrived at the schoolhouse just before nine o'clock in the morning. Carrie Bruvold, the teacher, was about to ring the bell. As an arithmetic assignment before the day was over, our class would measure the schoolhouse as to its width and length, the gray-painted floor, the thirteen desks, and the teacher's desk on the platform with the old, yellow yardstick. The schoolhouse length was thirty yards or ninety feet.

Van Buren School District 66 Country School now on the Vikingstad farm

As I walked home that afternoon, I was pleased that the bright sunshine helped to warm the day. Another day when it was raining "cats and dogs," a nice, shining, wet Ford coupe pulled up to me slowly and a man said, "Would you like a ride home?"

I hesitated as the rainwater steadily drenched me, and then I said, "Thank you. I don't think so." I was thinking about the Lindberg baby kidnapping. This event made front-page headlines, showing graphic details of the ladder going up to the second story window of the Lindberg home.

At the same time I heard the man say, "That's all right, I'm old man Gesche!"

My father had said that old man Gesche was the richest man in the community. As the water dripped down my back, I thought he wouldn't kidnap me, he's got enough money. I began the long climb up to the running board of the Ford Model A. I hoped that I would not make a mess of his beautiful automobile. It was such a nice car, and I was so thankful to be out of the cold rain.

Getting the paper for dad.
Georgette is about 7 years old.

At school my classmates Arden Olson and Evelyn Ristau made class interesting as they afforded a little competition. Arden was of Norwegian ancestry, and Evelyn was of German ancestry. What difference did ancestry make? It made a great deal of difference in a community comprised largely of Germans, interspersed with a few Norwegians. However, Arden, Evelyn, and I were compatible and became great friends.

The facts that my father was active in the Democratic Farmer Labor Party, we were poor, and we were Norwegians seemed to bear some relevance to numerous classmates. Many of the German families had inherited their farms, whereas we struggled with a large debt due to the Federal Land Bank and their loan. Our neighbors generally knew of our financial troubles through the "telephone party" line. Our "ring" was one short and two long rings. You could hear the click, click, click of the listeners to our calls. Sometimes a creditor wanted to be nasty as they hounded us with their telephone calls to remind us what my parents owed.

Perhaps because of the difficult financial times, my father sometimes landed with a hard judgment. I did not handle this with a great deal of understanding as I was super sensitive about trying to please my parents. Often there was a lump in my throat which crept up and the tears glistened in my eyes, but they did not fall. On one occasion I came home with new shoes that resembled a laced football and proudly told my father the shoes cost only four dollars. He exploded with a tirade about how much four dollars was worth and how we could not afford those shoes. I was devastated because I thought they were the "cat's meow!" After that I wore my shoes as long as possible. My feet grew so rapidly that I frequently had bloody toes from wearing shoes that were too short.

Little did I know that I would use the schoolhouse measuring lesson years later to measure the lot where my husband would build his dental office in Burien, Washington, and to measure the view lot of our first home in Normandy Park, Washington. Our house lot, which was pie-shaped, was the length of one school-house in the front and two schoolhouses in the back.

I would use my walking skills to attain one of my major goals in political life in Washington State. To be a strong candidate or incumbent, you must doorbell and think in terms of "a quarter of a mile," or another block, or another precinct.

The Years Fly By . . . . Graduating

I remember my teachers Miss Margaret Larson, Miss Carrie Bruvold, and Miss Verlow with warmth and thankfulness for the wonderful education that was and is so very important to me.

Quite a few daydreams floated around in my head during that quarter-of-a-mile trek to my country schoolhouse. I enjoyed history and geography. I dreamt about visiting distant lands and viewing for myself what was being revealed to me in these books I was toting back and forth.

Both my father and mother were willing to confront me with questions about history, geography, and our own politics. My father would read an article to us. I was glad to have my evening chores completed, so I could either study or relax with a good book for the remainder of the evening.

I was the tallest person in the entire school. I was neither the quickest, nor necessarily the smartest person in the class. That did not keep me from trying to attain these traits. I longed for privacy which did not exist in a country school with the "outdoor biffies" (outhouses). At eleven and a half years of age and at 5' 6½" tall. There were always giggles from the girls and taunts from the boys.

It was very easy for me to slip into a daydream of how life was going to be in high school. Evelyn Ristau, the one good friend that I had, would soon be leaving for the German Lutheran Church School up the road where nearly all the students were a part of her German Lutheran Church.

After Evelyn left I still had my friend Arden who was smart and polite. I loved being able to compete with him in the seventh and eighth grades. The students in the country school were required to take state exams in order to enter high school. In the seventh grade, the exam subject was geography. Exams on the rest of the subjects were given in the eighth grade. Both Arden and I both passed with flying colors (B+'s and A's). Arden Olson and I were the two that graduated from eighth grade from the Van Buren Country School in 1938.

The rural country schools would eventually close, and all the children would be sent to the Elmore School District. The small classes would be exchanged for better play equipment, an improved library, and maybe even an occasional educational trip to a museum.

When my little country schoolhouse closed, my father purchased the school building and lot for $1,000 and transported the school to the Vikingstad farm to store corn. In my daydreams, I probably could have envisioned creating a museum out of the Van Buren School building (named for President Van Buren).

No applause, comments, or remarks distinguished my eighth grade graduation day from Van Buren Country School in District 66. Arden and I went to a

Cousin Buddy Palmer, Georgette, and Astrid are back at the Vikingstad's Minnesota farm after Georgette's eighth grade graduation. Her new dress was slate blue in color.

graduating ceremony that had a distinguished county educational dignitary speaking to us about our educational future. Both our parents were pleased. I was excited about entering Elmore High School and the prospect of making new friends, studying new subjects, and new surroundings.

Elmore High School Rah Rah Rah!

As the warm days and cool nights of September of 1938 arrived, there was shopping to be done for some new clothes for school. Our family could not afford much, but maybe we would be able to buy one new outfit for Astrid and for me.

Astrid was about to enter first grade. She would be part of a big class and needed some new clothes to help keep her warm as she walked that quarter of a mile to the country school. Thank goodness for the egg money!

I still had to walk to the Van Buren Country School to catch the Elmore High School bus. I rode the bus with others to Elmore High School! Rah! Rah! Rah!

My high school classes started at least six weeks later in the school year for me because the rheumatic fever the year before put me behind and I had to catch up in my studies. But now it was all so exciting to be in high school! All of my dreams seemed to be coming true. New friends, classrooms, teachers, and subjects to study awaited me. I would have to study at night if I was to keep up with my classmates. I was prepared to have a "can do" attitude.

Georgette affectionately hugs Donna Ristau, two years younger and Evelyn Ristau's cousin

About two months after entering high school, I was called into Homer Musgrave's American History class. He said to me: "You are not applying yourself in history class. You can do better . . . ." With a big lump in my throat, I promised him I would do better in the following months. I kept that promise.

Evelyn Ristau and Georgette on Elmore High School graduation day in 1942

I could always study with my longtime friend Evelyn Ristau. She had left me at the Van Buren Country School to attend the German Lutheran Church School, but returned in high school. We made a good "studying couple." We did not study as much in the beginning years of high school, but in our third and fourth years, we were pretty regular about cramming before a test. No cheating for us. Graduation from Elmore High School was another high point in our young lives.

During my freshman year, I looked for that one special girlfriend. For some reason, I looked to the sophomore class and found a very pretty, smart, and friendly girl who responded to my eagerness as a freshman farm girl. That girl was Frances Yahnke, the youngest of five children from a family living close to Elmore. It seemed to me to be a great "find." We seemed to be pals from the moment we met. We could share our thoughts about boys, "girl" intimacies, and moments of class interaction that make for interesting elements of high school life.

Both Frances and I liked high school sports events. I had been watching my classmates with much interest, and one particular classmate, Richard Kerr, seemed to be very talented and smart. He was athletic and had a keen sense of humor. I'm sure his Irish mother and father had a great deal to do with his pleasant, easygoing attitude. I wasn't the only one interested in this new football star. He was setting records in various sports. He beat members of all other local schools with a record time of 10.4 seconds in the 100-yard dash!

Frances and I had a great time attending football games and watching our favorites playing their hearts and souls out for their fans. What was exciting was to be able to stay with my friend, Frances, at her home with her hospitable mother and father.

I was surprised to find myself selected as Miss Elmore and represented Elmore at the North Iowa Band Festival. Actually, I think the selection of Clarissa Thompson was more prob-able, but she was our baton twirler and was re-quired to lead the Elmore High School Band. I could think of several other good candidates for

Georgette's best high school friend, Frances Yahnke, in their Elmore High School days in 1941

Miss Elmore—my best friend, Frances Henke, but she too was needed in the band. She played the chimes. Another candidate, Mary Jane Emerson, would have made a splendid Miss Elmore, but she played the flute. Suddenly I found myself in a new pink dress, with silver buttons lined up in a design resembling a band uniform. My picture was on the front page of the *Elmore Eye*, along with a nice article about me. It filled me with a new sense of confidence about myself and my own sense of beauty. At the Bank Festival at Mason City, Iowa, I secretly played the part of a judge and found I agreed with the real judges' choice for band queen. The North Iowa Band Queen was a petite, dark-eyed beauty with long, beautiful, brown hair.

In my class of 1942 were the Ehrick girls, Viola and Violet, who were cousins and always together. They also challenged the rest of the class to match their A and B+ grades. They persevered and became the valedictorian and salutatorian of the class. I came out third in a class of seventeen. I was glad to have the Ehrick girls get these honors of our class. Arden Olson was a fraction of a point behind me.

Meet–Miss Elmore, Minn.

Entry No. 42 for Queen of North Iowa Band Festival June 17, 1941

Georgette Vikingstad was selected by the school band to represent Elmore, Minn., in the parade of bands and queens that will draw thousands to Mason City, June 17.

Miss Vikingstad, daughter of Mr. and Mrs. George Vikingstad, who live on a farm near Elmore, was a member of the junior class this past year. She has distinguished herself in music, scholarship and student leadership during her school career.

The Elmore candidate is first clarinetist in the band. She is interested in many sports, which include swimming, boating, archery, basketball, kittenball, fishing and travel. Her leisure hours also include gardening, floral gardens, reading and theatrical entertainments. She has appeared in several class plays during her high school career.

Miss Vikingstad, with other candidates, will be feted throughout the day of the festival.

GEORGETTE VIKINGSTAD
–Miss Elmore, Minn.

As the class of 1942, we could have fun, enjoy each others' company, and learn a great deal from each other. The boys in the class were in the minority, so they enjoyed a little boyish banter at the girls' expense. Jackie Vaughn, Dale Wise, and Wallace (Butch) Hagedorn were experts at playing pranks on others—often to the teachers' dismay. Bernadine Zerike had rheumatic fever and could not attend all our classes, but still managed to graduate with all of us. Mansel Mathison disappeared for a time, but resurfaced in time to graduate with us.

Two classmates I considered fashion plates were Mary Jane Emerson and Delores Hanks. They were inseparable, and it seemed "pals" forever. They added an air of sophistication to our class.

Others in the class who are pleasantly remembered in our world of Elmorites were Marie Cooan, Maxine Zeigler, Dorothy Risk, and Alice Thompson. Marie had a beautiful smile and naturally curly, blond hair. Maxine was a friendly person, always willing to lend a helping hand.

Some in our class did not survive. Alice Thompson died in a car accident in our freshman year. I will always remember a blue dress that Alice wore to class. I still think of her when I hear the song *In My Alice Blue Gown*. Dorothy Risk also died during our early high school years.

Class of 1942, After Graduation

Evelyn Ristau married a good-looking Norwegian fellow named Ivan Sansgard. They raised their four children on the Sansgard farm and enlarged Elmore and the surrounding farms with grandchildren and great-grandchildren. I was astonished when I saw a picture of all their offspring!

Frances Yahnke graduated from the Northwest School of Business and went to work for a Minneapolis bank after high school. In 1944 she married Kenneth Henke, and I was in her wedding. Our lives went in different directions and to different locations. We kept in contact and then lost touch with each other. Recently, I learned she and her husband were in the North Los Angeles area.

Arden Olson went on to graduate from the Minneapolis School of Business. Upon graduation, he was offered a position in Minneapolis. I saw him occasionally on the streets of Minneapolis.

Richard Kerr attended the University of Minnesota, where he graduated with a Bachelor of Science degree in Electrical Engineering. He worked for General Mills and Honeywell in the Minneapolis area. More recently, Richard had moved to Arizona, and the detective spirit within me was challenged. I located him in Sun City West. Sure enough, I heard the same Richard Kerr's voice on the other end of the phone answering my questions. After some years of not keeping in contact, we renewed our acquaintance. What a refreshing experience. It left me that old Elmore High School spirit!

Jackie Vaughn, Dale Wise, and Wallace (Butch) Hagedorn became successful businessmen in Elmore. Jackie Vaughn took over the poultry family business along with his older sister, Ardis Vaughn. All were very creative and added innovations to local businesses. Wallace (Butch) Hagedorn did very well in the local telephone company business. Dale took over his family's city garage business. Classmates Jackie Vaughn and Thelma Walton married and were happily married for many years. Classmates "Butch" Hagedorn and Bernadine Zerike also married. Dale Wise married Corrine Fenske, a girl from another class.

Mary Jane Emerson married Troy Rollins, a local physician, and they now reside in Portland, Oregon.

Over the years, many changes occurred in the little town of Elmore with a population of approximately a thousand people. Declining population on the farms surrounding Elmore caused major changes in the Elmore school system. Elmore High School closed its doors in 1990, forty-eight years after I graduated, with Vice President Walter Mondale, my second cousin, giving the major graduation address. Over a thousand people attended the final graduation in the Elmore High School gymnasium. It was inspirational to hear my cousin give the address, but sad to note the final death sentence for Elmore High School.

ALWAYS A REBEL AND NEVER WITHOUT A CAUSE

COLLEGE YEARS

A friend doesn't go on a diet because you are fat. A friend never defends a husband who gets an electric skillet for her birthday. A friend will tell you she saw your old boyfriend—and he's a priest.

Erma Bombeck

Waldorf Lutheran College Days
1942-1944

During the exciting days after my graduation from Elmore High School, I considered where I would attend college. I was impressed that my Grandfather Tenold felt that a college education for his daughters was important. I was determined to also get a college education and made it part of my goals in my life.

Georgette Vikingstad and cousin Carol Sue Johnson in Forest City, Iowa

I did not think I was ready to attend a large four-year college or university. Somehow, this farm girl wanted a short bridge to a four-year university. That short bridge turned out to be Waldorf Lutheran College located in Forest City, Iowa. My mother and her two sisters, Luella and Clara, had graduated from Waldorf and that gave me a certain comfort level about the college.

My relatives, Aunt Clara Tenold Johnson and Stanley Johnson and family, lived in Forest City. Their house was so modern and even included two indoor bathrooms. Uncle Stanley was the Editor of the *Forest City Summit* newspaper and could be such a prankster. I did not recognize his voice one day when he called me at the dorm pretending to be a suitor and asked me for a date.

Enrollment at the college was between 200 and 250 young students hailing from northern Iowa, the nearby Dakotas, Wisconsin, and Minnesota. Only seven male students were in attendance in 1942 because of all the young men serving in World War II. These young men were known as the "four F's." The fact that there only seven male students did not bother me. I was more interested in finding interesting people for friendships, and those days were memorable to those of us who were seeking our first

Cousins from left: Richard Johnson, Astrid Vikingstad, Georgette Vikingstad holding Carol Sue Johnson, and Duane Johnson

observations of the outside world without our parents' immediate supervision.

I did make a number of friends that I still correspond with today. Dorothy Querna, my roommate, was irrepressible with laughter at almost anything I said, so I figured we could survive any catastrophe, even the mumps which Dorothy came down with. The two Oppedahl cousins, Ruthie and Marguerite, were equally pleasant people with strong Norwegian roots. The fifth member of our female gang was Mavis Venji from Appleton, Iowa. She was our musical member who sang in the Waldorf Choir and had a beautiful contralto voice.

Eventually, I became a choir member and enjoyed the serious instruction of conductor Odvin Hagen. He was a very stern leader who seldom smiled. I was so frightened I could barely sing. He could smile, even laugh, but only after the choir had performed a magnificent song. Gradually I learned to relax, growing accustomed to his stern conducting.

At Waldorf I had decided a liberal arts course would lead me to my major at the next institution of higher learning. I was very enthusiastic about attending

Waldorf and happy to have the youthful Miss Prestegard as my German teacher. I enjoyed languages, and it seemed to reflect in my high grades.

Georgette Vikingstad, Mavis Vinji, and Dorothy Querna in happier days at Waldorf Lutheran College in 1943

Dean Folkedahl, our English teacher, was serious and thoughtful. She had a difficult job and did not think the students appreciated her disciplinary efforts as Dean of Students. I took Waldorf seriously, along with its admonitions for attendance at chapel (roll was taken), no dancing (even during summer vacation), and strict instructions to be in bed or in your room by 9 p.m. on weekday nights. I found that other classmates very quickly learned to climb the fire escape rather than go through the procedure of having Miss Folkedahl unlock the front door and subsequently finding several demerits ending up on their report card.

I had a job in the classroom, and also worked for Tillie Rasmussen, the school cook, waiting tables for all three meals. We got one weekend off per month which meant I could go home often. I once figured out how much I was making per hour and was so disgusted that I did not relate these figures to anyone in or out of Waldorf. I think it was something less than twenty-three cents an hour. We paid for our food, but only received thirty dollars per month.

Someone on our work crew visited several other Lutheran colleges in Iowa and Minnesota and discovered not only did these colleges provide free food for their workers, but they paid their waitresses and waiters a higher wage than we were receiving. We were surprised to learn we were so underpaid. Everyone began to say, "What can we do?"

I suggested that we could stop working, which we did. That was a bit of a shock for the college. When we appeared before our employee manager, our one male employee became tongue-tied and declined to speak. Suddenly I was pushed up front to speak for the group. I simply explained the situation to our manager. We were made aware of the other colleges' wealthy alumnae, and then he added that was the reason Waldorf could not pay its work force as generously as the other wealthy Lutheran colleges. We were told we would simply have to wait and see how much our checks would be at the end of the month. We waited eagerly and, low and behold, we did get a raise—a total of one dollar each month!

I was enjoying college life even though I thought we were all being underpaid, and even if the monetary result of our little work stoppage had not given us much of raise, I complemented us for doing what was right and honest to do. I'm sure if I had searched I could have found a verse in the *New Testament* that would have justified our actions, but that had to wait because I had to study for a German test!

A welcomed break was Bing Crosby's *I'm Dreaming of a White Christmas* being played over the loudspeaker while walking with Dorothy Querna as the snow gently fell in the evening hours in downtown Forest City.

Waiting tables was okay, but I thought perhaps I could aspire to something more intellectually challenging. Dr. Johnson, the chemistry teacher, was advertising for an assistant in his classroom. I applied for my sophomore year and was accepted.

Soon after applying for the assistant position, I was called into the office of Waldorf College President J. L. Rendahl. I wondered what the topic of discussion would be. We dispensed with the formalities of the day. He came right to the point and said that I could not have the job as assistant to Dr. Johnson, the chemistry teacher, because I had led the strike of waitresses and waiters the past year.

This was a great surprise to me. I explained that this was a group move and that I had done nothing wrong. I told him that unless I got the job working with Dr. Johnson, I would not be returning to Waldorf College and added that I would wait to hear from him before making any commitment to attend Waldorf for my sophomore year. With those words, I left the office.

The summer seemed to move slower than usual. I would run to the mailbox to see if I had any mail from Waldorf. Upon my return from a three-day trip to Omaha, Nebraska, my father told me that if I would help him shock the barley

Georgette
Vikingstad
and her 1929
Model A Ford at
Waldorf Lutheran College

field, he would pay me $90 so I could buy a 1929 Model A Ford. I thought that was quite a deal, and though I was "trip tired," I worked late in the day to get the barley field shocked before it rained that night.

The letter I had so anxiously awaited finally arrived in our mailbox in August of 1943. I was approved to become the assistant to Dr. Johnson, which was wonderful news for me. Now, in addition to sporting a Model A Ford as I drove to Waldorf from our Elmore farm, I would have a new job to pay for the gas, which was then about twenty-five cents a gallon.

Now that I had a new job as chemistry assistant to Dr. Johnson, I experienced a new sense of freedom as I entered my sophomore year. I was also learning more about the subject of chemistry. It was delightful not to have to wait tables anymore and enjoyed eating with my friends. It seemed I had more energy to attend chapel, and I was ready to crawl into bed by that anointed hour of 9 p.m.

I had religiously kept the Waldorf admonitions about dancing when, low and behold, Waldorf sponsored a square dance in January of 1944. Even square dancing had been taboo in previous Waldorf days. Somehow, I could not sport enough enthusiasm for this dance even though I had a beautiful yellow formal that I had worn at my best friend, Frances Yahnke Henke's, wedding. I sat in my Waldorf dorm room and looked wistfully at my yellow formal. Everyone else danced the night away at Waldorf's first square dance. My past faithfulness to the rigid rules of Waldorf College Campus left me unenthusiastic about the new college rules. It was the "rebel" in me that did not share in the change of attitude towards square dancing.

There were other areas where I could use my resources and talents. There were the snowy, icy trips to and from the Mason City train depot where I dropped off and picked up Miss Prestegard. I recall speeding along the country roads, viewing newer cars stuck in the ditch. Recalling the upright positioning of the Model A Ford makes me still appreciate the view one gains by sitting straight up while driving our newer cars of today.

It was not long before it was suggested that all five of us should visit our various families on the weekends. Our itineraries were arranged, and on our first trip we planned to visit Dorothy Querna's home located between Owatonna and Faribault, Minnesota. We were whizzing along the country road when a pheasant hit our glass windshield. Ruthie was sitting in the front seat beside me. The glass shattered everywhere in the car. We were near a small town where we located a physician who checked Ruth for injury. We patched up the hole in the windshield and continued our journey. Dorothy's parents were delighted to see us. We were treated to some wonderful Norwegian delicacies and *lefsa* (a salty Norwegian tortilla) with the Norwegian words of *Tussen takk og god tur!* (A thousand thanks and have a good trip!)

As a group, we were beginning to become nostalgic about our intertwined lives at Waldorf, our friendships, and special relationships between our religious lives. We were all reaching that fork in the road where we would be going in separate directions. The four of my friends were destined to become teachers, perhaps in Iowa or elsewhere in the United States. It was my choice to try my fortune at the University of Minnesota. With tears in our eyes and lumps in our throats, we all departed with commitments never to lose our sense of love and adventure for the future. Our desire to continue to remain in touch, especially during the Christmas seasons, still remains strong today.

Our lives were saddened by the death of two of our group of five friends. Mavis Vinji died within the first decade of Waldorf graduation. She was so young and ready to be married. All four friends were so distressed to have one of our own depart so early in life. Dorothy Querna Hoffman's health began to fail, and she died in Escondido, California, in 2005. We were devastated to learn of Dorothy's death.

In 1987, while I was a Washington State Representative, I was given a Distinguished Alumna Award from Waldorf College. The award read:

Georgette Vikingstad Valle

To Ms. Georgette Vikingstad Valle "44":

For political leadership
in the state of Washington
and dedication to church
and civic organizations.

Georgette's plaque below is on the wall at Waldorf College along with the other Distinguished Alumnae.

GEORGETTE VIKINGSTAD VALLE '44
POLITICS & PUBLIC AFFAIRS (1987)

The dream was always running ahead of one.
To catch up, to live for a moment in unison
with it, that was the miracle.

Anaïs Nin

The University of Minnesota

I had an Associate of Arts degree from Waldorf Lutheran College and was contemplating a nursing career, so decided to enroll at the University of Minnesota in a nursing course. I was to take my "pracical" nurses course at the Minneapolis General Hospital, a hospital that served the very poorest of the population of Hennipen County. I could have been described as a wide-eyed sophomore with the best of intentions for the patient population of Minnesota. I found that "square corners on the sheets" was the rule of every day. Plumping up pillows and a cheery greeting seemed to improve the patient's health. I was particularly drawn to an elderly gentleman who seemed unaware of the seriousness of his illness. As I retired to my nursing classes, I left a strong message with the nurses that he should be seen by his physician.

The next day I arrived with a burst of good intentions and greeted the nurses and nursing interns with "top-of-the-day enthusiasm." As I made my nursing rounds, I approached my elderly gentleman patient and thought he was very still. It did not take me long to discover he was not breathing; in fact, he was dead.

I could not believe that no one had told me of this disaster. Faint of heart, I quickly came to the conclusion that this profession was perhaps not meant for me. I took steps to transfer into the medical technology courses. A life of looking at test tubes was not terribly exciting, but I did meet a lot of nice young men studying to be medical technologists.

All in all, I did not think of consulting a career counselor. That would have served me well at this juncture of my life. Someone must have suggested that perhaps I might be interested in the Occupational Therapy profession. The science courses you took were with medical students. I was pleased with this aspect of medicine especially rehabilitation. This was it!

Now I could concentrate on the other parts of university life. I enjoyed being part of the World Federalist Organization. We had speakers of world status, and our leaders were often quoted in news articles. The University of Minnesota often complimented our programs with speakers once a week at Northrop Hall. It

Georgette attending the University of Minnesota and living at 225 Harvard Street in Minneapolis in 1945

was in front of this distinguished building that I learned of the death of Franklin Delano Roosevelt on April 12, 1945.

The Democratic Farmer Laborer Club (DFL) was relaxed and full of fun. Besides taking different stands on issues, they indulged themselves in choosing candidates for Miss University of Minnesota. One year I was selected as Miss DFL, competing for the title of Miss University of Minnesota. Former Governor Elmer Benson's daughter was a better bet and better looking too. I decided they must have preferred my politics. This was another special experience that boosted my self-esteem.

One of the more enjoyable glimpses of life at the university was the return of the veterans of World War II. There were men everywhere. There was a mixture of Army, Navy, and Marine uniforms worn on campus. Classes were now full of both genders. There were Waves (Navy women sailors) and Wacks (Army women soldiers), but they didn't seem to be so obvious. Occasionally there was a protest based on veterans' concerns. Our student numbers now swelled in the 1944-45 school year to about forty thousand students, with over ten thousand veterans enrolled.

It was obvious to me that I could not participate in too many extra curricular organizations because I was also working part time at the University Cafe on Washington Street, right across from my rooming house on Harvard Street. I got fifty cents an hour, tips, and my food when I worked. The cafe personnel were kind and willing to lend a hand when we were very busy. You could buy a meal for $1.25 with soup or salad, dessert, and your choice of beverage. And I did get tips. A $0.25 tip bought me one gallon of gas for my 1929 Model A.

Our chef was of Greek origin. He heard complaints about the serving of Spam one lunch hour and came out from the kitchen unceremoniously shouting, "I gotta no meat, so I serve Spam!"

At last I was graduating in 1948 in the first class Occupational Therapy with a Bachelor of Science in Occupational Therapy. My mother and Astrid were at the ceremony. My father was busy chairing the Progressive Party's Convention. (The Progressive Party was the embodiment of the former Farmer Labor Party and the Farm Holiday Party of the early history of Minnesota third-party politics.) Henry Wallace, former Vice President and Secretary of Agriculture, was to be a candidate for President this same year.

Georgette stands by two of her friends at the University of Minnesota on Harvard Street: Lorry Miller (center) and Inez Munson (right).

A sad day for me was when my 1929 "black and yellow wheeler" Model A (with "Gorgeous Georgus" written across the car visor) stopped running and my father had to tow it home from Mankato. Someone offered me $200 for the car, and I accepted the money because it would cost a good deal to fix the car.

My whole family had been so supportive of my days at the University of Minnesota. Those were the days when I could write a check on my father's bank by signing his name and my name below his. This came to an end, because now I could sign my own checks with my first job.

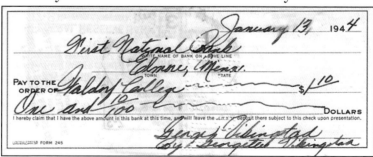

80

When I left the university, the mall was full of beautiful green grass on the long stretches of lawn. This was the student's moment of leisure to be able to relax on this "green" expanse.

I was honored and pleased to return to be the speaker at the graduation of a Senior Occupational Therapy class some forty years later. I was amazed and astonished at the many new buildings on campus. Although Miss Borghild Hanson was no longer the director, it was a great experience for me to return. In a short time, I had renewed my acquaintance with the university, thanking my alma mater for the education that helped my success in my political career and my life in general. I hoped that the young Occupational Therapist graduates would be able to say the same words of praise in the future.

> Challenges make you discover things about yourself that you never really knew. They're what make the instrument stretch—what make you go beyond the norm.
>
> Cycely Tyson

Fear in 1948

My first internship at Ventura, California, at a state psychiatric institution was interesting only to remember a little humor that occurred as several of our Occupational Therapist colleagues and interns were producing and putting on a puppet show for an audience of psychiatric patients. Several of the back stage psychiatric patients cut the strings on the puppets and escaped from the institution into the surrounding California hills. The patients in the audience were disappointed and may have been a little amused by the action of other patients at the same institution.

Then in 1948 I was assigned as a University of Minnesota Occupational Therapy intern to Fitzsimmons General Army Hospital in Denver, Colorado, doing tuberculosis internship training. As occupational therapy interns we were not told that the patients that we were working with were virulent infectious tuberculosis patients. I prepared craft projects for patients and worked close to them at their bedside. My colleagues did the same with infectious patients.

At this hospital I had personal experience with what I call a fearful injustice to my own civil rights. This was in the year of 1948—the presidential year of 1948, when Harry S. Truman of the Democratic Party, Thomas Dewey of the Republican Party, and Henry Wallace of the Progressive Party were the candidates. I came from a politically active family who were always ready to speak their minds and exercise their political rights in print at the local paper, in their political party, and even in church. Minnesota has a long history of third-party politics in order to protect the farmers and laborers from the corporate greed of the railroads, the banks, and even their state and federal governments.

Because it was a year of the presidential elections, I was eager to discover in my new internship position what I was allowed to do politically on a military base installation. I was informed I could not attend political meetings or make political speeches. That was agreeable with me, and I settled into the routine of serving my patients who had virulent infectious tuberculosis.

As interns, we were not informed that one medical intern had actually died. I discovered this tragedy three months into my internship. We were interns from every state university and college busily preparing our occupational therapy projects that patients could assemble at their bedside with their own artistic talent and have their own sense of accomplishment. I saw more than forty patients a day with projects ready for their artistic participation.

In a sense, both staff and patients at the hospital were isolated and eager to talk and talk about politics. And they did talk! Somehow the word must have been circulated that I was very interested in politics in general, and so everyone was interested in having discussions of the latest political news of theirs and mine. There were two supervisors who wanted to discuss political issues with me: one was a loquacious Emily Mills and the other a quiet staff sergeant who had been a Catholic priest. We were all interested in the world around us and particularly in the subject of peace. Our perspectives usually resolved crises in a peaceful manner.

One day I received a letter from my father and mother from our hometown in Elmore with the envelope barely sealed. My father related his activities as Chair of the Progressive Party in Minnesota, and my mother wrote about the farm and the harvest that had just been accomplished in that 1948 fall. My father wrote that his friend, Governor Elmer Benson, was coming to Denver and requested that I meet him at the Denver Airport. Governor Elmer Benson, Farmer Labor party, served the state of Minnesota for four years and was my father's friend. The Governor arrived and John Martin Abt from New York also arrived.

I was true to my father's instructions and delivered them to their hotel and left them for their evening of conversation. Later, I discovered that John Martin Abt was described as a Communist by *Time* magazine.

Fear is a frightening phenomenon. Circumstances, people around you, and your environment all contribute to fear. I had been very busy in my internship working my forty patients, providing them leather, watercolors, writing materials, and other art projects I thought appropriate and creative for their recovery. I was enjoying the spontaneity of the projects and the daily patient responses. In my work evaluation from my second lieutenant, I was surprised to hear from her that I was labeled mentally unstable, criticized for a lack of spontaneity in the projects I designed for the patients, and criticized for my general poor performance.

It was not long after that event that I was told by my friend Emily that I was being investigated by the Central Intelligence Agency (CIA). I was surprised and shocked to hear of these accusations. One thing I did immediately was curtail my conversations with everyone but Emily and the sergeant. It is very frightening not to have your own government have the decency to interview you personally. I was shocked, amazed, and indeed afraid. I did telephone my parents, but the connection with constant clicking on the telephone line was as if there was a listening device in operation. The telephone call was very unsatisfactory. I felt as the CIA was listening to our conversation.

I stopped seeing my patients regularly, stopped my conversation with staff members, and generally lost interest in my Occupational Therapy internship at Fitzsimmons General Army Hospital. The last interview I had with my second lieutenant was very interesting. According to her, I had regained my mental stability, suddenly my projects were excellent, and my performance had improved immeasurably.

So, after three months, I said goodbye to my dear friends Emily and my Catholic priest sergeant and gladly returned to my family and friends at the

University of Minnesota. Good news travels fast. When I returned to the University of Minnesota, I was informed by a friendly teacher, Mrs. Johnson, that the Director of Occupational Therapy, Borghild Hanson, had informed the CIA that I was not a Communist; that my family was very politically active; and that my father, George Vikingstad, Chair of the Progressive Party in Minnesota, also was not a Communist.

As a State Representative, under the Freedom of Information Act, I decided to get to the bottom of this politically inspired event that happened to me in 1948 at Fitzsimmons General Army Hospital. I instructed my secretary to write a letter to the Central Intelligence Agency and ask for a report on my activities as an intern at the hospital. I returned one day from a day of heavy legislative duties to find a letter from the CIA detailing Georgette Vikingstad's internship activities on my desk. The letter portion was three paragraphs long—all blacked out !!!!

I believed that there had been a severe injustice done to me as a student citizen voter at Fitzsimmons General Army Hospital. Since I now was aware that there must have been some intervening information that reached the CIA, I saw that I had to "zip my lips" and return to the University of Minnesota. There was no doubt that this episode in my life changed my personal trust in the demeanor of my own federal government. I saw my future as uncertain and unclear on that distant horizon of life. Perhaps, I would have changed my course to my many causes. ⚓

The story of love is not important—what
is important is that one is capable of love.
It is perhaps the only glimpse we are
permitted of eternity.

Helen Hayes

Occupational Therapy Internship and Meeting Norwegian Student Odd Valle

On a hot, muggy summer day in 1949, the Norwegian students drifted through the line at the University of Minnesota cafeteria. I was just beginning my Occupational Therapy Internship at the Children's Unit at the University of Minnesota Hospital. Food privileges were part of my internship. As I joined the line, I detected many different languages being spoken around me and heard a combination of English and Norwegian. It was always exciting to see and perhaps even meet foreign students. I was impressed with a very attractive man

Georgette *(center back)* working as an Occupational Therapist intern at a Minneapolis retirement home with various occupational therapy projects for elderly patients/clients.

speaking English with a Norwegian accent. I later learned that all of the Norwegian students had studied English for at least six years in Norway.

After my first two internships, I was glad they were finished—especially the Fitzsimmons intern experience. I was happy to be able to return to my family, friends, and to Minnesota. In a sense, the political investigation of the CIA had impacted my whole personal and physical self to a degree that even I did not detect while in Colorado. Returning to Minnesota, I was ready for a new life without the intrigues of an investigatory design of my own government.

As I stood in the cafeteria line scanning the friendly crowd of the lunch bunch, I thought sympathetically about the painful injuries of my five-year-old patient, who had experienced burns on nearly half of his body. I would have to be very ingenious to interest him in any kind of a project. I could see Hans Arstad and Torgeir Togstad at their table and remembered these two friendly, good looking, young Norwegians were dental students from Southern Norway and Bergen.

It was a busy day as I rushed through the cafeteria line only to drop my tray, breaking all the dishes and destroying my lunch. Suddenly, there was this very attractive, somber young man. He helped me pick up the broken pieces, setting them on my lunch tray. I had only seen this particular foreign student from afar, and I certainly wanted another encounter! He was a slender, tall Norwegian whose name was Odd Valle (right). The two Norwegian students that I knew ever so slightly, introduced us so we could at least say "hello."

It wasn't too long after our meeting in the cafeteria that Odd called me to ask for a date. We took the streetcar on our first date to see the movie *The Red Shoes*. It was a very pleasant evening spent talking about our families and what our lives had been like during the war years. It was peacetime now, but the war had influenced both of our lives.

Odd and I took long walks when we could find the time. There were parties at his Psi Omega Fraternity on the East River Road. I was out on a crisp, snowy Sunday morning in my red wool coat with its silver buttons glistening in sunlight. Suddenly a snowball hit the back of my right shoulder. I whirled around and saw Odd was already aiming another smaller one at my other shoulder. We were getting acquainted with each other with informal meetings such as Sunday snowballing in Minneapolis. It was a time when I could easily be distracted from my political thoughts.

We went out regularly for nine months until Odd graduated in 1950 from the Dental School of the University of Minnesota with a Doctor of Dental Surgery degree. He had to return to Norway to serve his year of military service in the Norwegian Army. We made a visit to the Elmore farm to meet my family before he left. There was uncertainty between us as to our relationship because of the great distance between the United States and Norway. I took him down to the Minneapolis Train Station in my 1939 red Chevy convertible when he left for New York to catch his ship back to Norway. We said goodbye with promises to write to each other.

ALWAYS A REBEL AND NEVER WITHOUT A CAUSE

Working and Engaged

Life is to be lived. You have to support yourself. You had bloody well find some way that is going to be interesting. And you don't do that by sitting around wondering about yourself.

Katherine Hepburn

My First Jobs in Occupational Therapy

After what seemed an eternity of time completing Occupational Therapy internships, I realized that I was finally qualified to search for a job. I owed no money for my education, and the plentiful job market assisted me in locating that special position.

With much anticipation in the fall of 1949, I applied for and received a job at the Minneapolis Rehabilitation Center in Minneapolis, Minnesota. I was sure this Rehabilitation Center would enlighten me about how to educate orthopedic patients in the skills of rehabilitation and recovery. I wasn't quite satisfied with what I learned during my internship training, so I was happy to have been able to refine my therapy skills. My starting salary was $180 per month. Benefits and vacation time were not mentioned. I was so eager that they were of no importance to me.

The Rehabilitation Center was located in a compact twenty-foot by forty-foot area which permitted for craft areas, orthopedic machinery, and exercise units for treatment. I wanted to be the best Occupational Therapist that I could be. My supervisor was self-confident and kind as she led new patients into the center. I knew I could learn from her as I watched her interact with the patients.

My supervisor was very critical of the notes that were written on the patients' charts. I was reminded of the importance of the patient's insurance and how carefully the notes detailing the patient's progress were scrutinized by insurance officials. As a young therapist, I thought these lessons were valuable tools for the future.

Occasionally, there were opportunities to assist patients in their homes during rehabilitation. A multiple sclerosis patient wanted to continue his weaving at home. By some quirk of fate, I located a floor loom for sale in the weekly newspaper. This patient needed financial assistance, and I was able to loan him money to buy the loom. His wife had a job in a nearby rug factory, so I thought she would help him repay me. Another patient with a truck delivered the loom. After assisting his wife with the set up of the loom, I had a real sense of satisfaction of helping him continue his rehabilitation at home and received a rag rug as partial payment for the loom.

I needed to write patient progress notes on the daily chart. Little did I realize how important this effort would be to our facility. As I prepared to teach a new male patient to walk with the assistance of crutches, I followed him as closely as I safely could as he progressed in his rehabilitation to become independent. He was beginning his third week of therapy when one day he faltered and began to fall backwards. I immediately stepped forward to stop the fall. I quickly grabbed him under the arms, but the weight of his body was too much to bear. We both fell backward. I was not injured and hoped the patient was not injured. Some time later, I learned that the patient had filed a lawsuit against the Minneapolis Rehabilitation Center in the amount of $175,000 for injuries that occurred. I was not asked to testify at any court proceeding, and the patient lost his case for remuneration for his injuries.

After about one year, I received an offer to become Director of Occupational Therapy at Swedish Hospital in Minneapolis rehabilitating polio patients. I had already been considering the job offer. This seemed like an appropriate time for a change. I had a certain amount of restless drive in my life at that time and felt I could use this time and energy to start a new professional career. My thoughts were centered on my Norwegian friend, Odd Valle, and whatever role he might play in my life. I also knew that I was responsible for making a living, so I accepted the job. I concentrated on acquiring exercise equipment to fit into the new Occupational Therapy Rehab Shop for the polio patients I would treat.

I was to work for Dr. Miland E. Knapp and receive $190 per month, with a $10 raise promised in six months. I discovered a beautiful hand printing press. This would be used for arm extension and flexibility with dexterity for hand and finger muscles. I purchased it on the spot for $75. A weaving floor loom and stationary bicycle rounded out the start of the shop.

Polio patients were much different than the orthopedic patients I had been assisting at the Minneapolis Rehabilitation Center. Here, I would have to work on strengthening the muscles that were left damaged by the polio virus. I saw patients that had flexion and extension of one arm and no extension and flexion in the other, but did have possession of hand flexion and extension with finger dexterity. I learned to work to strengthen the patients' muscles, both damaged and undamaged. There was also an assortment of supportive splints and slings I was able to design for the patients. I became very well acquainted with the patients' needs. During several occasions, the physical therapist and I designed an orthopedic device that served the special needs of one specific patient.

These polio patients had a very long period of recuperation and hospitalization before them. Many polio patients had survived the iron lung, which preserved their lives, but many of their muscles were left weak and paralyzed. Polio patients soon found their way to the Occupational Therapy Shop, arriving either with an orderly pushing them in their wheelchairs or slowly manipulating their wheelchairs themselves. They arrived eager and willing to try any of the new creative activities the center offered. Often they were disappointed to find their expectations were greater than their actual muscles could sustain. In that case, I tried to help them redesign their home to accommodate their difficulties as a polio patient. It was heartbreaking when patients could not qualify for a job because of their physical limitations. This was in the early 1950s when many patients survived the polio virus, but many were left with scars of physical limitations.

The patients and staff were excited the day we took the patients to the park across the street to play croquet. The patients were so grateful to be outside on a wonderful, sunny Minneapolis day. I marveled at their enthusiasm as they took long swings for measured distances to get the ball under the hoop. The game actually became competitive.

My personal life was measured by airmail letters. An additional ten or fifteen cents was paid to have that letter arrive sooner by several days. My letters from Odd Valle were saying that I should join him in beginning an interesting life in Hönefoss in Eastern Norway. He was stationed with the Norwegian Army in this small town. I decided that this was to be an exciting part of my life, and that I needed to live life to the fullest. On the day I had worked for exactly one year at the Swedish Polio Center, I quit my job as Director of Occupational Therapy and booked myself as a passenger on the *Stavangerfjord* ocean liner bound for Oslo, Norway. 🚢

> No pessimist ever discovered the secrets of the
> stars, or sailed to an uncharted land, or opened
> a new heaven to the human spirit.
>
> Helen Keller

Leaving the United States and Sailing to Norway on the *Stavangerfjord*

I was so excited and filled with great anticipation. On May 18, 1951, I was to set sail on the *Stavangerfjord*, leaving family, friends, and colleagues for an unknown period of time. I was consumed with so many thoughts about the future that it was difficult for me to concentrate on any one particular thought. My friends had met Odd Valle and were thrilled for me

Georgette, "Red" Anderson, and Joan Grimmett leaning on Georgette's beloved '39 red Chevy convertible in the spring of 1951

and my trip to Norway. I was looking forward to an ocean voyage with certainty that this event would possibly change my life forever.

Odd was serving as a First Lieutenant in the Norwegian Army working as a dentist. He had been very busy establishing records for his soldier patients, working regular hours at the Hönefoss Army Base, and completing the day by working with his private patients in the city of Hönefoss.

Reading *The Ugly American* convinced me that on my first trip abroad I would try to avoid the mistakes many Americans make when traveling outside of the United States. I had been taking conversational Norwegian to understand what was happening to me in this famous land.

Georgette and Astrid Vikingstad standing by Georgette's cherished '39 red Chevy convertible in the spring of 1951

The very first thing I did was to purchase a round-trip ticket to Oslo, Norway, for $325! It was possible to fly, but the flight would have been on an unpressurized cabin on a C-3 plane. Also, I know it would have been much more costly! I sold my beautiful, red Chevy convertible to my father for $250. He had been unhappy that I paid $325 for the car in the first place. I booked a double-room ticket (to include an unknown roommate) on the third deck in the front of the ship. I was quite willing to climb the steps to the second deck or even the first deck where the tickets were considerably more expensive.

In those days, letters were very important. I was fairly certain that Odd was quite serious about me coming to Norway. I certainly was serious about the relationship because I began asking myself all sorts of questions about whether I would like to live in Norway, whether I would give up my U.S. citizenship, and whether I could leave my parents for an extended period of time. I was not able to answer these questions. I did know, however, that I had very strong feelings for this Norwegian gentleman, so that was a good reason to plan a European trip.

Based on all these uncertain events, my friend, Joan Grimmett, gave me a lovely bridal shower. My eighteen-year-old sister, Astrid, was among the party givers.

Wanting to be completely prepared, I made a trip to the downtown Dayton store in Minneapolis and purchased a wedding dress on sale for $30. It was a beautiful, heavy satin gown with a small train. The dress had a unique cape jacket that, when shed, became strapless. This was a feature I never used. A short veil with a simple crown of orange blossoms made my bridal ensemble complete. I knew I was being practical. (Just in case I did not use my wedding dress, I had not invested a fortune—a resourceful rebel!)

After a few more purchases, I was ready to leave for my trip. My parents were very excited for me. They knew I was pretty headstrong at this point in my life, and even if they wanted to change my mind, they couldn't.

As I left for the first part of my trip on the train to Chicago, my mother said, "Don't forget you have parents and a sister here in the United States." Looking back on that part of my life, I think that I was a little sad, but the anticipation of a new adventure was the overwhelming emotion that I felt at that time.

After arriving in Chicago, I changed trains immediately for the trip to New York City. When I reached New York City at 10 a.m. on May 18, 1951, I discovered I had left my hat in Chicago. No respectable young lady would land in Norway without a hat and gloves. I had some free time as the *Stavangerfjord* was not scheduled to leave

Joan Grimmett celebrating her engagement to Ronald Gabrielson in 1951 with Georgette in Minneapolis.

New York until 2:30 p.m., so I boarded a bus for downtown. I'll never forget the truck drivers and their whistles and toots. I thought New York was a very friendly

To be sure I boarded the right bus, I asked a lady for directions to the *Stavangerfjord* ship. She said she was going there to say goodbye to her niece who was leaving on the same ship, so we rode together to the harbor. She was so gracious, listening to me and stopping at a flower vendor and purchasing two beautiful gardenia corsages—one for her niece and one for me to wear on my navy blue suit. The best part of all of this was that now I had someone to wave goodbye to as the ship left New York.

To my surprise, I had two roommates on board. They were what I considered to be a little on the elderly side, perhaps in their late fifties. I climbed to my top bunk hoping I would not wake them if I came in late at night. I did not have to worry about that because one night when I came into our cool cabin, they offered me a swig of bourbon from a welcome flask. After that, we all got along very well.

Perhaps one of the most interesting events about sailing on the *Stavangerfjord* was meeting the table partners at mealtime. I asked one lady with a Norwegian accent where she was from, and she said, "Brooklyn," with the accent on the "Brr." She further explained that she had spent many years in China as a missionary for the St, Mark Lutheran Church. She had not been to Norway for at least twenty years, so this was an exciting trip for her too.

One day a new guest came to our table, and when I asked where he worked on the ship, he said, "I am the Captain!" We were all invited to the bridge.

I soon learned that the second deck, or the B deck, was the most social section of the *Stavangerfjord*. The top deck was a little stuffy and stiff. The music, the dancing, and the young people were much more interesting on the middle deck!

Each morning as I walked to breakfast, I had to pass by the room where the fish were stored. I thought I'd better get used to this smell if I were going to live in Norway.

ALWAYS A REBEL AND NEVER WITHOUT A CAUSE

THE VALLE FAMILY

*Love is a game that two can play
and both win.*

Eva Gabor

Odd and Georgette Valle— Our Wedding and the Rest of the Valle Family

The subject of where we as a married couple were going to live came up very frequently. I was prepared to live in Norway or the United States, wherever Odd Valle, a dentist, could make a living. I had come to Norway to be married. This is not to deny that leaving the United States did not leave my heart a little "torn." However, I knew Norway was a democratic nation, with a strong and powerful history that I also cherished. We were to have thoughtful advice from important people in Norway about this subject. Meanwhile my parents were prepared to visit me wherever I lived and to pay for my ocean voyages to the United States if we lived in Norway.

It did not take Odd and I long before we found our way to the proper office to obtain a marriage license in Oslo. We were

Odd and Georgette at the Hönefoss Army Post

surprised to discover we had to wait almost one month for a marriage license. This period of time was to allow the marriage license to be posted so if anyone desired to object to our marriage, they could object. Thirty days was probably a historical Nordic custom so that other suitors could be considered. We looked at each other in an amused manner and thought that this time period was sufficient to get ourselves ready for the big event. I landed in Norway on May 23, 1951, and we now decided to be married on the June 30, 1951.

It was common in those days to rent a taxi to travel to Odda, Norway, where Odd's mother and father lived in their new house with Odd's sister and family. They built this house after the war when Odd was attending the University of Minnesota. Norway was much in need of housing, because when the war ended the last act of the Germans was to burn houses all along Norway's vast coastline.

Rut Valle, Eilif Valle, and Odd Valle at the Oslo port meeting Georgette Vikingstad arriving on the ship *Stavangerford*

Brother Arnulf and Odd near Odda, Norway

It was a very practical house in that it had a daylight basement, and two floors were built to accommodate the two families with bedrooms in the attic. Each floor contained a kitchen, dining room, bathroom, living room, and bedroom. I was amazed how the entire house was built so accommodating for families to live with each other. Odd's eldest sister, Aslaugh, and her two sons, Radar and Per Otto, lived on the second floor. Aslaugh's husband, Jacob, died while fishing in the Odda Harbor when German planes bombed the Odda waters during the war. Odd's parents lived on the first floor. I was learning how past events in Norway were influencing its present and future days.

Odda Lutheran Church

Othilie and Peder Valle with their son Odd Valle
in their Norway home in 1950. Odd had returned
from the U.S.A. to Norway.

Georgette in her
Navy Blue Suit

The Peder Valle family was always very cordial to me in their new house. Odd Valle was their pride and joy, the youngest son of ten siblings. He was born on November 23, 1923. The other sons (Heide, Arnulf, Valdemar, and Eilif) grew up and formed a strong Valle relationship working in Odda and surroundings areas. The daughters (Oddny, who died when she was sixteen; Aslaugh; Jennie; Elfrid; and Rut) finished their *gymas* (high school) in Norway. His family all lived, married, and worked in Norway.

As I look back on the event of our wedding, I realize that the role of the bride suddenly became Odd's role. He knew the language, the wedding would be in his Odda Lutheran Church, and the reception would be in the Valle house. In all of these events I could be helpful, but the planning would be have to done by Odd and his mother. As a result the actual wedding at times was surprising to me. Guess who lost weight? Usually it is the bride that loses weight, but in our case it was Odd who had the responsibility and lost weight!

Georgette Vikingstad having lunch at the Frognerseteren Restaurant in Norway in June of 1951.

Georgette Vikingstad viewing Odda Glacier in Norway in 1951.

Odd Valle above Odda Fjord in Norway in 1951

One item that was my responsibility was to get myself dressed and to the church on time. Odd's mother was very kind and considerate to me as a young bride in this new land, but it was natural for me to think of my own parents and my sister. My parents did consider sending Astrid to Norway by airplane. In 1951 it was unusual to travel by plane, so I'm thankful that she did not travel by air. It was not always as safe then as it is now.

Georgette Vikingstad, at the Odda Lutheran Church on June 30, 1951.

A taxi was ordered for me. I was so pleased to have the taxicab driver speak English. As we drove to the church in downtown Odda, he told me he had driven a taxicab in New York. I adjusted my veil slightly as we continued our ride to the church. I had a short veil which suited me fine. Mother Valle and others had suggested that I choose a long veil which was very fashionable in Norway. I was satisfied that the white satin wedding dress with a mini-train I brought with me was not ostentatious. I did not want to be labeled an "ugly American" with an extravagant wedding gown.

As we approached the church, I could see that there were people in the street watching me. The taxicab driver helped me out of the taxi and even straightened my veil. Afterwards Odd's brother Valdemar's wife, Edith Valle, assisted me with my dress as I entered the church.

A classmate of Odd's from the University of Minnesota, Dr. Torgier Togstad (right), was waiting for me to take his arm as we would march up the aisle together. I knew him from our university days, and now he was my substitute for my father, George Vikingstad. As we processed towards the minister, I

could see that Odd and his good friends, Dr. and Mrs. Jordal, were waiting for us at the alter. Odd looked very regal and grand in his tuxedo.

Georgette Vikingstad being assisted by Edith Valle

The church was a very attractive, small country church with a medium-blue paint being the dominant color and trimmings of red and white here and there to give it a Nordic touch. Norwegians ordinarily sit during their wedding ceremonies. Of course, I said I'd stand during the ceremony so everyone in the wedding party had to stand. But I did not know that the ceremony would be so lengthy. It seemed it was at least an hour or more! I did say *"Ja"* at the right moment, so there were no complications. As we marched down the aisle as Dr. and Mrs. Odd Valle, I could see that the balcony was packed with people. It was the custom to have guests only seated in the church proper.

We all returned to the Valle's home where "punch" was served. I was surprised that the punch was Manhattans and martinis on the second floor of the

Valle house. After about an hour and half, we descended the stairs to a beautiful table extended for twenty-some guests using both the dining area and the living room. With wine for everyone, a delicious two-course dinner of roast pork and halibut as entrees was consumed. Speeches were given and telegrams of congratulations with the last to be announced from my parents. I was nearly in tears as the transatlantic communication was read.

Aslaug, Elfrid, Jennie, og Rut sang to us:

To Georgette On wedding day 30 June 1951 Melody: Tiramtira – Tiramtira	Til Georgette På bryllupsdagen den 30 juni 1951 Melodi: Tiramtira – Tiramtir
We are together tonight with gladness, 　Tiramtira Tiramtira, a special celebrations shall occur . . . 　Tiramtira Hurra, for now two hearts in beautiful harmony have said yes to the priest and we said amen. 　Tiramtira, Tiramtira, Tiramtira, Hurra.	Vi er samlet i aften til glede og gam, 　Tiramtira - Tiramtira, en ekstra stor høytid skal feires med bram… 　Tiramtira – Hurra, for nu har to hjerter i skjøn harmoni, for presten gitt jaet og amen sa vi. 　Tiramtira, Tiramtira, Tiramtira, Hurra.
Gone from the lively a young miss, *ti* . . . you flee away with your newly baked man, *ti* . . . . Yes, now you shall work with him and cook potatoes and heat his water. *Ti*	Avsted fra din livlige ungpikestand, ti . . . . du flyver avsted med din nybakte mann, ti . . . . Ja, nu skal du styre og stelle for ham og koke poteter og varme hans vann. Ti . . . .
You mend his socks and repair his trousers, *ti* . . . and light his pipe and open his book, *ti* . . . . And if you really want to make him happy, you make meatballs for dinner every day. *Ti*	Du stopper hans strømper og lapper hans brok, ti . . . og tenner hans pipe og slår opp hans bok, ti . . . . Og vil du nu riktigen gjøre ham glad, hver eneste middag du kjøttkaker har. Ti . . . .
You know the duties of a married man, *ti* . . . . You have to be good to your wife at all times, *ti* . . . . But when she too often asks for money, then you play deaf, and start singing. *Ti*	Dine plikter som ektemann du kjenner til, ti . . . . At du mot din kone skal vært svært snild, ti . . . . Men når hun for ofte for mynt deg vil slå du straks bliver stokkdøv og nynner som så. Ti . . . .

And should the Mrs. one day treat you bad, ti . . . you slam the door and walk away from home, *ti*	*Og skulle madammen en dag blive slem, ti . . . du smeller med døren, går bort fra ditt hjem, ti. . . .*
When all is forgotten and your regrets appear, you shamefully return to your madam. *Ti*	*Når så alt er glemt og du angeren får, du liten og ydmyk til konen din går. Ti . . . .*
Yes, such is the symbol of married life, *ti* . . . from morning to evening a constant strife, *ti*	*Ja slik er symbolet på ekteskaps liv, ti . . . fra morgen til kveld er det stadig et kiv, ti . . . .*
And when you become a mother of the small, you get up in the night and start humming. *Ti*	*Og når du engang bliver mor for de små, du må opp om natten og nynne som så. Ti . . . .*
And as you sit as a bride here now tonight, ti . . . we wish you happiness and good luck on your way, *ti*	*Og når du som brud sitter her nu I kveld, ti . . . vi ønsker deg lykke og hell på din vei, ti . . . .*
And even if you travel so far away from here, please return soon to Odda.	*Og selv om du reiser så langt her i fra, en tur snart tilbake til Odda må ta.*
Tiramtira, Tiramtira, Tiramtira, Hurra	*Tiramtira, Tiramtira, Tiramtira, Hurra.*

We all adjourned to the second floor for dancing to the wonderful American jazz orchestra records that we were all so familiar with. It gave an international flavor for the wedding guests and for Odd and I. At midnight the wedding *kranse kaker* was served with coffee. *Kranse kaker* is made in a series of tins which are in the shape of a cone standing upside down. There is a ginger taste with coconut throughout the pastry. American and Norwegian flags adorned the cake. The Norwegian *blot kaker* was also served. This was a very light sponge cake with whipped cream with different jams in many layers. Delicious! The midnight sun was still providing us with warm light on our desserts, and on to more dancing. It seemed everyone had danced with the bride. At 3 a.m. there was a very special pea soup. Now some guests were saying good night, but Odd was saying that they must stay for breakfast. He sent the guests home in taxicabs.

It was an evening to remember. The midnight sun was just beginning to dim a bit into evening twilight. We spent the night together at the Valle home.

The next day we left for a honeymoon in Germany, courtesy of the Norwegian Army for Odd's work to establish dental records for the Norwegian soldiers at the Hönefoss Army Post.

Georgette Vikingstad Valle

Georgette and Odd on their honeymoon beside a train going to Germany

Georgette Valle and college friend Else Abshaugen stroll in Munich. Else had returned to her home in Munich from the University of Minnesota where they first met.

Georgette and Odd Valle on a boat trip on the Rhine River in Germany on their honeymoon trip

We enjoyed our honeymoon but were happy to return to Norway. 🚢

I was not looking for my dreams to interpret my life, but rather for my life to interpret my dreams.

Susan Sontag

Living in Norway, Back to the U.S., and Our Trip to Washington State

As a married couple, we had discussions about where we were going to live. Odd was thinking about Northern Norway because there were opportunities to begin a dental practice in that area. In Norway, we were assured that we could get an apartment with hot water. This was a major topic of conversation when we went to parties and talked with friends.

One night we were invited to a party where there were several important Norwegian state officials attending. We were introduced to the Minister of Social and Human Affairs, Ase Asland. Somehow she knew about us and Odd's talents and his life ambitions. She very quickly told us that rather than spend his time in Northern Norway, Odd should return to the United States and establish his dental practice in whatever state he had his dental license. We could make more money in the States than in Norway.

However, we were quite impressed with the lifestyles of dentists that we knew in Norway. I was very excited but did not encourage or discourage him in his decision as to where we would live. After all I had come to Norway, so I was game to try living wherever he could make a living. For a moment I thought about my relatives and what a difficult decision it must have been for them to decide to leave their beloved homeland. Perhaps they thought as I did, that wherever we were, we would be happy and have an interesting life.

Odd was working for local dentist Dr. Trygve Eriksen in downtown Odda. We were thankful for this job because it was so convenient for Odd to walk to work. Sometimes I waited in the dental office waiting room while Odd finished up with his patients. Torbjorg Solberg, a Norwegian American now in Seattle, remembers my reading a Norwegian newspaper in Dr. Eriksen's patient waiting room.

As Odd and I returned home after work, we climbed the hillside where the homes all had a view of the beautiful fjord of Odda. The ever-present raging river that tumbles down through the city is a gentle reminder of all the salmon that catapulted through the city into the fjord. The moving waters never sleep, always rushing, and a natural dividing line in the city.

One day as I walked to meet Odd, I was conscious of how politely people greeted me as if they had been introduced to me. As 1 walked down the hillside, I could see neighbors retreating behind their curtains, lest I catch them peaking out to see the walking traffic. I always liked to stop at the bakery to purchase some choice Norse delicacies. This Odda business owner had also loaned Odd money for his dental education, so I wanted him to understand we had appreciation for his benevolent gesture. We gradually and gratefully paid the dental education loans as time progressed.

It was not too long after the Norwegian Minister of Social and Human Affairs had made her suggestions to Odd that he said to me, "I think we should go to the United States to live."

I very quickly agreed and booked us on the new Norwegian ship, the

Odd and Georgette Valle on the *Oslofjord* setting sail on October 4, 1951.

Odd and Georgette Valle on the *Oslofjord* steaming to New York, October 6, 1951

Oslofjord, to sail to New York. After all I had my return ticket. It would take us five days to reach New York Harbor from Oslo.

It was wonderful to travel on a brand new ship, but I could tell this ship was not as seaworthy as the *Stavangerfjord*. The *Oslofjord* was built of metal and did not creak and groan or bend with the water like the wooden *Stavangerfjord* as it sailed the Atlantic. Somehow my stomach was churning in the wrong direction. We both spent one day in our cabin being seasick. I wasn't sick once on the *Stavangerfjord* voyage.

We were happy to see the skyline with the Statue of Liberty beckoning to us as we turned into the harbor of New York City. Odd's Uncle Olaf and Aunt Marie in Philadelphia wanted us to visit them, so our travel plans included a stop. Odd had stayed with them for six months while he made arrangements to attend the University of Minnesota Dental School. He had to make a change of plans as to which school he was to attend. In 1948 when he was traveling on a cargo ship from Norway to the United States, the ship ran out of fuel and had to stop in Bermuda and refuel. Odd therefore arrived late for his entrance into Northwestern University. This late entry also caused Odd to lose his four-year scholarship, which was a huge financial blow to a poor Norwegian student.

Although not at all rich, everyone in Odd's family was very supportive financially to help him in the reversal of his scholarship loss. For that he was very indebted to his whole family. Odd worked at his University of Minnesota cafeteria job plus in the summer doing construction work for the Gehlen Construction Company, a company owned by Norwegians. This St. Paul company had contracts with the University of Minnesota for the construction of buildings.

Olaf and Marie were busy in their retirement years but happy to see Odd again and to meet me. Their neighbor was planning to drive to Minnesota and wanted traveling partners. Within a few days, after saying farewell to Olaf and Marie, we were on our way to Minnesota to the Vikingstad farm in Elmore.

It certainly was exciting to see my parents and my sister again. I had never experienced the severe loneliness that some my friends reported and knew it was always because I could see them when I wanted to visit them. We talked and talked for hours.

My parents had prepared a welcome home party at the Elmore Lutheran Church. I again wore my wedding dress, and Astrid wore a white organdy dress, which fit this occasion. A good Norwegian chicken and mashed potato dinner was prepared and served to over sixty guests by the good ladies of the Ladies Aid Society. We all tasted another wedding cake!

With my parents' help, we borrowed $1,500 to purchase a four-door Nash sedan. It was a two-tone green and had room for our luggage and wedding presents. When it was serviced in the garage, someone forgot to check the transmission oil. To this day I can hear if there is transmission trouble in an automobile! It is the subtle sound of soft metal grinding against each metal part in the transmission. Can you hear the sound? The transmission was ruined. It took some time before we could afford a new car. After all, we had to pay my parents back the $1,500.

*Welcome home party for Odd and Georgette Valle
at the Elmore Lutheran Church*

There was a great deal of financial security for us to travel to Washington State. Before Odd left to return to Norway, he had traveled to Washington with his classmates Allen Watts, D.D.S., and Ted Bloomquist, D.D.S. All three took the dental examinations to set up dental practices in Washington.

We arrived in Washington State on November 17, 1951. In contrast to Minnesota winter weather, Washington State was shimmering in new rain with glistening green trees in the mountain passes as we approached Seattle. Seattle was spectacular with just one tall building, the Smith Tower. Before us was a view of the beautiful, blue Puget Sound with islands under the pink sunset. 🛶

It had long since come to my attention that people of accomplishment rarely sat back and let things happen to them. They went out and happened to things.

Elinor Smith

IRS and Success
The Birth of Peter Odd Valle

As a Norwegian student, Odd Valle graduated from the university with a Doctorate of Dental Surgery degree and was the only student in his class to pay his own tuition. The out-of-state student tuition at that time was $536 a quarter. The other students in his class were armed-service-related students who received G.I. benefits to pay for their classes. We, as a married couple, were happy to pay this tuition and did pay this debt off for several years.

Odd Valle, D.D.S., University of Minnesota graduate

At the end of graduation, the picture of Odd Valle, D.D.S., appeared in *Life* magazine with other students from all over the United States, earmarking these students as most likely to succeed. Since Odd left for Norway immediately after graduation, he was unaware that his photo was published in *Life* magazine. Others in the United States, however, did take note of the picture.

As we arrived in Washington, after several inquiries, we found an apartment which rented for eighty dollars at the Burien Garden Apartments. Orange crates made good bedside tables. Our trunk made a good table. One loaned chair from Odd's cousin, Ann Larsen, was gloriously comfortable. All in all, when Christmas came, we shoved all our furniture in the corner and brought in a Christmas tree. Everyone thought we had really settled into our apartment.

Family Gathering of Odd Valle's cousins
From to top to right around circle: Georgette
and Odd Valle, Julian and Frances Fullen, Edith
Christofferson, Charlene Fullen, Dale
Christofferson, Ann Larson, and Julie Fullen

Odd had his dental license so he could immediately seek employment. After a citywide search, he found a job with Dr. Homer Lockert in the White Center area, where he worked for three months.

We rented a small house in the Highline business area, which we redecorated into our first dental office. We discovered that a Highline dentist, Dr. Dodds, was retiring from this same dental office. He had dental equipment for sale that seemed very reasonable. We made some new purchases—two beautiful, tan naugahyde leather chairs, a maple table, and a lamp. We wallpapered with a beautiful rose-and-green-designed paper. A dark green rug made the waiting room very presentable. Meanwhile, Odd painted the rest of the dental office in a somber rose color. I must admit that I thought the colors were a bit bright for a dental office, but I was not about to suggest anything different at the time. An old-fashioned, black leather dental chair, which could be pumped up to the correct position, made the dental office complete.

Since I could not find employment as an occupational therapist, I was to be Dr. Valle's assistant, bookkeeper, appointment secretary, and janitor. I'll never forget the first day the office was open. Our first patient was a mother with her two small boys. While their mother was in the dental chair, the two boys remained in the waiting room. They did not seem to like the selection of children's books that I had purchased and proceeded to climb up and over onto the new furniture. I caught the lamp as it almost toppled to the floor. Soon it was their turn to have their examinations. Thankfully, the mother was now in charge, but she didn't have a great deal of discipline, so I watched apprehensively.

Our second patient could not stand the sight of blood. He was to have both upper and lower dentures made, which involved several tooth extractions. As a competent health professional, Odd checked with the patient's physician about his physical condition: blood pressure, any contraindications for this kind of surgery, and other medical factors related to the patient. The patient received a clean bill of health.

Although I prepared myself for surgery, I had never seen so much bleeding in my life! The only reason I did not faint was because I was needed to assist (in the very strongest sense of the word). We instructed the patient about what he should do after this surgery, and the Valle taxi took him home. To assist in his recovery, I continued to pick him up for his office visits and return him back to his home. In the end he was a very happy patient, enjoyed his dentures, and was able to smile and bite into an apple again.

We understood from Highline statistics that the Valle dentist office was the third dental office located in the Highline area. The patients poured into the office. For at least three months, we worked Monday through Saturday from 8 a.m. to 9 p.m.! We were very busy and happy to have so many patients. Soon we were able to relax when our patients could wait for about three weeks for an appointment. At the very beginning, however, patients seemed desperate for an immediate appointment. Perhaps, the fact that there were only two dentists practicing in the area before we arrived brought about this heavy dental patient activity.

Tax filing time was approaching. It seemed a good idea to hire an accountant, since I did not possess expertise in this area, nor did Odd. It was not long before we had a visit from the IRS wanting to know exactly what our income was and what our expenses were in detail. I could not remember my father ever having had a visitor from the IRS. I thought this visit was rather unusual, but then perhaps it was because Odd had applied for his citizenship or the fact that he was a new immigrant. Life went on as usual, and to our relief we had no mistakes in our accounting records according to the IRS.

The dental practice progressed, and we began to take time off for lunch. It was enjoyable going to the Highline Pharmacy to have Lois Hutton make her wonderful sandwiches. Ed Hutton, the pharmacist, was sometimes needed for prescriptions, so they were handy neighbors.

The Seattle Trust Bank and Savings was located on the corner of Ambaum and 152nd Streets where Hollis Ramsey, the president of bank, arranged for our first big loan. Our friendships continued to grow. Joe Owens had a realty office nearby. He was a friendly and aggressive realtor who always talked to me about the current political scene. He knew I was interested in the politics of the day, month, or year!

The second tax year arrived, and we enlisted Ken Christiansen as our accountant again. I was pregnant and was ready to quit the dental office due to nausea, but continued on because of my assisting responsibilities. Finally, after five months, the nausea ended. But again, we were being investigated by the IRS. Now they were being friendly like they were long, lost relatives looking over our shoulders. Whatever their reason for invading our business, we were being cooperative. We had what we thought were competent records, so there was a great deal of confidence about the audit since we were honest and our accountants were very professional. Our tax statements were eventually accepted by the IRS.

It was now time to quit the dental assistant role and become a real live mother. A month was enough time to get ready for the baby. I had some nice kimonos that I had hand-embroidered as I was crossing the ocean to Norway for my wedding. Some people thought this a little strange, but when you read about the rest of my life, you will think this is perfectly natural for me. It was so much fun to have a whole month to prepare the way for our baby to arrive. It seemed shear joy to go buy cotton diapers, a crib, and all of the little items for someone so small. Bell's store in the Highline district got to know me very well. The baby did not arrive quite on the predicted time. He was two weeks late, like many other first-time babies.

We had chosen Doctor's Hospital for the delivery because of the statistically "clean" nursery at the hospital. Hospitals at that time were having trouble with the sanitary conditions of their nurseries, and Doctors' Hospital was said to be the best. After twenty-four hours of labor, 9-pound-7-ounce Peter Odd Valle arrived. I was very happy to see him. He was a rambunctious baby who was anxious to come into this world, so he kicked a great deal. To our delight, he was a very healthy baby. I stayed in the hospital a total of six days before I was able to go home. Peter was a content baby. He was breast fed for eight months, gained weight, and prospered.

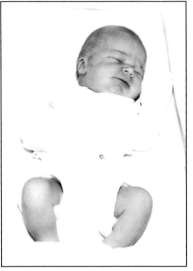

Peter Odd Valle was born August 17, 1953, at Doctors' Hospital in Seattle.

On May 13, 1954, we moved into our new home in Normandy Park. We came into the

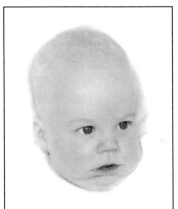

Peter Odd Valle at age three months

house with the baby crib all ready for occupancy. With brand new wood shavings on the floor, I put Peter into his crib where he finished his nap in his new home.

Another tax date had come and gone with the friendly IRS people emerging. I was amazed how patient Odd was. Of course, he had never lived in the United States without these friendly visits, so how would he know anything different. All along nothing was wrong with our tax statements.

The fourth time we were audited by the IRS was in 1956. We asked why they were so consistent in auditing us. Oh, hadn't anyone told us? The IRS was very noncommittal at this point. We never found out.

Caption to picture that appeared in the Sunday, May 13, 1956, edition of *The Seattle Times:*

"Mrs. Valle brought paintings to a meeting for discussion. A housewife and mother of two children, she was formerly an occupational therapist, which included teaching art. Now she takes lessons with her husband and finds it easier to inspire others than to do it herself.

Odd's parents, Peder Lindström and Othilie Valle, and Georgette, holding son Peter, are visiting Washington's Grand Coulee Dam in 1954.

This trip was a vacation from our new home in Normandy Park after I finished sewing 34 sheets together for living room drapes

They asked for extra data figures, and Odd said those figures were at the office. Both of the IRS agents said Odd could not retrieve them alone. One of the agents stayed with me, and the other agent accompanied Odd to the office. It took two days of auditing, and only a minor flaw was discovered in one of the documents costing us $36. Meanwhile, in the West Seattle Dental Office of Dr. Allen Watts, the IRS spent three days auditing the financial records of that office to the tune of $100. That was the last time that Dr. Watts was audited. For us, however, the IRS continued to monitor the Valle Dental office.

As the IRS continued to visit us Peter was growing up in our Normandy Park home. We found friends for him. Bill Schneebeli lived on an adjoining lot with no street in between our houses. His mother Joy Schneebeli, and I discovered this convenience. Peter and Bill were very compatible and became great friends.

Brian Harrison and Peter Sutherland joined Bill and Peter as they crossed Marine View Drive to go to Marvista Elementary School. They all played baseball together. When our lot became too small, then the boys moved to the Jack property across the street from our home to play their favorite game.

Peter and his friends enjoyed the Normandy Park Swim Club.

Peter was always an obedient child who arrived home after school for his "after school snack." One day, however, Peter was late and nowhere to be found. I called the Normandy Park police! Later he was found at a new friend's home on 200th Avenue in Normandy Park. Peter was strongly advised in the police presence that his mother should know where he was all the times. He was impressed that I called the police! From that moment on Peter was always very obedient. At about age ten to eleven years old, he would mow the lawn whenever I asked him. The task of mowing was a double job because we had two lots to mow.

Like all young boys Peter's musical desire was to play the drums. Eventually he chose the trombone to everyone's relief. We enjoyed his concerts at Olympia Junior High and later at Mount Rainier High school. I enjoyed his playing with the University of Washington band more than the football games.

Friends that he met along his school path, like Don Trotter, have remained friends at the University of Washington and in Peter's life today. Peter seemed to have grown up with all these IRS agents.

Odd's niece, Else Leona McClimans, and Johan Olav Bjerke on their May 17, 1997, wedding day. Odd and Georgette visited them in Maputo, Mozambique.

Odd's nieces and nephew, the McClimans children in Norway

In 1999 we decided to travel to Africa. Odd had a niece, Else Leona McClimans Bjerke, who was working as a young attorney for the United Nations on a gender equity program, and her husband, Johan Bjerke, was doing energy conservation and energy regeneration for the Mozambian government. They were living in a former ambassador's home with space for us should we want to travel to Mozambique.

We decided to fly to the capital on British Airlines. We arrived late, which caused some consternation, but we were repaid by receiving a free trip on British Air one year later. It was during that trip, while on a Nile tour in Egypt, that a gentleman approached Odd on a ferry boat and said to him, "I know you."

"You do?" Odd answered.

"Yes, your name is Odd Valle, and you are a dentist. I followed you for many years for the IRS."

"Really," Odd answered.

And the gentleman said it all began with his picture appearing in *Life* magazine!

Left: Statue of Ramses II in front of the Temple of Lexor situated very close to the Nile River

Below: Giza Pyriamids in Egypt

119

Peter Valle Gets New Baby Sister, Christine Georgette Valle

As a mother of Peter who was now twenty-three months, I thought it would be great to have a girl. I looked forward to finding the dresses and bonnets for a girl just in case a girl happened to come along.

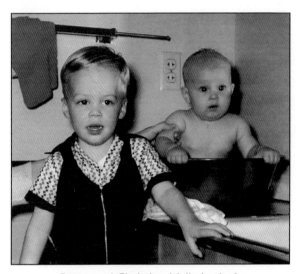

Peter and Christine Valle in their Normandy Park home. Peter is about two and a half years old with Christine about five months old.

It was almost as if all the Normandy Park mothers around me thought that it is time to have a baby girl now that they had a boy. Mothers listened to other mothers' tales that all said the second child would arrive in a very short time. Sure enough, Christine only took four short hours to be born, and she arrived on Monday, July 21, 1955. After I had examined her to see that she was equipped with all her fingers and toes, I remarked to Odd, as her dentist, he would have to correct her overbite. Wrapped in a pink blanket at 7 pounds 6 ounces, she looked pretty good to me.

In 1955 other mothers in the neighborhood had girls, and Christine's new friends were Joanne Schneebeli, Lynn Beardslee, Sherry Wold, and Susan Petterson.

We thought we were very fortunate to have our own house with bedrooms for each of the children. The house designed by Ralph Miller was beautiful with varnished wood beams in the ceiling, oak floors, and a view of the Puget Sound out of our bedroom, the kitchen, and the living room windows. We used the architect's drawings as wallpaper.

I could not always satisfy Christine with enough milk. I had nursed Peter for eight months, and so expected to do the same for Christine. On one occasion, as I was sleepily nursing Christine at 6 a.m., she bit me. I decided she really was not enjoying nursing. At the same time I thought she was a bit colicky. Dr. Smith said to put all her food in her milk bottle and crack the nipple. She seemed more satisfied, but she gained a lot of weight. Christine cried during much of the day but, thank goodness, she did sleep all night long. Peter seemed to be content with his new sister, always able to find a new toy to amuse her.

One day we went to Highline Jaffe's Shoe Store to buy Peter some shoes. It was important to me that Peter's shoes fit correctly. In those days the store had an X-ray machine to see that the shoes fit. I could now see that the shoes fit Peter. Within an instant, I missed Christine. Where could she be? She could not be far. She was only two years old. I found her busy outside the store directing traffic on 152nd Street. The shoe store was not too far from Odd's office, so we took her for a short stroll to see her father.

We located a kindergarten for Christine where she could be with her friends, who seemed to provide stability in that first bit of education. The class was full of talkative, energetic, and sweet young girls. Christine was a great actress and paraded her talents for her friends.

It seemed we could have had a kindergarten in our own yard. Odd put up a swing set. There was sufficient concrete so tricycles could coast over a small bridge and glide along a "playway" path. The children were remarkably accident free. I was ready for any catastrophe, but all my Band-Aids went unused.

Like her brother, Christine enjoyed the Normandy Park Swim Club and took home a trophy or two.

Christine loved ballet and enrolled in Delphin McDade's class with her other friends. Ballet classes taught her grace, agility, and gave her confidence in her body. However, she grew tall very quickly and so grew beyond her ballet chorus line roles. She quit her classes in the eighth grade. Mrs. McDade was so disappointed and so was I.

Christine had a knack for getting her picture in the newspapers, as we see next:

Tuesday, November 5, 1963   **The Seattle Times** B

Little Ballerinas Seek Spotlight

HOPEFULS: Three little ballerinas prepared for their tryout yesterday. They were among 100 youngsters who vied for the 30 dancing roles for children in "Ballet School" to be presented Friday night and Saturday afternoon by the Stars of the Bolshoi Ballet. From left — Lynn Murata, 7; Charmel Puckett, 8; and Christine Valle, 8. Those selected began intensive training today.

POLITICAL JOURNEY

Nobody can make you feel inferior without your consent.

Eleanor Roosevelt
(I approve this message. H. H. Humphrey— author's note)

1960 Presidential Election
Humphrey/Stevenson/Kennedy

Hubert Humphrey for President

Presidential campaigning is probably the most exciting form of political campaigning in which a person can be involved. It all began with Hubert Humphrey and his announcement that he was running for President in the 1960 presidential election. He was the Democratic Farmer Labor (DFL) party candidate and senior senator from Minnesota, the land of ten thousand lakes.

My father, George Vikingstad, was a DFL party leader in southern Minnesota for many years. It seemed the Vikingstad family had endured many a financial hardship, but being part of a presidential campaign didn't seem to be difficult for one of your own, Senator Hubert Humphrey. My father and mother gladly donated money to support Hubert Humphrey's presidential campaign. At least they were at the point of retirement, so their income was stable and comfortable in contrast to past depression years.

There seemed to be such a sense of exhilaration to be able to support and work for a Minnesota DFL'r while living in the state of Washington. It was not long before I was a committed part of the Humphrey presidential campaign in its early stages. I knew Luke Graham, the Washington Chair of the Democratic Party.

Senator Hubert Humphrey being greeted by Christine Valle.
Georgette and Peter Valle are on the far left.

In this picture I was at a "Humphrey for President Rally" with my children, Peter and Christine. Christine climbed up on a two-by-four sawhorse to tell Senator Humphrey that her mother was Georgette Valle.

Dinner at the Valles for Senator Humphrey

What better way to rally the Democratic group behind Hubert Humphrey than to host a dinner party for the important political people in the state of Washington? I had tried out the Minnesota chicken and gravy on mashed potatoes recipe from my mother's church cookbook and served it along with assorted appetizers for the Seattle Dental Wives with success at a Monday luncheon. I doubled the recipe on Saturday night for the politicians. If the recipe was good enough for the Minnesota Lutherans, it certainly should be satisfactory for the Washington State Democratic politicians.

There were about fifty to sixty important Democratic Party officials gathered in our home. Humphrey's legislative record was one I was comfortable with, both on international and domestic issues. I was beginning to choose my candidates for President based on those who encompassed peace agendas. Senator Humphrey and his aides arrived at our home after a long plane ride from Juneau, Alaska, and Salt Lake City, Utah. They were hungry and thirsty. We welcomed them with appetizers and Canadian Club whiskey, Humphrey's favorite. I was carrying our young daughter, Christine, on my right hip because she had a sore throat. Senator Humphrey was quick to inquire about her health and within moments had dispatched one of his aides to the nearest pharmacy to get the best cough medicine in the world—Cheracol. After a couple of teaspoons of Cheracol, Christine fell fast asleep and never awoke with a cough during the whole night.

Senator Humphrey could never resist talking a little longer than other politicians did, and he was true to form that evening. Virginia Burnside, one of Washington State's young Democratic critics, wanted him to stop talking, and I wanted him to have dessert.

This meeting was an important part of Washington State's presidential campaign because earlier in the evening, Hugh Sidey, one of the nation's best presidential biographers, asked if he could put his typewriter on our fireplace extension to begin his description of Humphrey's presidential campaign.

I hurriedly said, "Yes, of course." It seems remarkable to recall and to cherish the memories of all the reporters and media personnel that I have come into contact with over the years. I often think in very enduring terms of the many hours that are spent recording an event only to have it rejected by the superior of that lone reporter.

The Humphrey Campaign Defeated in West Virginia

The Humphrey campaign seemed to be going well throughout the nation until West Virginia and its "Appalachian poverty-ridden folk" came into national view. The West Virginia campaign with its poverty and lack of jobs was a fertile primary political battle. Humphrey's progressive legislation on employment, the eradication of poverty, and health care for the poor was an ideal legislative record for West Virginia. But the campaign of Hubert Humphrey was no match for the Kennedy wealth, which was very evident in that campaign. Senator Humphrey lost that presidential primary in West Virginia to Senator Kennedy. It was heartbreaking to watch Senator Humphrey during the evening news and see that somehow his campaign was not able to compete with the glamour and wealth of the Kennedy family. It was shortly after this West Virginia campaign that Senator Humphrey withdrew his name from the 1960 presidential campaign.

It was very difficult to admit to friends that I had no presidential candidate to support now that Senator Humphrey had withdrawn from the race. In reality, the next best option I had was to return to my perennial favorite, Adlai Stevenson, who was considered the favorite of many of those who supported Senator Humphrey.

Meeting Jackie at the Kennedy Presidential Campaign Luncheon

Senator Kennedy's presidential campaign had finally reached Washington State in the early spring of 1960. He was a featured speaker at a Washington State Democratic luncheon at the Mayflower Hotel in Seattle. Senator Kennedy was in his prime that day. He was an affable speaker, always articulate, with that Irish sense of humor. There was the feeling that he would become a very popular candidate.

I was seated at the head table when Jeannette Williams, King County Democratic Chair, came over to me and asked if I would accompany Jacqueline Kennedy to the bathroom. Of course, I agreed and immediately asked the desk clerk in the hotel lobby where the nearest restroom was located. As Jackie Kennedy and I slowly climbed three flights of stairs, I prayed all the way in Norwegian fashion that the bathroom was clean. Jackie was not very talkative and I realized she might be still suffering from morning sickness.

1960 Democratic National Convention

Miracles do happen. When Russ Carter (my neighbor Joy Schneebeli's brother) offered me a ride to California to attend the Democratic National Convention, I immediately accepted. A hotel room in Los Angeles and a baby sitter to stay with the children were obtained easily, much to my surprise. Some students moved out of a hotel and gave me their room and our regular baby sitter accepted the baby sitting job.

At the National Democratic Convention, I was an alternate delegate. I could attend all the meetings but could not officially speak or vote in the Washington State Democratic meetings unless a delegate was absent.

The considering of the rules and regulations was time-consuming and arduous for Chair Luke Graham. The Washington State Democratic delegation was the most evenly divided in the nation, with the result that their half of a vote ended up being cast for Albert Rosellini! Delegates declared that they had come this far and would cast their vote for their favorite candidate. As a result, Washington State lost its chance to be the state to declare Senator John F.

Kennedy the victorious nominee at the 1960 Democratic Presidential Convention. Even I could see the handwriting on the political wall. As a result, Hawaii, which had declined to announce when called upon alphabetically, became the state to make John F. Kennedy the presidential nominee.

I received an invitation from Senator Humphrey to attend a reception at the famous Coconut Grove Night Club in Los Angeles. It was quite an evening watching the political stars being wowed by show business stars! Tony Bennett sang, with the assistance of some beautiful young starlets. Former First Lady Eleanor Roosevelt signed autographs for many enthusiastic fans. I danced with Georgie Jessel who hopped around the dance floor in his enthusiastic personal style.

Marilyn Monroe, in her breathy, sexy style, sang *Happy Birthday* to the next President of the United States. It occurred to me that she did not have a very powerful voice, so she must have other attributes that gave her that honor. Of course, the crowd went wild. As I watched the crowd's frenzy over Marilyn Monroe's *Happy Birthday Senator Kennedy*, I caught Luke Graham's sleeve and told him I wanted to run for the Legislature.

Luke looked at me and said, "Why don't you become Washington Voter Registration Chair?" Isn't that how women have always been considered—as assistants to power? But I needed to prepare myself to make my run for the Legislature.

I looked on child rearing not only as a work of love and duty, but as a profession that was fully as interesting and challenging as any honorable profession in the world and one that demanded the best that I could bring to it.

Rose Kennedy

The Kennedy Era and Voter Registration

I could not gather enthusiasm for the Kennedy/Johnson slate for the Presidential ticket. I had to agree with people in the Northwest that we really didn't know the Kennedys well. As I walked through the streets of Los Angeles, I told myself that I should not have shed so many tears over the Stevenson loss. My eyes were smarting in the Los Angeles air. Later, I realized that it was the Los Angeles smog which was irritating my eyes.

Voter Registration Road Trip

It took me three days to make up my mind, and then I called Luke Graham to accept his offer to chair the Washington Voter Registration Drive. I found there was plenty of work to be done. Arrangements for a sixteen-city visit had been set up by the Washington State Democratic Party. Meetings had been arranged with local Democratic officials in each city. Meals for my family were made ahead of

time, so it was easy for the baby sitter to take over the Valle household. The children liked being with the baby sitter and were happy as long as they were fed and read that special story at night. My expenses were to be paid for, but I can't remember if baby sitting expenses were included in my stipend. I do remember the "Register and Vote" sign that I made for our black-and-white Chrysler.

With all my preparation completed, I set forth on my Washington Voter Registration trip to register 100,000 new voters. I could leave no potential voter out whether Democrat, Republican or Independent. But it was known that the majority of those unregistered voters were potential Democrats. The Washington League of Women Voters, the Parent Teacher Association, and the Washington Labor Unions were all to be contacted, and I was to publicize our meetings. The matter of publicity was a little tricky, because it did become known that the Washington State Democratic party was the instigator of these events. It soon became known that this was one of the strategies the Kennedys would use to win the Presidential race for the White House. All of my home planning was done as I began to phase in the absent days on the calendar. Now I could relax and watch the national scene.

Thank goodness the Kennedys and the Johnsons were good at garnering publicity. Both also seemed to be serious at the right moment. John Kennedy appeared to have a sense of humor which suited the nation. Jackie Kennedy's sense of fashion with a distinctive new style seemed a little unusual for Democrats, but that, too, seemed to energize the Democratic Party. Lyndon Johnson fit in well with his Southern drawl.

As the delegation neared the city, I was to call the appropriate city's leading newspapers. A picture story usually resulted.

As a relatively young person in politics, I was welcomed to these events as if I were some sort of celebrity. Admittedly, I was very enthusiastic and sometimes a little naive. To some party politicians this was a welcome quality. I kept true to my schedule and didn't receive any speeding tickets. I always checked in at home. When I received the report that all was going well, then I could relax and get a good night's sleep.

John, Ted, and Bobby Kennedy Campaigning in Washington

All of the Kennedy brothers visited the state of Washington. Both the Democratic State Party Chair Luke Graham and the Democratic King County Chair Jeanette Williams called me to come to the airport and meet and greet Bobby and Teddy Kennedy. I was asked to explain the Washington State Primary Voter system to them. I was from Minnesota. I got busy and studied the Primary Voter System. I did discover was that the Washington State Grange was responsible for writing the present system into an initiative, supporting and passing it with money and people power.

Luke Graham and Jeanette Williams, along with Bobby Kennedy, were in the back seat of the car. I was in the front seat, between Teddy Kennedy and the driver of the car, but to my surprise not a single question was raised about the Primary Voter System in the state of Washington. We talked about every subject —the weather, the Kennedy campaign and our families, but not the Primary Voter System.

The Washington Armory was full. Tin cans were passed to collect money for the Kennedy campaign. Kennedy's message was well received in the Boeing City of Seattle. The media was concentrating on John Kennedy's charisma, and there was an added feature about his whole being, that of projecting a sexual element into the candidate's persona.

Voter Registration and the Presidential Campaigning Continues

The Democratic Party was now concentrating on voter registration in mostly the Democratic King County, the state's largest county. We would need to register at least 33,000 new voters in King County. I counted on my friends in the League of Women Voters and the Labor Unions to register many voters. We worked long, late hours. We did not have the comfort of knowing whether we were registering Democrats or Republicans, as was the case in some states.

The campaign was heating up with the primaries approaching when I received a call one morning from Democratic headquarters to go to Boeing Field. Having just washed my hair, I had to leave the house with wet hair. I was dressed in my bright red suit, and five-year-old Christine was in the backseat of our black-and-white Chrysler. She was not quite as excited to see Senator John Kennedy as she had been to see Senator Hubert Humphrey.

On September 6, 1960, John F. Kennedy landed at Boeing Field in Seattle. Luke Graham and other dignitaries were all there to greet the candidate. Senator Kennedy walked up to our black-and-white Chrysler and said, "Well, how is it going?"

I said, "Fine," and stood proudly beside the beautiful sign that still said "Register and Vote." Meanwhile, in the car, Christine ducked as the cameraman shot a few pictures of Luke Graham, Senator John Kennedy, and me.

Senator Kennedy won Washington State in the November election. Newly-registered voters totaled over 100,000! A majority had been contacted by our Democratic workers who were now celebrating— not to feel their exhaustion until later.

But there was more to come!

Georgette Valle greets Senator John F. Kennedy as Washington Voter Registration Chair. Christine is ducking in the front seat of the Valle car.

So, let us not be blind to our differences—but let us also direct attention to our common interests and to the means by which those differences can be resolved.

John F. Kennedy

The Kennedy Inauguration

In December of 1960 a very large envelope arrived for me that turned out to be an official invitation to the 1961 Kennedy Presidential Inauguration in January of 1961. Odd thought it would be a great opportunity for me to meet and greet lots of Democrats from all over the nation—but without him. I found out his schedule of patients for December and called. They were very supportive of my cause. His patients quickly convinced him that he should accompany me to the inaugural festivities.

Odd said we could go to Washington, D.C. Now I could purchase our airline tickets, arrange for a baby sitter, and do some shopping for the trip. It was a joy to be able to work for months for the Democratic Party and finally realize that, indeed, I could enjoy such a momentous occasion as the inauguration of a President.

I selected Nordstrom's as the store to purchase the gown that I would wear to the Inaugural Ball. It was probably pure fantasy to think that this gown would be the only one like it at this event. I did surmise that even paying more for a beautiful gown would not ensure that I would be the only one there dressed in a deep magenta gown with spaghetti straps. It was really a very lovely dress for only $49.95 and was what we could afford. I hoped that everyone else had more money to spend on their gowns than I did. In the eventuality that I saw myself too many times, I knew what I would do. I would simply walk across the floor and compliment the lady on what a beautiful gown she was wearing. Of course, I hoped I would not have to repeat that process too many times during the course of the evening.

There was one outfit that I knew would not be duplicated. This was a suit made from blue serge wool, which was crafted into a beautiful skirt and a three-quarters length coat with a nice stand-up collar. There was not adequate material available for a suit for Odd, so I decided to use it for myself. It was a great outfit, as it did not wrinkle and beautifully held its shape. We were not going to be in Washington, D.C., for very long, so I didn't even consider taking warm clothing with me.

I informed my long-lost cousin, Leslie Tenold, and his wife, Jonnie, of Arlington, Virginia, that we would be coming to their house for a few days in January. This was a wonderful opportunity for me to become reacquainted with my mother's nephew, Leslie Tenold.

My uncle Clarence, Leslie's father, was involved in a divorce with Leslie's mother, Rosalyn. As a result of family friction, Leslie and I did not see each other much during our

This is Leslie "Les" Tenold. Look at his leather gloves and shoes.

Leslie Tenold with his scooter

childhood years. In any case, Leslie resembled his father, and I totally enjoyed meeting him again. It was fun to renew acquaintances and have the opportunity to meet his wife, Jonnie, who was a very cordial hostess.

The Tenolds happened to live beside the Captain of the Guards of the House of Representatives. This proved to be a big asset in obtaining a ride to the Capitol for a tea being held at the National Art Museum with various famous politicians' wives in attendance. Odd and I arrived at the National Art Museum. I delayed my exit from the taxi until Odd focused his 16-millimeter camera on the cab and filmed my entrance into the Museum. Odd was pursued by several young ladies who wanted to know who he was photographing. He probably said, "Oh, she's just my wife."

It was so exciting to meet Muriel Humphrey, Senator Hubert Humphrey's wife. That evening we were invited to a party at the Shoreham Hotel hosted by Senator Warren G. Magnuson. Actress Tippy Hedron, wife of NBC News Commentator Chet Huntley, was entertaining at the Shoreham that particular evening. It was a wonderful time of meeting new friends and greeting old ones. As the evening wore on, the outside weather grew very threatening. A blustery snowstorm was brewing, so Senator Magnuson called upon an Army sergeant to give us a ride back to the Tenold home. We were thankful to be able to crawl into a warm bed when we arrived back in Arlington.

At 6 a.m. the next morning, we again caught a ride to the Capitol with the Captain of the Guards. This was also an important and busy day for the Captain.

John F. Kennedy in his top hat

Because he was accompanying us, we were able to enter the Capitol which was open to the public only by invitation. It was freezing cold outside. We found our seats which were front and center, but some distance from the festive Inaugural stands built for the swearing in of the President.

Odd took movies. I flipped the snow away from my seat and put newspapers down to protect my elegant Deleso Deb pumps from the snow. I introduced myself to a man who was brimming full of Massachusetts' pride because a native son was being sworn in as President of the nation. By the time the ceremonies were underway, I had consumed only one doughnut from the Tenold residence in Arlington, Virginia,
along with three swigs of bourbon for breakfast, the hospitality offered from the folks from Massachusetts!

Meanwhile, Odd came back to his seat because the Bollix camera he was using became frozen. In the midst of the festivities, with Marion Anderson having sung, Robert Frost began to read his poem, and then discovered the cold fogged up his glasses and prevented him from seeing the written version, so he recited another poem from memory. As the new President approached the podium, smoke broke forth. The fire was soon put out by Army personnel. We will always remember the Kennedy inaugural speech for its "ask not" message:

> And so, my fellow Americans: Ask not what your country can do for you—ask what you can do for your country. My fellow citizens of the world: ask not what America will do for you, but what together we can do for the freedom of man.

> —John F. Kennedy, *Inaugural Address, January 20, 1961*

We watched the swearing-in ceremony with a sobering respect for the toil, time, and tenacity of the presidential campaign that had preceded the moment. It was all real because we were there.

Somehow we were able to wrangle an invitation to a luncheon inside the Capitol hosted by the Speaker of House, Sam Rayburn. Could we ask for anything more? I am remembering that I was in some sort of "political heaven." I'm sure that people from Texas would agree with me.

Of immediate concern to us was getting back to my cousin's house so that we could have time to get dressed and prepare for the Inaugural Ball. I was eager to try on the new white kid gloves that I had purchased in Washington, D.C., for $27.50. I thought they were a terrific addition to my ball gown.

After arriving at the Armory, along with hundreds of other Democrats to attend the gala occasion, we enjoyed dancing to the music of the magnificent Paul Whiteman orchestra beside celebrities from the political world who didn't know my husband or me, but I kept nodding to them anyway. And, yes, I only saw the ball gown I had chosen once during the evening and immediately approached the lady and congratulated her on her unique gown. She concurred.

All of a sudden the orchestra stage spun around and the United States Marine Band was center stage in front of us with their beautiful uniforms and instruments. They announced the entrance of President John F. Kennedy, his wife, Jackie, and their respective families. *Hail to the Chief* was played! The Kennedys looked like the grand family they were with a smiling Jackie in a beautiful white sleeveless gown with sequins placed appropriately on her slim, beautiful silhouette.

Her long white gloves added to her beauty. The applause was polite, but enthusiastic. It did seem as if we were entering a new, magical era of Camelot.

The day after the Inaugural Ball we bade farewell to my newly-found cousin and his wife. We vowed we would find time to see more of each other. Our future contacts consisted of their visit to our Washington home and both of us keeping in touch via Christmas cards. We returned to the state of Washington with a new-found hope and fresh vision for the nation. Our trip made the *Highline Times:*

Strictly for Women

BY LETTIE GUDMESTAD

Highline Times Women's Editor

CH. 2-0100

THE KENNEDY INAUGURATION may be just another page in the history books now, but for at least three Highliners, the recent festivities in Washington, D.C., will be a memory bright for a lifetime.

The three localites, Dr. and Mrs. Odd Valle and Mrs. Murray Gamrath, were back in town last week, with many a glowing tale to tell of the big events in the nation's capitol.

The Valles arrived in Washington early in inauguration week, in time to attend many of the glamorous affairs. Georgette remembers with special pleasure the lovely tea given for Democratic women in the National Art Gallery.

The high point of the trip for all of them was, of course, the inauguration on Friday. "We sat with our feet in the snow and our heads in the clouds," Georgette reports.

After the ceremonies, the Valles lunched at the Capitol with House Speaker Sam Rayburn's staff, and that evening attended the Inaugural Ball at the National Armory.

Georgette's ball gown was a simple design in deep-pink faille. With it, she wore pearls and a capelet of Norwegian blue fox.

"Frankie" Gamrath's choice for the ball was a bouffant formal gown of white satin, bodice banded with folds of red satin which fell into the skirt panel. Her stole was of autumn haze mink.

For these ladies, the inaugural week was the culmination of months of hard work in behalf of their party, Georgette as state voter registration chairman, and "Frankie" as president of the Seventh Congressional District of the Democratic Federated Women's Club.

Mrs. G. was also a delegate to the national convention in Los Angeles in July, and has just been elected Democratic State Committeewoman for King County.

The Valles, by the way, stopped off for visits in Philadelphia and Minneapolis on their way back to Seattle.

*   *   *

Beginning New Lives

Returning to normal after the 1961 Kennedy Inauguration presented challenges and changes in our own lives. We were delighted to hear the baby sitter stories from Peter, who was eight years old, and from Christine, six. Both the children were old enough to help the Mrs. Perry find the breakfast food, and the neighbors had volunteered to acquire any needed groceries. They had watched television but didn't see us in the crowds or in the Washington, D.C., parade.

All seemed well. Our baby sitter, Mrs. Perry, and her son, a pilot for Northwest Airlines, were Odd's dental patients. The kids loved her like a grandmother. Her son and Odd were members of a morning Toastmaster Club.

There were plenty of the usual household duties for me to do. Odd had agreed I could run for office while in the car in a downtown Seattle traffic jam. It was only $12 to file for State Representative.

Since I had made up my mind that I would run for State Representative in the 31st District, there was plenty of groundwork to lay. It was more important than ever to attend the League of Women Voters, the Garden Club, and the 31st Precinct meetings. I didn't think I had made very much of an impact on these meetings as far as demonstrating my political skills, so there was a lot to be accomplished. I knew I had a lot to learn about the political process of running for state representative. There were no Democratic Party workshops to teach me how to run for political office. I would have to teach myself!

But for now I could relax a bit, I thought, as I rushed to do the laundry.

My First Campaign in 1962 for 31st District Representative in the House of Representatives

In the 1962 campaign, I ran for state representative because I thought I could do a better job at representing the 31st District than some of the people who were elected as state representatives. There did not seem to be anyone who had leadership qualities. Senator Andy Hess was in my estimation a public servant of integrity and leadership. I'll have to admit that I had a tremendous "liking" for politics both state and national.

Choosing a Campaign Chair and Executive Secretary-Treasurer was very important, and I set out to accomplish that task immediately. Florence McMullin was a Democratic colleague and a League of Women Voter who was smart, had a good sense of humor, and dependable. She had a wonderful winning personality that allowed her to influence people with her ideas and quick wit. Her husband, Dick, was also friendly and supportive. I knew both of them would be a positive asset to my campaign.

I appeared before the Seattle Municipal League and received a "Superior" rating. The Municipal League was and is a private organization that tends to be Republican and sometimes those ratings are used against you in a race. They were at that time a little anti-Democrat, but they did give me a good rating. Either Superior or outstanding were good ratings.

My campaign Committee to Support Georgette Valle for State Representative was comprised of friends and neighbors—some Democrats and some Republicans. Everyone seemed to be pleased they had been asked to join the Committee.

The Valle family belonged to the Normandy Park United Church of Christ. This church had a religious philosophy that fit our family. I particularly liked the Sunday School curriculum offered for Peter and Christine. I think Odd would have liked to have attended a Norwegian Lutheran Church so he could *snakke Norsk* (speak Norwegian) every Sunday. I chose this church because of its active attitude toward current events on the national, state and local scene, with many forums and discussions offered that focused on events in our state.

The Valle Family in 1962. *From left:* Peter, Georgette, Christine, and Odd

The Ballard family, whom we met at church, was key to my 1962 state representative campaign. They had a growing family with lots of spirit and fun interspersed with activities both in the church and with the family. Dr. Jack Ballard was a well-known local physician who was a Democrat and very active in the community. Merlene Ballard became my enthusiastic supporter and hosted fund raisers and coffee parties for me. Their children, Randy, Jackie, and Judy were friendly and looked upon me as a novelty from whom they could learn about their community and politics in general.

Both Randy and Jackie Ballard added to my list of supporters as they door-belled for me in their old neighborhood of West Seattle. I watched as they raced from door to door chanting my slogan "Rally to Valle" in their old neighborhoods. The slogan was designed to help the voter understand the pronunciation of the Valle name.

Judy Ballard, the Ballard's eldest daughter, was watching and making mental notes on the politics of the moment for her future.

> Her mother has since related to me her interest in politics at the City of Mercer Island, an incorporated city of suburbanites interested in good living, schools, and government. When Judy became the new Mayor of Mercer

Island, I was not surprised. But when she ran for State Representative and won that position in 2003, I was ecstatic! I visited with her in Olympia and found her to be on all the right sides of the issues in the Democratic Caucus! Judy Ballard Clibborn is still serving as State Representative.

As I reflected on the 1962 campaign, I thought of the 500 signs we had purchased for the campaign and the intensive labor that was involved in putting them up. The lathe had to be cut to the right size and the stakes had to be sturdy to withstand the pounding of the signs into the good earth. Herr Lumber Company seemed to offer the best prices to us. At last we were prepared, and our sign crews went out to install the signs. I was devastated that all the signs were torn down by my opponents!

I spent $3,240 during that campaign, and contributions to my campaign totaled $300. Florence McMullin and Dr. Ballard did a great job for me, but I lost that campaign by 320 votes.

> *The men who create power make an indispensable contribution to the Nation's greatness, but the men that question power make a contribution just as indispensable, especially when that questioning is disinterested, for they determine whether we use of power or power uses us.*
>
> President John F. Kennedy
> Amherst College, October 26, 1963

Loss of a Beloved Young President

Watching the Kennedy family in the White House was like viewing a brand new soap opera, but this one was named *Camelot* and it was real and interesting to me since I had seen both of them on the real stage in Washington, D.C.

For the nation it was a time to listen and appreciate this new young president as he grasped the presidency with his well spoken, articulate words. President Kennedy said, "When we got into office, the thing that surprised me the most was that things were as bad as we'd been saying they were."

Jacqueline Kennedy was welcoming foreign visitors in their own languages with the President standing by her side beaming with pride. President Dwight Eisenhower left office as the oldest president, and the next president was John F. Kennedy, the youngest at forty-three years of age.

Jacqueline Kennedy went about the task of the restoration of the White House. We were all interested in seeing pictures of the Kennedy children. Sometimes there was a released photo from the White House, and everyone enjoyed these precious moments. Jacqueline was a mother who protected the privacy of her family so not too many photos were released. Our nation's imagination raced ahead of the Kennedy presidency, expecting our handsome, eloquent leader to perform presidential miracles.

President John F. Kennedy speaks at a gathering of citizens in Pasco, Washington on September 28, 1963.

While protecting her children, Jacqueline Kennedy traveled in Europe; went horseback riding in Hyannis port; played touch football with the Kennedys, which resulted in a broken ankle; and listened to classical music with Joe Kennedy. On a trip to France, the President and Jacqueline were a great hit with President de Gaulle. Jackie spoke fluent French to him and dazzled the French people with her wardrobe and striking beauty. The President afterwards laughingly said he felt ignored. The trip was, however, considered a diplomatic triumph.

But with this Presidential optimism, there was cynicism brought on by the Vietnam War and the Watergate scandal. "One of the things President Kennedy did was to instill in the American people the idea that they could make a difference," said Deborah Leff, director of the Kennedy Library and Museum. "It was a time when you saw America striving to be its best."

It was also a time of testing—testing President Kennedy's youthful leadership. Premier Khrushchev involved the nation in a confrontation with the Soviet Union during the Cuban missile crisis that could have led to nuclear war. I well remember this crisis because I believed my family and I would not live to see my next birthday, October 31, 1963. We were seventeen miles from the center of Seattle, so I was sure that our lives would be severely affected. But President Kennedy was able to lead the nation through that missile confrontation. We learned by watching the evening newscasts that Khrushchev had withdrawn the missiles from Cuba and the Cuban missile crisis passed.

According to biographers of Jacqueline Kennedy, she suspected her husband of marital infidelity. Jacqueline was a very private person, and she held herself in a very reserved manner. In 1963 Jacqueline became pregnant with Patrick, and he lived only forty hours after birth. This incident brought the presidential couple together in a healing process, so much so that Jacqueline agreed to accompany her husband on a presidential political trip to Texas scheduled for November 22, 1963.

Although the politicians were surprised and pleased at Jacqueline Kennedy's decision to accompany the President to Forth Worth, Texas, and then on to Dallas, Texas, I was frightened by a Texas newspaper containing warnings to the President.

Yellow roses of Texas were given to the First Lady Jacqueline at the Fort Worth breakfast. In a thirteen-minute Air Force One flight to Dallas, the presidential couple relaxed even to the point of holding hands. When the plane landed in Dallas, the first lady was presented with red roses. They both looked happy and vibrant as they greeted the Dallas Democrats. Jacqueline was dressed in a pink wool suit with a matching pillbox hat. The President wore a green khaki-colored suit with blue-striped shirt and matching narrow blue tie. It was a perfect day to win the hearts of Texans.

For President Jack Kennedy and Jacqueline Kennedy this was a glorious midday in Dallas, Texas. The streets were lined with friendly, waving people waiting to see this vibrant, young presidential couple visit their city. The

Presidential limousine with the President and the first lady proceeded with Governor and Mrs. John Connelly down the streets of Dallas in the motorcade. Among cheers and whistles from the crowd, Mrs. Connelly said to the President, "You can't say Dallas doesn't love you Mr. President!"

In a later Theodore White interview with Jacqueline Kennedy, she remembered as the motorcade neared the overpass that she thought she heard a motor backfire. She had no recollection of climbing onto the back of the limousine to assist her bleeding husband. Three and a half hours later she was still wearing the blood-stained suit.

As the Kennedy Presidential limousine sped away to the hospital, the Valle phone rang with our friend, Gloria Jobs, on the phone. She said, "I have terrible news for you, Georgette. The President has just been shot in Dallas." It was not too long before I heard Walter Cronkite announce that the President was pronounced dead at 1:30 p.m., Texas time.

It was reported that the swearing-in ceremony for Lyndon Johnson to become the new President of the United States would be held on Air Force One. Phone calls were made to Washington, D.C., to assure officials that the correct words would be administered for the presidential oath by Judge Sarah T. Hughes. A Bible was found in the President's sleeping compartment. Merriman Smith of the UPI reported there were twenty-seven people in the center compartment, including Lyndon and Lady Bird Johnson and Jacqueline Kennedy. Jacqueline Kennedy appeared in the same blood-stained suit she had worn earlier in the day. Sid Davis of UPI reported:

> What you had was a new President of the United States in the airplane, the body of the fallen President in a casket in the back, and the wife of the new President on this plane going back to Washington after such a glorious day in the politics of John F. Kennedy. It said something about the strength of this country, the fact we had this thing happen, we didn't know who did it or why they did it, but the transition from one man to another was done in an orderly way.

Jacqueline Kennedy retired to the Presidential compartment and stayed with the President's casket until Air Force One landed in Washington. The nation was still in deep shock as people took time off to go to church, be with their families, and simply reflect on their own lives here in the United States. Messages arrived from all over the world with other nations sending their best wishes and condolences upon the death of President John F. Kennedy.

We in the Valle family spent a quiet weekend reflecting the week's events. November 23, 1963, was a very sad, sobering birthday for Odd. The presents were opened and the children went back to playing their games.

Jacqueline Kennedy expressed the *Camelot* theme with an iron-willed attitude, still protecting her children. She wanted John-John to hold his head high like a soldier as she stood silently in her veil of mourning during the funeral procession. Mrs. Kennedy and her children moved out of the White House eleven days later.

The Lyndon Johnson Era—1964 Campaign for the 31st District Representative

The events of 1963 seemed to propel us into the new years of 1964 and 1965. We were glued to the news admiring how quickly President Johnson was moving to pass the Voting Rights Act of 1965. The new President was doing what he did best and that was to work with Congress with speed to take full advantage of his first one hundred days in office. Some of us had a little difficulty listening to a soft southern accent in contrast to the articulate Boston accent of the recent past.

Protests were beginning in the south, and northern citizens were heading south to protest. In the state of Washington, Governor Albert Rossellini was passing legislation to build institutions for the mentally ill, for schools, and for building highways across the state to connect Western and Eastern Washington.

It seemed that I could take a breather to focus some thoughts on my political future. Running a household, watching over the children, Peter (9) and Christine (7), and keeping our active schedules uninterrupted was a task challenging enough for a full-time manager. But unless I could do this job well, I could not possibly attempt to succeed in public office.

Campaigning—1964

In my bid to be elected as State Representative I chose Richard "Dick" Smith, a local architect who was a smart and savvy politician, to be my Campaign Chair. Florence McMullin again agreed to be my Secretary-Treasurer.

I reviewed what I had done in the past legislative race when I had only lost by 320 votes and realized the campaign had to be run differently. I would have my signs redesigned and would be made using the silk-screen process. Odd, my Sign Chair, had more artistic ability than I did, so with his expertise and my political know-how we could design a sign that would be attractive, emphasize my name, and my party. Since we needed a sufficient crew of sign makers, the neighbors were recruited and friends of Peter and Christine also participated. A large basement with little furniture came in handy as large drying spaces for the signs. Each sign went through two processes with two colors of ink used—blue and orange. My husband would dutifully inspect each sign as if it were a work of art.

Odd was also making wine from Oregon grape bushes that grew on our property. It was tested with some frequency after a busy day of sign making. Someone jested one evening as we retired from a long day of campaigning that Odd was certainly the "Best Sign and Wine Maker" in the 31st District.

As I doorbelled, it was my job not only to ask for a person's vote but to ask their permission for a sign placement. In my enthusiasm I often forgot about the placement of a sign. Odd didn't forget, so signs sprung up and the campaign took on a new look. The public interpreted a very visible sign with a successful candidate.

Four Candidates

In 1964 when a candidate filed for the office of State Representative in Washington State, the filing was held at large in the district. This meant that in the primary, as a Democrat seeking a State Representative position, the candidate ran against all the Democrats who were incumbents.

Norm Ackley resigned from the Legislature and ran for Congress in the 7th District. I did not have any political differences with either Senator Andy Hess or Representative Norm Ackley. I thought both of them represented the district well. I entered this race with the understanding that I was to perform in a manner which did not embarrass my family, friends, or campaign. There seemed to be an unwritten code that I could not exactly pinpoint, but I knew I had to walk a straight line that was honest and above board.

Campaign Publicity

The *Highline Times* told me I could run short stories about coffee parties that were held discussing state legislative issues. In seventeen weeks I ran seventeen consecutive news articles, mostly about funding of K-12 education, local transportation issues, and environmental issues in the 31st District, as well as including my personal resume.

The *Highline Times* helped me to design my brochure costing nine-tenths of one cent to print. It was rumored to have been designed at a poker party. Al Sneed and Reid Hale of the *Highline Times* were the principal conspirators of this "news." The brochure was printed on blue paper and featured our family photo, as well as my picture with John F. Kennedy, with the caption on the back of the brochure stating, "A Woman Around the House?"

The *Seattle Times* ran an article entitled, "Dental Wife Runs for Rep." A few people thought that was gender discrimination, but I was thankful for the publicity.

Vice President Hubert Humphrey examines Georgette Valle's campaign brochure in 1964

Florence McMullin gathered crews of women to go to the King County Courthouse and copy the lists of people who had voted in the last primary. This required a lot of work, and then people had to type the labels and place them on the literature for mailing. Florence's house was always busy with campaigners working diligently.

Close Call

Odd and I busied ourselves by putting a huge sign on the top of our little yellow Opel. One night, after leaving the 31st District meeting at the Epicure Restaurant in White Center, a white panel van driving beside me on First Avenue stopped alongside my small Opel bearing my big GEORGETTE VALLE sign. I was in the right-hand lane and the driver motioned to me. I rolled down my window to see if I could help. He uttered a string of four-letter words. He was bigger than I, and his van was much larger than my small Opel. I proceeded with caution until I was within sight of the intersection of 152nd and Ambaum Street. I made the decision I would have to run a red light to lose the van if there wasn't any 152nd Street traffic.

I quickly drove to the Lewis and Clark Drive-In on First Avenue in Burien. I phoned the local police. They followed me to my home. As I approached 160th and First Avenue, I spotted the white panel van containing the foul-mouthed driver. It was with a great deal of relief that I crawled safely into my bed that evening.

Georgette Valle campaigning in 1964

Pitfalls and Gossip

My Campaign Chair, Dick Smith, was out with the sign crew, along with Odd, placing the signs. King County crews would take the signs down if they were found on county property, and we had to have permission to place a sign on private property.

Various methods are used to defeat a candidate. One day someone in my campaign told me she had heard that I was having an affair with Richard Smith, my Campaign Chair. I immediately contacted his wife, Elizabeth, and asked her if she was aware of this story. There was one way to counteract this rumor, and that was for her to accompany Dick and me to meetings. We both laughed, and all three of us ended up attending political meetings together.

Primary and General Elections

There were meetings, news conferences, coffee hours, interviews, and long hours of doorbelling. Seattle Municipal League ratings were important. I had fallen from "Superior" to "Outstanding." I never could understand how I could fall so fast since 1962! I knew several precinct committee workers that supported me. When they doorbelled their precinct in the primary, I was encouraged.

In those days of electioneering, the votes were first counted by the poll workers. The results were posted at voting places. As a candidate, one frequently went to bed on election night not knowing if one had been elected.

There was a tremendous feeling of exhilaration on the part of all my campaign workers when I won the primary nomination. I was now one of the nominees. Now there was the task to win the general election, but it was a Democratic district.

The 31st District had three representatives and one senator: C. G. Witherbee, Wayne Angevine, and I were the three Democratic nominees. I could now relax and garner advice from my Democratic colleague candidates. We all worked together and won that election of 1964. This 31st District was a huge district, and this win was a significant victory.

Manners are a sensitive awareness of the feelings of others. If you have that awareness you have good manners, no matter what fork you use.

Emily Post

Careful Campaigning With My Father

My parents were very helpful in my campaigns. First they contributed $1,500, which was a nice campaign nest egg. That money was always a nice amount to start my campaign rolling with small essentials such as signs, stakes, staples, ink and cardboard. My father was a great asset in helping me doorbell in the 1962, 1964, and the late 1960s campaigns. He had a set speech about how his daughter would make the best representative for the state of Washington and all she needed was their vote.

One day I lost my father as we were campaigning in Georgetown. After reviewing all the latest crime statistics of the area and after ten minutes of driving, I found him in a blackberry patch. Blackberries are bigger and better in Washington than in Minnesota.

On another occasion, we were doorbelling in an older part of Georgetown. I was trying to convince the woman that I was the best person for the state representative job. She heard the back doorbell ring and excused herself to answer it. Then I heard my father give his fiftieth campaign speech of the day about his daughter, Georgette Valle.

It was a warm autumn day, as my father and I headed out in the little yellow Opel with the big "Georgette Valle" sign on top. We were to campaign in an area close to our Normandy Park home. We had just enjoyed a wonderful lunch and good cup of coffee prepared by my mother. A tasty lunch and a good cup of coffee were as necessary for campaigning as they were when farming in Minnesota.

I gave my father a hand-drawn map of the precinct and enough brochures for each house for a four-block area, along with some political analysis of the area adjacent to the Manhattan business district on 180th and First Avenue South. I then drove on to start my own campaigning.

*Georgette Valle doorbelling with her father, George Vikingstad, in 1963
during her 1964 campaign for 31st District Representative.*

While doorbelling I met friendly women who were preparing their yards for winter, children coming home from school hungry for that afternoon snack, and occasionally the man of the house picking ripe fruit from heavily-laden trees. I made an effort to engage all of these people in campaign conversation, registering them to vote with the hope that all would vote for me. The voters seemed pleased to have someone asking their opinions about affairs of the state. At this point, no one knew me, but they were pleased that I was a Normandy Park resident. A number of times I was asked if I were related to Dr. Valle, the dentist, and I happily said, "Yes. He is my husband."

My father was unusually quiet as I picked him up from an afternoon of campaigning. I had an evening meeting, so I rushed into the house to help my mother with the dinner preparation.

We finally sat down to dinner. The dining room was quiet as we enjoyed the meal. "How did the day of campaigning go?" Odd asked.

My father replied, "The first house was on the south side of 180th S.W., and there was no one home. I hurried on to the next house and rang the doorbell. I waited a good amount of time and was ready to leave as the door quickly opened."

"Please pass the peas," Christine said quietly.

My father resumed the conversation. "The lady came to the opened door with a very pleasant smile. She was very well dressed to the waist, but below her waist she was completely naked."

"What did you do, Grandpa?" Peter asked.

"What was I going to do? I finally came to the conclusion that I was there to campaign for Georgette, so I proceeded to say what a fine daughter Emily and I had and what a decent and honest State Representative she would be and handed her the brochure."

My father said he left very quickly, not asking her if she were a registered voter. He looked back at the house after he ran down the steps only to discover he had left his beloved walking stick on the side of the steps. He recovered the stick and walked to the next house, hoping he was not in the midst of a nudist colony.

By this time, my mother had enough time to digest the conversation and asked, "Are you sure about this incident, George?" My father was very positive as he again began to relate details of the incident. I cleared my throat and declared it was time for me to leave for my meeting. I must confess that my meeting was not nearly as interesting as my father's afternoon of campaigning.

More often than not my father took real life stories that revealed people's tendencies to be serious and twisted their motives (which he often agreed with) slightly to make the actions they were taking humorous. My mother and I didn't always know how to take his humor, but we would talk about his remarks later when he had gone to the fields to work. I can remember Mother flipping her apron and laughing to herself about some humorous remark he had made over lunch. In the case of the humorous quotes, these torn and worn clippings were found in his billfold.

Humor from *George Vikings ted*

Arizona Mountains without vegetation
Clouds without rain
Women without virtue,
Men without brains

           Mark Twain

Campaign Story: I have learned that you can't kill a rat with a feather-duster clipping.

Said the Judge: I wish to commend you two drunken drivers for running into each other instead of some innocent person. If this thing can be encouraged, I think we may have hit upon the solution of a serious problem.

A nervous bridegroom appealed to the minister in a loud whisper, "It is kisstomary to cuss the bride?"

"Not yet," replied the minister, "but soon."

Arizona people are very irreligious —
Winter spoils for them the charms of Heaven,
Summer takes away their fear of Hell!

Unless you choose to do great things with it, it makes no difference how much you are rewarded, or how much power you have.

Oprah Winfrey

Service in Washington State's 31st Legislative District in Session in 1965

To put it mildly, this was a very exciting time for a Minnesota farm girl who had won the 1964 election in Washington State's 31st District. Strange as it seems, my mind was preoccupied with the more important business of hiring a housekeeper. This arrangement had to meet with the approval of my Norwegian husband, Odd. I would cook for one week and the housekeeper would then cook the extras that were last minute additions to the Valle menu.

Thank goodness this was only going to be a sixty-day legislative session. Mrs. Smith, the housekeeper, lived at the south end of Normandy Park, was Catholic, and seemed quite reliable. Odd was pleased with the appetizers she made, and the children looked upon this arrangement as a new opportunity for new snacks and exciting desserts.

The Washington State Capitol in Olympia was sixty miles south of Normandy Park—about an hour's drive from our home. The legislative session usually began on the second Monday in January. The selection of this date and time was to accommodate the farmers of our state since this was their dormant season. There were other citizens in the state who said that even the cows had more voting power than the city folks. "One reason to redistrict the state," I thought.

Redistricting and reapportionment of the state of Washington was not a new issue. People in the populous cities had long complained that the larger areas with less population had greater voting power. In Washington State it was Eastern Washington that had greater voting power. This amounted to less money for our K-12 students, transportation, and other budgetary matters. The decision in Washington State on redistricting and reapportionment would also affect other legislatures from other states. Sometimes when a decision is handed down from a state high court, then it is taken to the Supreme Court and affects all states. So issues that affect one state may frequently affect other states. One state may learn of solutions through the National Legislators Conference.

Representative Curley Witherbee, with outgoing Governor Albert Rosellini *(1957-1964)*, and Representatives Georgette Valle and Wayne Angevine begin their 31st District terms in 1965.

As I arrived in Olympia to be sworn in as the 31st State Representative, I discovered that the legislature was under a court mandate to redistrict and reapportion the state into new legislative districts before conducting any legislative business. We could not even organize ourselves. I was happy to collect the $25 per day stipend and the $100 per month salary, but I wanted to earn my pay by working on the state's problems.

There were sixty-five newly-elected Democratic representatives and thirty-

Representative Georgette Valle greets Senator Scoop Jackson as she begins her 31st District Legislative 1965 term in Olympia, Washington.

four Republicans in the House. This was an unprecedented majority of Democrats serving in the Washington House of Representatives. What was even more surprising was the fact that I was one of seventeen newly-elected representatives. This class of newcomers decided to elect their own Speaker of the House of Representatives. As freshmen legislators, we were required to meet off campus to make our decision.

In the past legislative session, the House of Representatives had a powerful struggle with the issue of public versus private power. It culminated with a split in the Democratic Caucus resulting in Representative "Daddy" Day of Spokane being elected Speaker of the House. He defeated longtime Speaker of the House of Representatives John O'Brien, who was a public power fan. The courts consented to allow us to elect a Speaker. Subsequently, Representative Bob Schaffer of Vancouver, a public power advocate and attorney, was elected Speaker of the House of Representatives.

As legislators, we had neither offices nor secretaries available to us. Any correspondence we had to have typed was to be prepared by the pool of secretaries located in the basement of the Capitol. Representative Doris Johnson and I discovered that in order to get letters typed, one also had to bear gifts. The male representatives offered liquor and candy. Doris and I shared the cost of one bottle of liquor and two boxes of candy. Presto —our letters were finished!

Mary and John O'Brien on their wedding day October 4, 1952. Speaker John O'Brien served eight years as Speaker of the House of Representatives.

As a Democrat and a League of Women Voters member, I knew that Washington State was in need of tax reform, including a more equitable tax structure. This would mean the introduction of a graduated state income tax, reduction of the sales tax, and more equitable property taxes.

When asked what committees I wished to serve on, I listed Revenue, Education, and Local Government. The court's mandate was to first redistrict and reapportion the state. After several weeks of haggling with the court, we were finally granted permission to organize our committees. In 1965, committee meetings were closed to the public. When public testimony was given, the meetings were open.

In a closed committee meeting, Representative Henry Backstrom, Chair of the Revenue Committee, asked what the

GEORGETTE VALLE, King, part

In 1966 Peter and Christina Valle visited their mother in Olympia during Representative Valle's first term

desires of the committee were. When it came to me, I announced that since we, as Democrats, had a majority of sixty-five Democrats in the Legislature, this number was only one shy of the sixty-six needed for a constitutional amendment to be passed for a graduated income tax. Therefore, I was very interested in working on a proposal for a graduated income tax. The rest of the committee had less ambitious desires, naming some tax changes for local government and adjustments of other tax rates.

I was immediately removed from the Revenue Committee and became Vice Chair of the Appropriations Committee. Representative Wes Uhlmann from Seattle was Chair—so much for my lofty ideas.

Meanwhile, back at the Valle household, Mrs. Smith was getting rave reviews. I was home on Friday nights to relay all my legislative tales. While I was gone I checked in with the children and Odd each night.

On the weekends, our family always attended Sunday School and church at the Normandy Park Cove United Church of Christ, a church which embraced people with different religious points of view. That suited me just fine. I especially liked the Sunday School curriculum and began to teach a fourth grade Sunday School class.

An impressive ceremony always opened the beginning of each legislative session. We repeated the Pledge of Allegiance followed by a prayer. The process of "Redistricting and Reapportionment" was a very tedious one because each individual representative and senator had to sign off on their own district. The Governor could always veto the entire plan. Experts on redistricting were saying that the 31st District's senator represented more people than the other senators in the Senate and that amounted to unequal representation.

Representative Georgette Valle was a member of Governor Daniel J. Evans' (1965-1976) Temporary Committee for Higher Education who interviewed all applicants for a new four-year college. Evergreen State College in Olympia was selected and built in 1967.

This legislative session was very chaotic since neither the House of Representatives nor the Senate was managed with a great deal of order. Members attended their committee meetings and waited for action. No orientation classes were held. There were a total of ninety-nine Representatives in the House, including eight women. The Democratic Caucus met in the largest room of the Capitol and represented every part of the state and almost all nationalities.

One late night there was discussion on a motion to adjourn the body. I rose to make a statement as to why I would support a motion to adjourn.

There was a thunderous shout of "Go to Hell" from the Republican side of the House. The House was restored to order with a demand for an apology from

Republican Representative Charles Neuschwander. But, at the moment, he was nowhere to be found.

Within moments, Representative Mark Litchman, a Seattle Democrat, rose to his feet and acknowledged he would vote for the Redistricting Act if certain changes were made. With that remark, pandemonium broke out in the House. The atmosphere was charged with partisan politics and personal vendettas against the Redistricting Act. Order was restored by the Speaker without breaking the gavel.

The next day everyone was on the floor of the House of Representatives ready to make their speeches. Representative Newschwander gave a muffled apology, which no one seemed to understand.

Senator Shirley Winsley and Representative Georgette Valle welcome former Representative Doris Johnson from Pasco to the House of Representatives.

I rose to give a polite "thank you" and went on to say, "I have been to Hell, Norway. It is a small railway stop in the beautiful mountains, very scenic, and full of nice, polite Norwegians." KING television was covering my remarks. When I later saw the tape of the broadcast, my remarks were cut after I said, "I have been to Hell." From then on, as a new politician, I had to watch every word I said and when I said it.

The Redistricting and Reapportion Act was passed that day resulting in my now being located in a Republican District, the 30th District.

Representative Doris Johnson, a K-12 teacher, and I formed a lasting friendship. We were not always elected simultaneously but managed to keep in touch over the years. We were of like political minds despite the fact that she was from Pasco in Eastern Washington. For over twenty-four years, I represented West Seattle, White Center, Burien, Normandy Park, and parts of unincorporated King

County. (I served the 31st District from 1965 to 1967 and 1972 to 1983. I served the 34th District from 1985 to 1997.)

There were other outstanding new legislators. Representative Alan R Thompson was nicknamed "Landslide Thompson" because he won his position by seven votes. Later he went on to become a member of the Senate and then came back as Clerk of the House. Representative Mary Lux represented the Olympia area and gave legislators good advice on tax reform. Representative Dick King presented the Democratic Caucus with information about the workings of both labor and community colleges.

I had so much to learn in order to catch up with my colleagues. I thank the League of Women Voters for the knowledge they gave me through their organization. I had a basis of primary knowledge to begin my legislative career because of the League. I was prepared and could speak on many topics pertaining to the state of Washington. However, to my colleagues' relief, I resisted the temptation.

Wes Uhlmann, Appropriations Chair, called meetings before the final date of decision-making for the Appropriations budget. Only one staff person assisted the chair, and the two of them sat up each night until after midnight studying the budget so they would be knowledgeable about every fact and figure. Today, a staff member is provided for every major area of government.

Since sessions often lasted late into the night, it was too dangerous trying to commute to my home and back each day so I rented an apartment during the Regular Session.

Julian Bond visits with Representative Georgette Valle at an Olympia reception given in his honor.

The Regular Session ended with a Special Session being called by Governor Dan Evans. On May 6, 1965, I set out for Olympia to begin another day of that

Special Session. It was a rather windy day and difficult to keep the Opel on the road. The newscasters were talking about how all the pictures on the walls were falling down. I thought that they were presenting an Orson Wells comedy relief news broadcast. When I got to the Capitol, I discovered we had experienced an earthquake with a seismic count of 6.5. I phoned home immediately and found Odd had taken the children to the Marvista Elementary School after the quake. During the earthquake the house and the fireplace were moving, with the outside ground rolling for a matter of several seconds.

A story about Representative Sam Smith indicated he had never made such a fast exit from the Capitol! The Capitol Rotunda was damaged and closed off for a full year. The cost for reconstruction was approximately $100,000.

Seventeen new legislators had survived the 31st Session, the Redistricting and Reapportionment Act, the travails of their own personal legislation, as well as an unexpected earthquake.

IN OLYMPIA — State Rep. Georgette Valle (D-31 District) received a warm handshake from Ralph Nader, consumer advocate. Nader was in Olympia to address the Legislature regarding current consumer and environmental projects. Rep. Valle, also a strong advocate for consumer protection, is a member of Nader's citizen consumer affairs group.

The Valle family in 1965:
Peter (10) and Christine (8)

The Years Following the 1965 Session
The 30th District Campaign

I called home and Christine answered the phone and began to cry. I said, "What's the matter?"

Christine said, "Dad wants to take away my kitty!"

As quickly as I could I said, "Don't worry—I will be right home!"

I arrived home in time to relieve Christine's anxiety about her kitty.

Christine convinced her father that she would be able to resolve the differences between the big kitty and the little one. Big kitty had been the big cheese with the Valle family for some time, so we all had to make an effort to make peace between the two. Christine was determined to keep her little kitty.

There was much catching up to be done with the children. I could now attend PTA meetings and parent-teacher conferences. We had always found Peter to be a very easygoing child. However, he had several responsibilities as a fourth grader which he did not take seriously. At the parent-teacher conference with his teacher Al Reamer, I discovered he had not been handing in his daily assignments in a timely manner. Mr. Reamer and I discovered many of Peter's assignments in his desk. The result was that Peter's grades suffered. With thirty some other students, I felt the teacher did not have the time to allot to individual students. I promptly enlisted a tutor for Peter, and the tutoring continued for the next four months.

At the end of three months, I asked Peter how he was responding to his tutor. His answer was that now he could concentrate on his studies and did not even think about going out to play at recess.

Valle Campaign in 30th District

The 30th Legislative District included the cities of Kent, Federal Way, Des Moines, and the unincorporated areas of Normandy Park and Highline. There were different areas with varying needs, so the district comprised a tangled geographical mass of demands and desires of many divergent groups of Democrats, Independents, and Republicans.

One of the tasks that I saw as important to my legislative future was to let people know what I had accomplished in the new 31st Legislative District. As a result, I asked for postage monies for mailings and was granted that privilege by the House of Representatives. I was attacked immediately in the South King County local newspaper by Representative Frank Warnke, Democrat, and portrayed as acting in an illegal manner because the Redistricting Act was not yet in effect. It was a case of my sending a mailing to my future constituents. I had included my picture and my letter stating that in many instances I did not only represent my future constituents but the whole state of Washington. It made the front page.

As I doorbelled the different areas, I met many women who were unregistered voters. As I registered them to vote, I reiterated my qualifications as a legislator in the past legislative session. When I queried these newly-registered voters, many said to me, "I have to wait for my husband and see which candidate he is going to vote for." From then on, if the husband was home, I would spend some time with both of the voters on specific issues or simply give pleasant remarks about the weather, their home, or garden. If children were in the vicinity, there was always a possibility of emphasizing my support for educational measures.

This was the day of the six-cent first-class postage stamp. My opponent was mailing his materials with six-cent postage, while I was using a postal bulk mail permit which was much cheaper for mass mailings. My opponent was Paul Barden, a former police officer, who was a pleasant, good looking Republican with a very charming wife, Jamel Barden. She was an asset using her smile and persuasive powers to win votes for her husband.

I had my charming Norwegian husband who constructed and positioned our signs in this very large legislative district. The van-

Odd and Georgette Valle in 1965

dalism of my signs in the district was rampant. However, I could not participate in such campaign practices. I again put the word out to my supporters that we would not resort to these destructive tactics.

I had a picture taken of me positioned in the middle of all the destroyed signs. This was published in the *Highline Times*. We almost caught the destroyer of our signs on camera one night. At the end of the campaign, before election day, my husband and Vance Carroll took down all the signs and subsequently arose at 6 a.m. to put the signs back up for the voters to see.

As a doorbeller, I risked my personal safety. Dogs of all varieties that saw you as a threat to the homeowners' safety could be vicious. I learned to look for big, empty dog dishes on porches. My father carried a big stick when doorbelling for me. I learned to run fast if a dog looked hungry. You could not take any chances. I did not take my children with me when campaigning. It was too dangerous!

The sitting Republican Governor Dan Evans had vowed to raise $100,000 in order to take back the House of Representatives. He raised much more money than expected and spent it accordingly.

The public was not aware of campaign costs, nor was I as a candidate. My supporters arranged the first fund raiser in a small church in Federal Way. The Teamsters Union hosted a meatball and spaghetti dinner for me. Before the dinner, people within the 30th District rose to tell their recollections of my public service. They stepped up and spoke while standing on the church pews. It was just like a revival meeting. The red wine created an atmosphere of warmth and congeniality. Mixing red wine and politics in a church setting became one of my most impressive fund raisers.

This campaign was conducted before the "Campaign Right to Know" legislation was passed. There were no reports of contributions received or any expenditure made. There was also no way of knowing how much my opponent was spending. During that campaign, I raised and spent about $10,500. I later discovered through a local educational association that my opponent, Paul Barden, spent $32,000. Although the campaigning was a tremendous family effort with my supporters doorbelling their precincts, I lost the campaign by about 1,500 votes. It was considered a highly-contested race with much public interest.

After this exhausting campaign, the next morning, I performed the task that required the most physical energy. I grabbed the garbage cans and proceeded to scrub them clean with a vengeance.

Christine Valle, age 13, in 1968

In February 1969 Peter, almost 16, and Christine, almost 14, were riding the ferry to Vashon Island, Washington

Doorbelling Moments
In My Campaigns

Doorbelling during a political campaign encompasses many memorable moments. It gives the candidate a chance to relax in the pleasant weather during the summer season. On the other hand, if it is raining and the candidate looks like a wet cat lost in a storm, the voter is usually very impressed with the candidate's doorbelling tenacity.

When I first began to doorbell, I was petrified to approach a homeowner's property. I began in my own neighborhood with trepidations about the fact it was a Republican precinct.

If I doorbelled after 5:30 p.m. my Normandy Park area neighbors were generous and would often invite me to join them for a Manhattan, but I would always decline, understanding that having liquor on my breath and a slur in my speech would not add up to a good beginning for my campaign. I also knew that these were good Republicans offering me a drink.

As I thanked them for their kind invitation, I extended my literature to them hoping they would not throw it immediately into the garbage. I hoped they would read it and make up their mind accordingly. My literature was usually written and designed by me with a homespun quality rather than a slick public relations quality.

In the early days the so-called "man of the house" often determined the politics of the household. People invited the candidate inside, and you tried to be as succinct as possible. At this point the man did become curious so you could capture two votes. Today women have learned to trust their own judgment and often add valuable ideas and issues to the candidate's own platform.

As a Democrat, I needed to pursue the voters in Democratic precincts. This, of course, meant that I had to doorbell in some very poor areas of the 31st Legislative District. It was not always easy for me since my own family of origin had struggled for so many years trying to make ends meet on the farm which had a sizable mortgage. I found that I could only doorbell these poor families for half a day.

Very often, the doorbelling candidate is the first real, live candidate a voter has ever seen. Many of these voters were unregistered. Sometimes those I met became volunteers in my campaign or would put up a sign or even promise to vote for me. Once I re-registered a couple from Kent into the 34th District in West Seattle. They reminded me that I had doorbelled them in another campaign.

One bright, sunny day I approached a man in his doorway, and I introduced myself with my literature. With a grimace that revealed a loss of a few teeth, he announced he was a Republican. I asked if he had ever heard of Georgette Valle. "Yeah, I voted for him!"

One evening I approached a home and rang the doorbell. The little gated opening in the door flew open so I could give my pitch for Mayor Wes Uhlmann and Georgette Valle. Mayor Wes Uhlmann was being recalled as Mayor, and I wanted to be reelected. The voice thundered out of this small aperture and said, "This is a very dangerous neighborhood. You are going to be reelected and Uhlmann will probably survive this election. You better get back to your car!" With that I decided to call it a night and ran all the way back to the car.

There were moments when I could actually help a constituent. One person told me he was presently unemployed. He talked about how difficult it was for him to successfully apply for a certain job. With a few more particulars about his background and education, I suggested that if he wished me to write a letter of recommendation, I would gladly do that. The letter was written and he got the job.

Today candidates work with a list of registered voters and often can rely on these voters actually going to the polls. However, you may not be assured that they will vote for you. For many years I carried voter registration materials with me and registered many people. Today, a citizen can register by mail. If it were a presidential election year, people would usually register. I always stressed the fact that every vote is important.

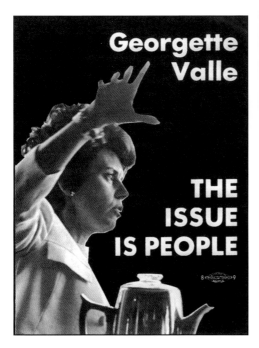

Georgette Valle

THE ISSUE IS PEOPLE

FAMILY FIRST...

With the Valles, the family comes first. Georgette Valle, her husband, Odd; son, Peter, and daughter, Christine, are involved in church and community affairs. Dr. Valle is a Burien dentist. Peter Valle is a University of Washington student and is spending the summer in Japan as part of the Lions Youth Exchange Program. The Valles will also host a Japanese student, Hisayuki Kaseki.

.....THEN PUBLIC SERVICE!

Georgette Valle is a graduate of the University of Minnesota with a Bachelor of Science Degree in Occupational Therapy. She is Director of the Occupational Therapy Department at the Valley General Hospital.

She has been active in the America Association of University Women, the Highline League of Women Voters, PTA, Normandy Park United Church of Christ, Washington Environmental Council, the Board of King County TB and Respiratory Diseases, Puget Sound Youth Foundation, Legislative Chairman of the Washington Occupational Therapy Association, and many other civic organizations.

As a former state representative - (term of office 1965-1967)- she is the only candidate running in the 31st Legislative District that has served the entire area in the new 31st Legislative District - new precincts and old precincts.

Elect

Georgette VALLE

**State Representative
31st District**

Democrat

Position No. 1

BULK RATE
U.S. POSTAGE
PAID
SEATTLE, WASH.
PERMIT NO 9954

Return Georgette Valle to the Legislature Jim Duggan, Chairman

Rally to . . .

Georgette **Valle**

Committee to Elect **Georgette Valle**
Lorraine Bonnell, Executive Secretary-Treasurer
13023 15th S.W. Seattle, WA 98146

34th District ○ **Democrat** ○ **House of Representatives** ○ **Position 2**

Re-Elect
Georgette
Valle

34th District • Position 2
House of Representatives • Democrat

C753

Yesterday ...

EXPERIENCE COUNTS

Georgette Valle has served as state representative for fourteen years. She knows
that it takes more than talk to get the job
done — it takes hard work and most
importantly, it takes experience.

First elected in 1964, Georgette has
worked on and found solutions to dozens
of problems facing our state and its
citizens. Here are just a few of the good
ideas that Georgette turned into state law:

- Limits on out-of-state nuclear waste
- Basic Education Act
- Washington Indoor Clear Air Act
- Senior Citizens Services Act
- Dam safety legislation
- Shoreline management protection
- Worker health and safety laws
- Funding for West Seattle Bridge
- Funding for mental health programs

President John F. Kennedy and Representative Georgette Valle

Today ...

Governor Booth Gardner and Representative Georgette Valle

MOVING FORWARD

Never one to rest on past accomplishments, Georgette Valle hit the ground running when the Legislature reconvened in January, 1985.

Georgette worked hard to improve our state's public education system, fought for an accessible toxic waste information office, and tackled one of the toughest issues of the session — funding for the clean-up of Puget Sound.

In 1986, Georgette's string of successes grew. She and Senator Talmadge teamed up to secure funding for a West Seattle group home. Working with West Seattle business leaders, Georgette was able to push through legislation designed to help keep ship-building jobs here in Washington.

Recognizing that crime is a serious and growing problem, Georgette turned her attention to one of the most serious flaws in our criminal justice system — the controversial sex offender program at Western State Hospital. Citing ineffective treatment and a long list of escapes, Georgette introduced legislation that would put the program back behind prison walls. Georgette's bill is now state law.

Tomorrow ...

THE FUTURE

As your legislator, Georgette Valle knows that much more remains to be done.

Acknowledging that state government must be constantly reviewed to keep costs down, Georgette will continue to push for a leaner, more efficient state government.

She will continue to fight for a welfare system designed to move people off welfare and into productive employment. She will continue in her effort to control the state's use of expensive outside consultants. She will continue to fight for an improved public education system and more equitable teacher salaries. And, she will continue to make sure that the interests of the elderly are protected, not bargained away for the benefit of narrow special interest groups.

Yes, whatever the issue, one thing remains constant — Georgette Valle puts **your** interest first — yesterday, today, and tomorrow!

Representative Georgette Valle and Frank Merritt, Page

Quotes

● *It's always a pleasure working on issues relating to the 34th District with as capable a representative as Georgette Valle.*

Senator Phil Talmadge

● *Facing tough issues takes experience. Georgette Valle is one of the few legislators with the energy and knowledge to deal effectively with the complex challenges that lie ahead. She deserves your support.*

Governor Booth Gardner

● *Georgette Valle is sensitive to the needs of the 34th District. She's a hardworking and tireless advocate for the people of this community. She has my enthusiastic endorsement.*

Mayor Charles Royer

● *As Vice Chair of the Education Committee, Georgette Valle's energy, years of experience, and command of the complex issues facing our state, make her one of the most respected members of the House of Representatives. She's an outstanding state legislator.*

State Representative Brian Ebersole
Chair, House Education Committee

AWARDS

★ Award of Merit —
Washington Education Association

★ Flammable Fabrics Award —
West Seattle Jaycees

★ Save Our Local Farmlands —
Seattle Municipal League

★ Public Official of 1980 —
Washington Environmental Council

★ Friend of Education Award —
Highline Education Association

★ Outstanding Public Contribution —
Washington Occupational Therapy Association

★ Outstanding Service Award —
Southwest Youth Service Bureau

★ Washington Indoor Clean Air Act —
American Lung Association

★ Woman of the Year —
West Seattle Business & Professional Women

Ed Hanson

The Committee to Re-Elect

Georgette Valle

34th DISTRICT   REPRESENTATIVE   DEMOCRAT

Nanci Colbert, Executive Secretary - Treasurer
3525 · S.W. 97th   Seattle, Washington 98126

 C753

You can't go around hoping that most people have sterling characters. The most you can hope for is that people will pretend that they do.
                              Fran Lebowitz

The Politics of Money
Who Gave, Who Got, Issues Won
and Lost, 1967 and On . . .

Who gave, who got, the issues won and lost are really what partisan politics is all about. Unless, as a politician, you controlled the press, the issues won and lost are rarely that evident to the public. An issue between Paul Barden and me in the 1967 campaign was the governance of community colleges and whether it was to be a local or state issue. I had supporters who switched their loyalty to Paul Barden because he sided with the numerous local school officials who wished to control the community colleges at the local level. On the other hand, I could see that the most effective control of community colleges was at the state level and included state accountability, standards of education, and institution costs. All of these controls would foster the growth of community colleges for the benefit of the taxpayer and the student. Barden won the election and went to the Capitol and voted for the Community College Act of 1967, which included state accountability, standards, and cost.

Campaigns are greatly influenced by the strength of the campaign organization. The unpaid volunteers, the jeweled saints, are dedicated, intelligent, and loyal and work night

Odd and Georgette Valle wish Vice President Hubert Humphrey good luck in his presidential race in 1969. We each paid $5,000 for this fund raiser for Humphrey.

and day for the candidate. If I were a political god, there would be a political heaven where these saints saunter into richly-furnished mansions with the latest lavish computer systems which can easily transmit communication news into political universes throughout the galaxies. This *"political saint heaven"* is the very least that they deserved. Some such heroes are my executive secretaries: Florence McMullin, Jean Hueston, Lorraine Bonnell, Norma Kragtorp, Ellen Fawcett, Flora Belle Key, and Lucia Burrows. Campaign Chairs are also considered "hallowed saints." These include Dr. Jack Ballard, Dick Smith, Odd Valle, Vance Carroll, Allen Munro, William Taylor, Walt Bowen, and Bill Cole. The Sign Chair, Odd Valle, can still recall where signs were placed and how long they stayed up. Eric Matheson, now Editor of *Highline Times*, also made signs for my campaigns.

On the home front, my teenage children grew by leaps and bounds. Peter grew a phenomenal six inches one summer and continued to grow another three to four inches during the winter season. He enjoyed playing his trombone, and Christine practiced her *plies* for ballet. Christine continued to grow to be 5' 8" tall.

The race between Paul Barden and me proved to be futile because the district was largely Republican.

Jamel Barden, Paul Barden's wife said that my father told her it was too bad that two such nice people were running for the same spot in this legislative race. I began to think that I would have to do what other politicians did, and that was to move into my "old" district—the 31st District—in order to be reelected. My family was very supportive of the move to the 31st District. There were, however, problems. Since the Equal Rights Act had not passed in Washington, I would have to move all the beds too.

We found an apartment in the Highline area and settled in for the political season. The Normandy Park house was put on the market.

I kept hearing that there was some kind of legal challenge coming my way. Sure enough, a legal challenge against my 31st District candidacy was filed against me by Eleanor Lee, a Republican, and even one Democrat.

When I sought help to find a Democratic attorney who was familiar with legal challenges involving legislative races, all the attorneys I contacted were otherwise occupied. Finally, I chose an attorney who had worked for the Washington State League of Women Voters.

There was nothing in the Washington Constitution that stated I could not move into a legislative district, live there a prescribed amount of time, register to vote, and file for candidacy as a state representative. But some partisan politicians were going to try to prevent this.

I continued to doorbell for the position of State Representative in the 31st Legislative District. I enjoyed being back in my old district, working for and with a Democratic base. My friends, new and old, were very supportive.

The trial date arrived. On that day I wore a white outfit. I thought the color white was as far as I could get from "dirty" politics. Odd was called to testify at the trial. He could not remember the name of the realtor who was going to sell our house. I had written an extensive history about my political experiences for my attorney. In the end, Judge Walterskirchen ruled that my name was ineligible for the fall primary ballot of 1972 because my moving to an apartment did not qualify for legal domicile. Only the man of the house could establish such legal domicile. It was like a nightmare. And indeed I did dream about the trial! I was true to the promise I had made to myself that I would not mention this to anyone.

The headlines in the *White Center News* were the largest I had ever seen, even larger than when the Lindberg baby was kidnapped. But life went on as our realtor, Florence McMullin, located a house for us in Hurstwood in the Highline area. The house had a beautiful view of Puget Sound waters, Vashon Island, and the Olympic Mountains. It satisfied almost all of our family's needs.

Our needs were not very extensive, but naturally Peter and Christine wanted to finish their high school studies at Mount Rainier High School. Administration officials permitted Peter to finish his senior year high school studies at Mount

Rainier. We helped Peter purchase an older car, and he enjoyed the freedom of having a car as he graduated from Mount Rainier High School.

The new Hurstwood House

Unfortunately, Christine was denied permission to attend Mount Rainier. If she had been a "problem" child, then she could have gone to Mount Rainier High School with her all her school chums. All of this was very distressing to Christine as she did not want to move. Now it is legal to request permission to attend another school rather than the school that is closest to the student's home.

Harold and Trudy Sanders, good friends, agreed to let Christine stay at their home in the Mount Baker area and attend Franklin High School in the Seattle School District. They had a young daughter, Diane, who enjoyed Christine's company. Franklin High School had a wonderful group of teachers, so I breathed a sigh of relief. She would go Franklin High School and come home on the weekends, which was great with us.

Christine was very interested in drama and the arts and wanted to apply for acceptance at the American Academy of Drama in New York. She learned that she had enough credits to graduate from high school in December.

After graduation, she managed to land a job in the state Capitol in Olympia as a tour guide. She saved her salary (which was over a thousand dollars) for her future New York experience. Lots of cards and letters of congratulations on her job performance were received from everyone, even lobbyists.

Cousins Stephanie Connel and Christine Valle in the summer of 1972

Christine and Peter Valle visit their mother in Olympia. Christine is working as a Capitol Tour Guide, and Peter takes a little break from his University of Washington classes.

GEORGETTE VALLE, District No. 31

She was enrolled in the American Academy of Drama in New York City. During her training there she received muscular manipulations known as "rolfing." Ever since then she has had excellent posture and carries herself with an air of "tall" confidence.

Christine Valle poses for a "model" picture at the American Academy of Drama in New York.

Christine stayed in New York eleven years and had enough experiences to fill another book. I made an annual effort to visit her in wonderful "New York, New York."

She worked in famous restaurants, continued her acting training, and served as editor of *It's Me* magazine. Her New York apartment building was converting to condos, so when she vacated her apartment as the last tenant, she was given a check for $4,000, which she used to finance her move across the country to a warmer climate in California.

Two years later, in 1974, I ran for the House position in the 31st Legislative District and was elected by a majority of voters. After political losses in the 30th Legislative District, a devastating political trial, and a move of residency, I sensed a real feeling of jubilation after winning the 31st Legislative District position. Now I was in a position of strength, my supporters were jubilant, and my posi-

GEORGETTE VALLE, District No. 31

tion as State Representative was likely to be retained for some years. I wondered if I could ever truly thank all the people who have helped in my campaigns.

Florence McMullin and Debbie McMullin join Representative Georgette Valle on House floor.

Sarah Miller served as a page for Representative Georgette Valle

Representative Georgette Valle and Page Carl Erickson on February 11, 1976

FORTY-FIRST LEGISLATURE
1969-71

SESSIONS SERVED:
SENATE: 1967, '67 EX., '69.

COMMITTEES

CHAIRMAN: EDUCATION
CITIES, TOWNS AND COUNTIES
HIGHWAYS
JUDICIARY
LABOR AND SOCIAL SECURITY
WAYS AND MEANS (APPROPRIATIONS)

Washington State Senate

SENATOR
ROBERT C. (BOB) RIDDER
THIRTY-FIFTH DISTRICT
5604 SOUTH ROXBURY
SEATTLE, WASHINGTON 98118

Dear Georgette:

Tuesday, September 19th is "Decision Day". The people will again have a choice on that day to select the candidates for the final ballot in November.

You know me and my record in the legislature. It is for this reason I write to offer you my support as Representative, Position I in the newly redistricted 31st District.

It was sad to see how you were cheated out of the chance to run in the last election. The legality of your ability to run came long after the election was over - a bitter pill indeed.

You stand for those things that I stood for in the 35th. A perfect labor record when you served in the house two sessions ago; a driving interest in Consumer Protection; Fair Taxation; Aid to the Elderly; State Financed Education with emphasis on Accountability; and Vocational Opportunity with an end to those distasteful Special Levys.

You have proven yourself to be a fine, hard-working legislator. Now, with a grown family, I know you will devote even more of yourself to that end.

When I hear the voter complain about the caliber of Legislators it brings me to write this letter to you, Georgette, which you may use in any way you wish. You are honest, hard-working, thorough and above all, interested in just plain people. I've never known of your bowing to special interests in your pursuit of what is best for the people - The voters in the new 31st need you and about 50 others just like you in Olympia when the session starts.

God bless you in your efforts for re-election to the State House of Representatives. If there is anything more I can do to help in the election of excellent candidates such as yourself just call on me.

Robert Ridder, Senator
Thirty-Fifth District

Paid for and distributed by the Committee to Elect Georgette Valle to the Legislature · Jim Duggan · Chairman

George Vikingstad's Final Days and Funeral

In the later 1960s and into the 1970s we were not really aware of the mental slide that our father was experiencing in Arizona and in Minnesota. Unfortunately, unless someone brings this memory loss to your attention daily or weekly in letters, this slide can happen very slowly and without notice. Mother was probably aware, but as you get older it's normal to not readily remember everything.

On an earlier 1974 trip to Phoenix to see them, my mother told me she was really noticing his memory failings or dementia, but we did not speak of it in his presence. Her frustration was sufficient to call and ask me to come to Arizona again and drive them home to Minnesota. I quickly flew down to Phoenix and made my way to their home in the Loren Green Estates in Mesa. I drove very quickly back to Blue Earth, Minnesota, with my mother encouraging me not to drive too fast!

So we watched as the husband of Emily; the father of Georgette and Astrid; and the grandfather to Peter, Christine, Stephanie, and Camille declined in his mental health and general participation in our lives. He once had been prominent in so many

George and Emily Vikingstad with daughter Astrid Alexander at their home in Blue Earth, Minnesota

avenues of our lives, but now he was passing us by. It was always a difficult task to tell my father anything, let alone tell him to take his blood pressure pills. His present and past anger at the American Medical Association was enough for him to disregard the doctor's prescription. I am sure that as a result of this inaction, my father had small strokes and his dementia became worse.

After being raised in and attending the Norwegian Lutheran Church most of his life, my father was really a Unitarian at heart after attending Unitarian Churches in Minneapolis, Arizona, and California. When he was safely home, he had several visits from Reverend Thompson from the Trinity Lutheran Church in Blue Earth. My father really expected some kind of resentment from Reverend Thompson over his Unitarian Church preference. Instead the man was very cordial and pleasant with no sense of resentment towards him. My father was surprised and pleased.

My father received this special card and poem:

Get Well Card to George Vikingstad	The Farmer
Astrid told me you were in the hospital.	Let the wealthy and great
May it give you the least pain and least worry while you are under "average" nurse's care.	Roll in splendor and state I envy them not, I declare it; I eat my own lamb, My chickens and ham,
It will be lonesome without your radiant personality in places I have so often enjoyed it, and been inspired, more than any paid preacher, by it. The best things are free, as air, water, and politicians before election!	I shear my own fleece and I wear it. I have lawns, I have bowers, I have fruits, I have flowers; The lark is my morning alarmer So jolly boys,
Another great thing that is free as air is the love of men like you who have worked faithfully to make others happy in doing their duty and making this crazy world more fit for *homo sapiens* to live by.	Here's God speed the plow, Long life and success to the farmer. *Anonymous*
Best Wishes to a real friend to man.	
Oscar	

Not long after returning to Minnesota, my father wandered from the house and was lost. This was difficult for the family, friends, and my mother to realize the time has come to place our father in St. Luke's Nursing Home.

The nurses in the nursing home seemed to be amazed at my father's vocabulary. Everyone said he uttered such huge words. He also expected everyone to answer him and ask him some questions. They responded by asking a multitude of questions, which he usually answered with more questions.

He gradually became bedridden. Astrid came as often as her school teaching routine and the care of her children would allow. I came less frequently, but he did recognize me. It was not too long after my last visit that I got a call from Mother that our father had died at St. Luke's Nursing Home on August 3, 1974.

He was buried in the Blue Earth Cemetery after the funeral service attended by many who respected the life my father had lived—his long-standing campaigns for the farmer's fights to retain their farmland, for the people's right to rural electrification, and for the general commitment to an end of rural and small town poverty. I said a few words to remind people to remember our father as he wished to be remembered.

After the services, two people shared some moments in the past that were important to the Vikingstad family. One person remembered when Reverend Nels J. Vikingstad had preached a sermon on the possibility of there not being a Hell in the eternal process of salvation. I thought possibly he was a "rebel" in the Norwegian Lutheran Church.

A former student at the Dell School District where my mother taught was there when my parents became engaged in the school hallway.

As the service ended at the Blue Earth Cemetery, I heard the whistle of the train as the caboose rushed by the city station. I felt it was in honor of our father who had wanted so much to be a railroad engineer, but instead returned to the Elmore farm to please his parents, especially his mother. 🚢

 ## Emily Vikingstad's Last Days and Final Struggles

In the early 1980s my mother was having difficulties fixing her own meals and just plain "being" at home. Since my father's death, she had lived well, traveled by plane alone to visit us in Seattle, had visits from Astrid and Camille, and had enjoyed the freedom of being with her friends. But now, her health began to falter. She was accustomed to taking care of herself by resting each afternoon, taking her medication, and getting "Meals on Wheels" to come to her door occasionally.

At this point Astrid could not care for her because she was still working as a kindergarten teacher in Minneapolis. Between the two of them they decided that she would have to go into a nursing home. As St. Luke's Nursing Home in Blue Earth was full, the Winnebago Nursing Home was her destination for several weeks. My mother was reluctant to become a full-time resident of any nursing home.

Today there is another solution which is much more fulfilling to the disabled person and that is the choice of "assisted living." Assisted living legislation was one of the last bills that I sponsored and passed in 1996 at the Washington State House of Representatives. In an assisted living situation, a designated professional comes in to help the resident take medication, to assist in baths.

Mother was becoming frail at this stage of her life and grew unhappy about the nursing home care she was receiving. One day she was so dissatisfied that she checked herself out of the Winnebago Nursing Home.

Eventually she called me in Seattle to tell me she was back at home. It was decided to send her granddaughter Stephanie to Minnesota to help

A picture that Stephanie Connel gave to her Grandma Emily on September 1, 1980

her grandmother, since Stephanie was between jobs on the West Coast. She was happy to be of service. We decided that she would be in charge of hiring a practical nurse that could assist Mother in eating her meals at the dinner table, bathing, and taking her blood pressure and medications.

Stephanie shopped for food, cooked the meals, and did the general housework. My mother was grateful to be back in her own home.

Stephanie arranged for a hospital bed to be brought into the house and set up in Mother's bedroom. Dr. Anderson, who had been such a loyal professional, now came to the house to see Emily Vikingstad as a patient in her very own house. He was not as optimistic about Emily's health as he had been in the past. After all, he had saved Emily's life many times over a multitude of years. Once she had even driven herself to the Blue Earth Hospital!

At last Stephanie called and told me perhaps I should consider coming home to see Mother. I made arrangements with the family and came as quickly as I could, arriving in Blue Earth during the middle of July 1983. I was aware of the Dr. Anderson's pessimistic views about Mother's health, still I was surprised to see how thin and frail she had become over the last months.

We were all determined to make Mother's last days as comfortable as possible. She was now being fed by the nurse. I telephoned Astrid to let her know about Mother's health. All this time Mother was as sharp as she ever was. She made the effort to tell me she wanted to die, that she wanted to "go home to George." I thought at that moment that she was pretty tired of having to fight for her life with so little energy. Reverend Thompson of the Blue Earth Trinity Lutheran Church visited weekly with Mother.

Emily Tenold Vikingstad was the eldest of two of the last surviving sisters of nine children. All her sisters and brothers had succumbed to heart trouble with the exception of Clara Amanda who died in 1904 of tuberculosis at age twelve.

Mother was now eighty-seven years old. The doctor had wanted to provide her with a pacemaker, but it was not certain that she could withstand the operation. Dr. Anderson came to see her that last day in her Blue Earth home. He gave me, Stephanie, and the nurse the sad news that Mother would probably die that evening. The nurse telephoned Astrid when her blood pressure was falling in the early evening of August 29, 1983.

At 8:30 p.m. Mother's hand slipped away from my hand. It is still my only experience of witnessing death. Even with the terrible shock, I was glad to have been at her side. Stephanie was out for the evening, but returned home about 9 p.m. When I broke the sad news to her, she rushed to Mother's bedroom and simultaneously the mortuary people arrived. Stephanie noticed that Mother did not have any stockings on, so she insisted on carefully putting warm socks on her grandmother's feet. I will always remember this as a final and loving gesture.

The removal of her rings and jewelry, the shopping for the coffin, and selection of Mother's last clothing are difficult tasks to be performed, but that is the part of the final things that had to be done. Mother wanted her wedding ring to be given to Astrid.

Odd arrived the night before the funeral, so I was relieved he was going to be on time. Odd said to me, "Too bad about Henry Jackson's death, isn't it?" With that I nearly had a heart attack. I had not had time to review the news or listen to the television. I reminded myself that we are only here for a short time, and sometimes it goes much too quickly.

Mother's funeral was on September 3, 1983, at the Blue Earth Trinity Lutheran Church. We all appreciated how peaceful our mother—grandmother looked in her pink dress with a quiet facial expression on her face. She was as if in a deep sleep.

After Mother's internment, we gathered in the basement of the Blue Earth Trinity Lutheran Church over healing cups coffee and freshly baked cakes and cookies from the Ladies Aid.

Georgette and Astrid with children. *From left:* Peter Valle,
Christine Valle, Georgette Valle, Camille Connel, Astrid Alexander,
and Stephanie Connel

Scoop Jackson Presidential Fever

Remembering what "presidential fever" was like in the 1970s has helped me focus on the Washington Democratic Party's role in Scoop Jackson's bid for President. Senator Henry "Scoop" Jackson had been our United States Senator since 1941. There were some Democrats like myself who would have preferred Scoop Jackson to support initiatives to solve the Cold War problems. On the other hand, Scoop Jackson's overtures to help Jewish refugees escape from the U.S.S.R. Communist control were very popular with the Jewish block of voters in this country. It was nice to have one of our own Senators running for President.

Washington State supported Washington's "Golden Boys" Senate Team— Scoop Jackson/Warren G. Magnuson. They repeatedly brought more revenue back to "this" Washington from the "other" Washington than we taxpayers sent.

In 1975, the Valles and the Jacksons had a lot in common—both with a son and daughter named Peter and Christine and Dr. Odd Valle and Senator Henry Jackson were both members of the Sons of Norway Lodge in Ballard.

Ballard is a part of Seattle, but Ballard took over all of Seattle's limelight during the May 17 Norwegian Consti-

Odd and Georgette Valle and Senator Scoop and Helen Jackson at a gala dinner for Scoop's presidential bid

tution Day celebrations, the second in size in the nation.

Helen Jackson would have been a superb First Lady. If you dropped in for a cup of coffee at the White House, she probably would have graciously served homemade *krumkake* and *tyttebear* jelly. Visions of Scandinavian goodies surrounded my taste buds as I speculated on the future President of the United States.

I worked with Senator Jackson for the Academy of Peace, an institution which many of us in the Northwest were involved. I didn't always agree with him on foreign policy, but Senator Jackson's positions and record on domestic issues, the environment, working people, education, and labor were very good to excellent.

During this same time, our son, Peter, was finishing his senior year at the University of Washington, completing his Bachelor of Arts degree in anticipation of teaching elementary school. He was very organized and first researched which school districts passed their local levies and proceeded to apply for teaching positions in those districts if any were available. Salary was a consideration, but beginning teachers did not earn very big salaries. Still he had the natural enthusiasm of a young teacher ready to accomplish the task before him. Peter had several interviews in different parts of the state and finally accepted a teaching position with the Vancouver, Washington, School District. He appreciated the help and assistance of Mrs. Peterson who was an experienced elementary school teacher in the district.

Peter loved to work with young children during his university days and had a part-time job at the

Odd Valle, Peter Valle, and Georgette Valle
during Christmas 1978

University of Washington Educational and Professional Preschool Center.

University professors were allowed to enroll their children in this center by paying a fee of $1,000. It was a center based on research on child development.

Peter enjoyed his teaching experience in the Vancouver School District, but realized after taxes he received less than $500 dollars of take-home pay each month. Reluctantly, Peter made the decision to go back to the University of Washington and obtain a Master of Business Administration degree. He has been able to provide good life choices and many comforts for himself and his family.

In the United States' South, Jimmy Carter, former Georgia Governor, was being heard on issues that affected our nation's morality. I've always supported the "bird in hand" theory in the selection of presidential candidates.

President Richard Nixon had resigned with a new President Gerald Ford issuing a Nixon pardon. We were ready for a little "national morality."

The South was very supportive of Jimmy Carter as a Democratic Presidential candidate. We as Northwest Democrats were listening, but in a presidential bid for attention, another area such as the "South" seemed very far off.

The National Democratic Convention picked Jimmy Carter, with his wife, Rosalynn, and their young daughter, Amy, at his side. I was delighted with Jimmy Carter's choice for Vice President, Senator Walter "Fritz" Mondale, who was related to us and the Tenolds by the marriage of Aunt Anna (my mother's eldest sister) to Ed Mondale, who was the brother of Fritz's dad Reverend Mondale.

A winning combination of Carter-Mondale swept the country bringing Democrats once again to the White House. President Carter offered leadership during the energy crisis and brought truth-telling to the presidency. Vice President Mondale was the first Vice President to be totally informed of all international and national events with an important role to play for the benefit of the nation.

One can never consent to creep when one feels an impulse to soar.

Helen Keller

Vice President Mondale and Georgette's Valle's Candidacy for 34th District Representative

Reverend Mondale and my father were very good friends. The Mondale boys were very smart students in Elmore High School. Walter F. "Fritz" Mondale was four years younger than I, and his brother, Peter Mondale, was a year older. The family lived in a big, white, square house, which was the Methodist parsonage. Mother Mondale was a gregarious minister's wife who dutifully fulfilled the obligations thought necessary for their congregation.

There was always pressure for preachers' kids to be perfect. Parents who were ministers were frequently too strict in disciplining their children, so

inevitably a parental/child clash occurred. It occurred in the N. J. Vikingstad family.)

Peter Mondale became a university professor, another became a law professor, and another son became a medical doctor. Fritz Mondale (left) became Vice President of the United States on November 2, 1976, running on the Democratic ticket with President Jimmy Carter.

Fritz Mondale was courteous and passionate about the Democratic issues of the day. He possessed a quick wit and demonstrated great intellect during debates and public lectures. He drew on the moral convictions of his father and the political knowledge of Senator Hubert Humphrey.

After graduating from the Minnesota School of Law in 1956, and being admitted to the bar in 1956, he began his law practice in Minneapolis. He quickly jumped into the political fray of the Minnesota Attorney General's race and was elected in 1960 and reelected in 1962. On December 30, 1964, he was appointed to the United States Senate to fill the vacancy left by the resignation of Hubert

Vice President Walter "Fritz" Mondale and President Jimmy Carter

Humphrey, whose term was to end in 1967. Fritz was reelected in 1972 and served continuously as the Chair of the Select Committee on Equal Education Opportunity.

Jimmy Carter was a President who deeply believed in solving problems with nonviolent solutions. The hostage-taking episode in Iran near the end of his term was a troublesome situation, which resulted in behind-the-scenes dealing by Republicans which may have cost Carter the reelection.

U.S. voters had a deep sense of trust in the all-American "good guy" image. And that "good guy" wore a cowboy hat and rode a western horse in Ronnie Reagan's movies every night for three weeks before the general election of 1980.

Redistricting had occurred in 1980, and now there was an overabundance of legislators in the newly-formed 34th District. The 31st Legislative District was moved from our area. All six incumbents were now located in one district. One incumbent, Senator King Lysen, dropped out of the race. Senator Phil Talmadge ran a solid race for the Senate spot. Phil was a smart young attorney who was politically ambi-

Georgette laughs at a Minnesota joke that her cousin Vice President Fritz Mondale.

tious. There were two Republicans incumbents, Bruce Addison and Jeannette Burrage.

The race was now between Bruce Addison and me. Redistricting is a strange phenomenon with little public understanding as to its impact on the voters or the politicians. Paul Pruitt was an incumbent Democrat and Congregational minister with positive public recognition. He defeated Republican Jeannette Burrage with little difficulty. Bruce Addison had served several terms in the 34th District, therefore his name was better known to the voting public. I was new to the district and felt that I was swimming upstream with a lot of sharp rocks in my way. Both Bruce and I raised about the same amount of money, approximately $75,000. I lost the race, but I had been impacted before by redistricting. The next morning, guess what, I was out scrubbing those garbage cans again.

On the national scene in 1980, Fritz Mondale had chosen Geraldine Ferraro (seen left) as his running mate. This was history or "her story" in the making.

I intended to try to attain a position in the 34th District. I was an active precinct worker, bringing in new precinct people. All of this activity helped to promote my future candidacy. I continued to build my political organization with reliable and trustworthy workers. Lorraine Bonnell and Norma Kragtorp were always at my side, which was a testimony of their tremendous faith in me. These women were active Democrats and knew what had to be done during arduous campaigns.

There were others in the 34th District who wished to become the 34th District Representative. Liz Pierini was a League of Women Voters member, a Democrat, and a recognized public figure in the 34th District. She and her husband, Bruno, were gracious enough to host a fund-raising party for me and EVERYONE came. Washington's United States Senator Scoop Jackson and Seattle's Mayor Charles Royer were there to give me and all our campaign workers encouraging words. Subsequently, more campaign workers emerged to help.

I spent the next two years testifying for needed legislation and worked for the League of Women Voters and for other causes that were important to me. Then, suddenly, Representative Reverend Paul Pruitt announced he was not going to seek reelection in 1980. That would mean there would be an open spot. I immediately put out a press release that I was going to seek that position.

By this time, it had become known that John Carlson, a conservative Republican, was also going to run for this same position. I did not underestimate the challenge John Carlson presented and quickly got to work on my own organization. I could see that my valuable helpers were arguing and bickering about minutia at this point. I knew that I could not solve this mini-campaign war. I asked Tim Ceis for assistance. I knew he cared deeply about the district.

Some years earlier, I had sought the counsel of his mother, Margaret Ceis, who was wise beyond her years, giving me needed advice.

Tim did a great job reorganizing my campaign. Everyone responded positively, and I felt very energized to be able to return to my doorbelling. Tim organized Democratic Truth Squads that followed meetings, particularly functions where both John Carlson and I were speaking.

When active Democrats heard that Carlson was running against me, there

was a general snarl and uproar from organized groups, such as higher education. I looked upon John as an honest, conservative Republican, but I realized we needed to defeat him now so we don't have to contend with him later. I offered my experience in Olympia, but had to admit John was hugging some of my issues. Well, get out and doorbell, I told myself!

Georgette in front of her campaign billboard

We used all the resources at our disposal. Our recreational vehicles were used to deliver coffee and goodies as precinct workers took coffee breaks. Even Seattle Mayor Charlie Royer stopped by to congratulate us on our vigorous campaign.

Tim Cies and Odd Valle are by our truck and motor home
adorned with Valle campaign signs in 1980.

One late afternoon as I was approaching a home on the corner of 41st S.W. and Angeline, I encountered a man I knew who spoke Norwegian, so I prepared myself. *"God dag!"* (Good day!) *"Hvorden står det til?"* (How are you?)

"Bare Bra!" (Just fine!) "Say, vhat is the name of det fellow running against you?"

"Oh, his name is John Carlson."

He said right back to me, "Oh, ve'll beat that Svede!"

John and I would occasionally be working in the same precinct and exchange pleasantries of the day. At the very end of the campaign, John's literature depicted the West Seattle area as in a lavender color—where he lived—and where I lived a gray color, as if I were not even a resident in the 34th District.

Some overactive campaign chair, I thought. At the close of the campaign, I received the endorsement of the *West Seattle Herald*. Thank goodness for that endorsement! Subsequently, I saw that John's literature and advertisement listed him as the person the paper endorsed. I literally slumped home.

The morning after the election, the phone rang shortly after 9 a.m., and I gave a tired "Hello."

The voice said, "Congratulations!"

"You mean I won? Who is this speaking?"

The voice on the other end of the phone said, "This is John."

"John who?"

"John Carlson!"

Three Georgettes, *left to right:* Georgette Logan, Representative Georgette Valle, and Sister Georgette Vayless of St. Joseph Hospital in April of 1990

WALTER F. MONDALE

2550 M STREET, N.W., SUITE 500
WASHINGTON, D.C. 20037

March 11, 1983

The Honorable Georgette Valle
1434 S.W. 137th Street
Seattle, Washington 98166

Dear Georgette:

I have been traveling so am only now able to take a minute to write and say how much I enjoyed our visit in Seattle in January.

I appreciated your joining me at the luncheon, and I enjoyed our conversation about your son, Peter, and the state of the Party in Washington. I hope we will have other such opportunities to visit, and I will have my campaign staff contact Peter in New York so that we might involve him in our efforts.

I am grateful for your offer of help and look forward to receiving your advice and counsel as we progress in the days ahead. In the meanwhile, let's keep in touch. Warmest personal regards.

Sincerely,

Pitching a Mondale bumper strip, Georgette talks about her cousin's expertise to become President to Bob Fithian and Senator Bob Ridder.

Mistakes are part of the dues one pays for a full life.
Sophia Loren

Pranks and Pranksters

We, as legislators were always cautioned to behave as serious legislators with no other thoughts than talking and thinking about legislative business twenty-four hours a day. After all, there were cameras around us all the time: morning, noon, and night. Very often, if leadership wanted an issue to be passed, they would keep us there until the light of the next day. This was true of either political party.

The "sunshine laws" did help to protect the public's right to know when hearings were going to be held, public notice when they would be voted upon in one legislative body, and the cutoff point for the introduction of bills.

When more women of both parties were elected to the legislature, we got together and convinced leadership to pass the ten o'clock rule. One of our colleagues from Snohomish County had fallen asleep in the House of Representatives at 3 a.m., and on the following election saw a picture published of herself in a hit piece with the caption "Asleep on the Job." Needless to say, she was defeated. We did not think that we were a productive body when performing our legislative duties beyond the hour of 10 p.m.

When I was first elected State Representative in 1965, Governor Albert Rossellini, a Democrat, was just leaving office and Governor Daniel Evans, a Republican, was entering the office of Governor. I was a cautious Democrat and viewed him critically. I was to discover that on most issues I agreed with him. He might have crafted his legislation for a democratically-controlled legislature, but on the environment, education, and in fiscal issues I did agree with him.

No Smoking Bill Pranks

Legislators worked very hard. I felt this was true of both political parties. However, at the moment, there were legislators who had no serious items of business on the floor of the House. That certainly must have been the case when a fire was set in my wastebasket as I was discussing what was known as the "No Smoking Bill." I was deeply engrossed in detailing the parts of the bill and did not even notice the billowing smoke. I think a supporter of the Anti-tobacco Bill finally put the fire out.

A good sense of humor provided a better chance to stand the pranks played by my legislative colleagues and an ability to laugh at myself. I received the letters full of cigarette ashes, cigarettes left still burning in the ashtrays on my desk, and more. When I was sure that the Washington Indoor Clean Air Act was going to pass, I asked a good Republican friend of mine, Dick Barnes from the 30th District, to light up a big, long cigar during my speech. He was very obliging and lit it up, to the consternation of our colleagues. I leaped to my feet, seized the cigar, put it out in a glass of water, and gave him an equally long toothbrush! (I was famous for giving out

Representative Dick Barnes receives a huge toothbrush in exchange for the burning cigar. Representative Delores Teutsch looks on in support of Representative Valle's move.

toothbrushes for the Washington Dental Society every two years.) The House of Representatives roared with applause.

Another member, Representative Alan Thompson, spoke with mock jest with an upside-down corncob pipe smoking through his supportive speech. On another occasion, I was treated by two of my Democratic colleagues, seated immediately behind me, with less than professional courtesy and continual banter while I was speaking on the floor of the House of Representatives. One day I entreated them to speak for me during one of my speeches. They were quiet for some days and finally approached me with a solution. The galleries were packed with over four hundred people. I was to be recognized by Speaker Pro Tem John O'Brien. The

As a prank, Representative Valle was doing a ONE-TIME research test on how bad a cigar tasted and smelled at a social event. Someone took this damaging picture and threatened to release it during a campaign, but never did.

entire House of Representatives was very still as I silently mouthed my procedural request into the microphone. Instead of my voice, the deep resonant voice of Representative G. K. Douthwaite thundered into the mike: "Mr. Speaker, I request the previous question."

The gallery crowd roared with surprised laughter while the perplexed Speaker O'Brien was left wondering who he really recognized. (This contrived operation was managed by the electronic assistant having me speak into a dead mike while Representative Douthwaite spoke the words into my mike. The Speaker had to recognize me, which he did.) My colleagues never troubled me again with their incessant banter.

Double Standards

I always wanted to be seen in fashion and appear well-groomed. I used to hear my male colleagues say they would be right back and then in a soft tone say, "I have to go for a haircut!" I was told I could go for a haircut at the salon, third floor, Democratic side of the House, which I finally found located in a closet. The barber had no customers. I decided not to have my hair cut and was offered an alcoholic drink. I declined that, too. The women legislators heard about the male barbershop and said we needed equal rights! For a time we had a beautician in our ladies lounge. Hairdos were relaxing. That was very convenient for quite a few of us women until Adele Ferguson reported our activities in *The Bremerton Sun* as frivolous.

Henry Called

As the cool rain slid down the kitchen window, I thought about the letter I had written to Henry Fonda asking if he could come to a Democratic fund raiser at the home of David Sprague. I wondered if Henry Fonda had received the letter. David Sprague was a very active member of the Metropolitan Democratic Club. As I was mulling over all of these thoughts, the phone rang. I used my best modulated voice as I said, "Hello."

An inquiring voice said, "Georgette Valle?"

And I said, "HENRY FONDA!"

On the other end of the line Henry Fonda said, "I'm pleased that you asked me to come for a Democratic fund raiser. I am taking it easy because I just had a pacemaker put in my heart. I'm returning to my wife today. I am not doing any special events."

As I recovered my voice, I said, "Thank you for calling."

After repeating this story, several male legislators called me saying they were Henry Fonda.

Jail Prank

Playing a prank on myself resulted in my arrest by the Seattle Police on May 24, 1989. Two of my constituents, Jean Hueston and Art McDonald, were riding with me to a legislative meeting on Jail Rehabilitation. Not being quite sure of my destination, I moved the car from one lane to the right-hand lane with no difficulty because at the moment there was no traffic. As I made a right-hand turn, I heard the musical *tootle* of a police motorcycle.

I asked for the ordinance that the police officer was using to cite me. When I read that moving from one lane to the right-hand lane was actually illegal on First Avenue, I refused to sign the ticket. I was subsequently arrested, fingerprinted, and photographed. Within the hour, I was actually lobbied to introduce legislation for more funding for the King County Jail. We hurried to the Jail Rehabilitation meeting knowing a little more of jail procedure than earlier in the evening.

These activities are not to impugn any legislator's motives or actions. It is to suggest that legislators are human, too.

*Life is so constructed that the event does not ,
cannot, will not, match the expectations.*

Charlotte Bronte

Legislative Process:
The Story of Personal Service Contracts

The governor has three choices: sign the bill, veto the bill, or ignore it and let it become law in ninety days.

If a bill I introduced reached the governor, it was usually signed. However, one day Governor Booth Gardiner called me to his office. I obliged, with the happy expectation that Governor Gardiner was going to sign my bill. It was not a bill of great consequence, but I had worked the legislative process, which is grueling and time consuming.

When I arrived a photographer was present, but none of the co-sponsors of the bill were there. The governor announced that he was going to veto the bill. I was astounded and asked him why. He gave me several explanations which did not please me. When I saw that the photographer taking pictures of me, I really exploded! When I saw it was truly a losing cause, I gave up and returned to my busy schedule.

Representative Georgette Valle discusses with Governor Booth Gardiner the State Investment Board legislation. Governor Gardiner *(1985-1992)* later instituted auditing rules and regulations by Executive Order to the State Investment Board similar to Valle's bill.

Legislators were interested in the activities of the State Investment Board and had been watching the actions of the Board. We were concerned with their business practices, so a consultant was hired and made good recommendations to the Board. The Board was not following the recommendations, so I introduced a bill with the recommendations to the Board as mandatory practice. Governor Gardiner looked at the bill and created an Executive Order with those recommendations incorporated.

Bionic Legislator, always in a cast (1980s)

One day I paused to take in the architectural beauty of the marble walls, the vastness of the dome, and grandeur of the stairs leading up to the floors of the legislative building and then continued on. As I heard my heels clicking behind me, I thought I should be a little more careful as there were no railings in the building. Representative Marion Kyle Sherman had fallen down the marble stairs on her way out of the Capitol to her office. We had discussed the possibilities of having a gold banister installed down the middle of the stairs. Marion, who was known for her quick wit and intellect in her remarks on the floor of the House, could have promoted some kind of action, but since her fall had not resulted in broken bones, there is still no gold banister.

1993 Women Legislators

A fiscal issue that involved a lot of government money was the practice of directors of Washington State agencies engaging personal service contractors to perform certain specified tasks for specific sums of money. Many of these personal service contracts were extremely costly. I always figured there was a connection between the governors' campaigns and the many personal service contracts. However, I never had the time to delve into the public disclosure records of Governors Evans, Ray, Spellman, Gardiner, or Lowry.

Odd Valle and Representative Georgette Valle in her last session in 1996

I was overworking one of my secretaries, Lavona, on this particular issue. Alan Thompson, Clerk of the House of Representatives, facilitated my obtaining the services of an eager intern who was very diligent about completing the research that I needed. I could then develop the legislation that would effectively govern the fiscal relationship between personal service contractors and the state of Washington government agencies. I had no quarrel with what directors were asking in these contracts, but I questioned the amounts of money that were paid.

Governor Gary Locke *(1997-2000)* stops to speak to Georgette Valle on September 10, 1999.

Over the years, changes were taking place. Professional women were entering the field as lobbyists, directors of agencies, and as personal service contractors. Not only were they engaged as contractors, but often charging much less than their male counterparts. Oversight is very important in state government with accountability and the quality of products considered. I left this subject with the Chair of the Appropriations Committee, Representative Gary Locke. In my last session as Representative in 1996, I took my last look at the report on these state contracts, hoping that since Gary Locke, who became governor, would be accountable in this time of fiscal crisis. 🚢

These and other protesters found out about the impending closure of the Admiral Theater with just a few days' notice, but they scrambled to launch a demonstration on closing night, January 29, 1991. (*Seattle Times* newspaper clipping)

SECRETARY OF STATE

March 14, 1996

The Honorable Georgette Valle
Washington State Representative
1434 Southwest 137th
Burien, Washington 98166

Dear Georgette:

How can I thank you enough? You have been simply superb, and offered
so much support to the proposals from this office. You are very highly
appreciated by our entire team. This session, a special thank you for
your work on the International Education and Exchange Bill.

We will miss you immensely in the legislative arena. You have worked so
hard on international programs and world trade. It will be very difficult to
replace your interest, involvement, talents, and skills.

I hope you will keep in close touch. You are the very best.

Sincerely,

RALPH MUNRO
Secretary of State

RM:jn

6 Wednesday, October 9, 1996 West Seattle Herald/White Center News

COMMENT

Valle set tone for successor

Say what you will about Georgette Valle. Many already have. They've called her crazy, vacuous, soft, clueless.

But criticism's as integral as yard signs when you spend 24 years of your life in the public spotlight. And say what you will, Valle has persevered. Anyone willing to risk holding their private x-rays to the public glare deserves a special medal in this day and age.

Valle blazed the trail for female legislators, enduring ridicule in the male-dominated capitol to pass the 1985 Clean Indoor Air Act. She also battled for recycling plastic diapers, mentor-teacher programs and college savings bonds.

The lifetime Democrat never wavered from her core beliefs. She was a consistent advocate for children, the elderly, personal health and the environment. Even after she retires from the state House of Representative in December, she'll continue to be an activist for an environmental learning center in Burien's Seahurst Park.

She has served her Westside constituents gracefully and well, setting a tone of conduct we hope her successor follows. Her retirement adds a classy topping to a distinguished career.

We wish she and her family well. We suspect we'll still see her around.

204

Representative Georgette Valle presents a Norwegian *blöt kake* to the legislature on May 17, 1989. Georgette is in her Norwegian Hardanger *bunad*. Rep. Dick Nelson is standing to her left. (*Kake* made by the Burien Danish Bakery)

Representatives Rob Johnson, Ken Jacobsen, Tracey Eide, and Julia Patterson join Representative Georgette Valle in May 1994 to celebrate their Scandinavian ancestry.

President William Jefferson
Clinton at the swearing in for
his second term as President
of the United States in
January 1993

Odd, Georgette, and Peter Valle at President
William Jefferson Clinton's second Inaugural
Ball in January 1993

Representative Doris
Johnson at Senator
Cantwell's President
Clinton luncheon

Running for 7th Congressional Seat in 1993

This picture used in the Congressional campaign when Brock Adams was Secretary of Transportation. *From left:* Ethel Kennedy (Mrs. Bobby Kennedy), James Whittaker (Mt. Everest Climber), and Representative Georgette Valle.

Representative Alan Thompson and Barbara discuss Georgette's candidacy for the 7th Congressional seat. Congressman Brock Adams resigned to become Secretary of Transportation.

Representative Rich Bender talks with Representative Georgette Valle about her race for the 7th Congressional seat. Representative Bender became President of the Washington Labor Council in 1993.

Ellie, Our Scottish Terrier

A PLEASANT ENCOUNTER WITH ELLIE

A pleasant encounter
Meeting a curly-haired puppy
So dark you'd miss her
On a black night.
But in the sunlight
She'd sparkle personality.
And a solid quality,
Feet so near the earth,
Her tail so proud,
Wagging fast and quick.
Proof of her
Scottish terrier kin
And her FDR Falla cousin.
Her affection never wavered.
Her direction now and then tarried.
Her attraction to us—
Our selection of her,
Our devoted dog, Ellie.

One rather slow day while working in the Washington State Legislature in 1986, I was invited by a legislative colleague to meet a relative of Falla, FDR's famous inimitable Scottish terrier pet. At that time I was not a dog fancier, and so I ambled along with an "I won't be impressed" attitude. The legislator, Representative Alan Thompson, was a newspaper editor who prided himself on being a dog fancier, having raised several breeds of dogs. As I approached his office doorway, I saw he was busy teaching the Scottish terrier puppies to read the best editorial papers in the state of Washington—*The Seattle Times, The Post-Intelligencer,* and the *Cowlitz Inquirer*. Little did I realize then that one of the puppies would soon be my pet. I placed a $100 deposit for one irresistible ball of fur. She was chosen for her straight back, stand-up tail, and just plain perkiness. Her black,

shiny coat curled as if she had just exited from the beauty parlor. Her eyes were full of expectation of the new life that was awaiting her. Two weeks later I was invited by the Thompsons to come and transport Ellie from Castle Rock to her new home in Burien. After a delicious dinner at the Thompsons, Ellie was carried to my car in a special box decorated with a Scottish tartan cloth and then promptly plopped down beside me as I drove home. Ellie soon settled down and stirred slightly as we drove through Tacoma's bright lights.

As we reached her new home, I placed her carefully in her new Scottish decorated box with a clock ticking beneath the pillow. I had been told that the ticking clock was to represent the sound of her absent mother. I hoped that at six weeks of age she would not miss her mother too much. The next morning at 6 a.m., as I struggled to awaken, I heard Ellie whimper and bark. I jumped out of bed and ran downstairs to carry her up to our kitchen. There the latest editorial pages were carefully distributed on the kitchen floor to continue her education in the Valle home. Ellie was busy wagging her tail when my husband, Odd, introduced himself to her. Ellie was very impressed with his presence, making short little noises as her head bounced from side to side.

In retrospect, Ellie had been named by me in the two-week interval after I first met her. I decided that since she was a relative of Falla that her name would be Eleanor Falla Valle. I also realized that I could not be calling her Eleanor as her days progressed at our home. It was our three-year-old neighbor, Melinda Ford, who first called her Ellie. That name seemed appropriate, and the veterinarian also liked it. She was always known as "Ellie Dog" to Melinda.

I took her to dog obedience lessons (and I think I learned to obey her). Ellie learned to sit, bark, and let us know when she was hungry. However, to walk obediently at the end of a leash did not seem to be her style at all. We met a lot of new friends, because Ellie did not like to stay home unless she was busy playing with us. She loved to run up the hill to the apartments because there were plenty of children to give her attention or accompany my husband to the mailbox.

It's true I was a new dog owner, but there were things I should have watched out for. Ellie was good playing by herself on the fenced porch. We could leave her for a few hours, or so I thought. There were roaming male dogs who would actually take advantage of a six-month-old puppy. Sometime later, when Ellie was having a check up at the vet's office, I learned she was pregnant! Ellie was an excellent mother and took good care of her pups. When they were old enough, we gratefully gave them away. We had learned a good lesson.

Later in her life she was bred with a much respected Scottish terrier. We continued to be watchful parents. This time around my husband made her a birthing bed. Ellie again turned out to be a very good mother, giving birth to four beautiful Scottish terrier puppies! We charged $100 for each puppy, the same amount we paid for Ellie.

Ellie was occupied with exploring her surroundings. She sniffed all things up, down, and around. It was a warm spring day and life was a little bit boring for an active dog like Ellie. Both Odd and I were watching her and were about to say "No, Ellie!" when she snapped up a huge slug. Her reaction was a stifled and muffled whimper. My dentist husband sprang into action, grabbed Ellie's mouth, forced it open, and dug the huge slug out of her mouth. Ellie gave a whimper of relief and slumped into an ambulatory pose.

We thought that Ellie was the "cat's pajamas," but not everyone agreed with us. When we moved her outside into the garage, we did not hear her bark, but unfortunately the neighbors did. One day when I was in the Legislature, a call came from my husband saying we had been threatened with a lawsuit if we didn't debark our dog. Of course veterinarians didn't think the dog would suffer any pain, but I thought it was cruel and unusual punishment for Ellie. Finally we agreed to have the surgery done.

When Ellie came home from her debarking operation, every time she barked, she looked around to see who was making such a funny high-pitched sound. We

didn't hear complaints from any neighbors after that, but if there was a dog barking, I would get an anonymous call telling me, "Stop your dog from barking!"

Ellie loved to travel and jumped into everyone's car to go with them. So, we
decided to take her with us on a trip. Taking her to a kennel was expensive, and I
didn't think she enjoyed our vacations that much when we left her there. We
found a hotel-motel that would accommodate pets. The elevator was glassed in,
and Ellie thought was it was grand to watch people disappear as she barked with
amazement. When we got to our room, we would always feed her, but she didn't
always eat. One day as we were having a snack in our room, Ellie scurried over to
the corner of the room where she had carefully hidden some of her food. It was
very comforting to see that she wanted to enjoy her food at the same time we
were having our dinner.

Ellie didn't seem to be aging and even enjoyed gardening with my husband.
She watched him as he weeded, planted, and picked the strawberries. He would
tell her that it would not be long before they could both rest on the patio.

Ellie was a very trusting dog, stopping for water and food up the hill from the
apartments. Then one day I noticed that Ellie was growing larger—larger than
was appropriate for a dog of her size. I knew it was time to take her to the vet.
We got in the car, but this time Ellie was not capable of jumping up into the car,
so I lovingly lifted her up to the seat. The veterinarian shook his head. He didn't
know what was ailing Ellie and wanted to keep her to do tests on her. A few days
later I got a call from the vet telling me that Ellie had died. That same afternoon,
flowers arrived on our doorstep from the vet. Now I know that Ellie has sprouted
angel wings, because I can still hear her bark with her funny high-pitched bark!

Wedding Bells Are Ringing
Peter and Junko Valle's Wedding

1990 was a busy year for Peter. The long-term friendship that had began on Mount Rainier through the Lions' Student Exchange culminated in two students, Peter Valle and Junko Kajikawa, becoming engaged on July 28, 1990. Peter had nicknamed Junko—CoCo—and the engagement ring was especially designed to read CoCo in diamonds.

One year later, on July 28, 1991, they were married at the Plymouth Congregational Church in Seattle by Pastor Susan Yarrow Morris with Japanese and American guests in attendance.

The reception for the new Valle couple was held at the Valle residence in Hurstwood in Burien. A small musical group played and Japanese cuisine and Norwegian sandwiches were served to guests. Their wedding cake was baked by the Burien Danish Bakery. Junko has a beautiful singing voice, and she fervently sang two or three joyful songs for our guests.

The happy couple began their honeymoon in a white convertible to enjoy the sunny weather ordered for their wedding day. They honeymooned in San Martin in the Caribbean.

Junko and Peter Valle at their
reception at the Valle home

Junko's parents, Hiroyshi and Takako Kajikawa, very generously paid for their Japanese guests' flights and hotel stays at the Seattle Embassy Suites Hotel. The hotel bill cost Papa Kajikawa over $6,000. He had a little difficulty with his key, and I didn't think the Embassy Suites Hotel was accommodating to him over this incident, so I wrote to them from my Olympia office and suggested they should have given him a gold key for that kind of hotel bill. Sure enough, the next time we visited the Kajikawas in Kobe, Japan, there was a gold key displayed in with other valuables in a beautiful glass case in their residence.

Christine Goonetilleke and Georgette
in the Valle house garden on
Peter and Junko's wedding day

Fortunately for children, the uncertainties of the present always give way to the enchanted possibilities of the future.

Gelsey Kirkland

Russian Junior Achievement in a Moscow High School

Superintendent Kendrick and the Seattle School Board were taking a trip to the U.S.S.R. to view the Junior Achievement process in Russian schools in Moscow in 1991. I was serving on the Education Committee of the Washington House of Representatives at that time. I thought this would be a valuable trip for me to take. I was under no illusion that my trip would be paid for by the state of Washington, but I thought that this educational opportunity would not present itself again. It would be financially worthwhile for me to absorb the cost.

I asked my secretary, Leslie, to arrange for me to accompany the Seattle School Board and the Superintendent on the trip. The trip took place in November, about a year after Boris Yeltsin was elected to succeed Mikhail Gorbachev. I knew the weather was likely to be cold, so I packed all my winter clothes. I had good boots with Cuban heels, so as Nancy Sinatra sang *My Boots Are Made for Walking*, I was ready for Moscow weather. I had a nice brown-suede coat with fur around the wrists, the neck, and the skirt of the coat. I bought myself a fur hat that matched the coat to ensure everyone would think that I was Russian. The coat was very stylish, good for bracing me from the wind, but not necessarily warm.

If anything can put a snarl in your day, speaking only English in the U.S.S.R. can complicate your activities. On a previous trip to Moscow, I wanted to say hello on the telephone to Governor Dan Evans, who was staying in another hotel in Moscow. Within minutes, I was connected to the capitol of the United States in Washington, D.C. I gave up the idea of speaking with Governor Evans.

The Seattle delegation was in a distant hotel. There was no communication with me. I did not let that bother me. All the taxi drivers spoke some English. Some of the time I could walk to the meetings.

Arriving at the conference in the morning, I was nowhere near the Seattle School District delegation, nor could I find anyone who was aware of their whereabouts. Thank goodness I had a program. At least I could point to the buildings so I could attend the panel presentations. I walked to and from meet-ings while admiring the Kremlin in the distance. It was a spectacular site as the colorful spires pointed skyward. The reds, the bluish purples, and the golden yellows on the spires all sparkled in the sunlight.

At one of the meetings, the United States Assistant Secretary of Education and Labor Lynn Martin was

Various dignitaries address the participants and the guests at the 1991 Junior Achievement Conference.

in attendance. I was very impressed by her presentation, because the current Republican administration was not presenting the same views on Labor and Edu-cation back home as they were here in Moscow. She had previously served in Congress as a Republican. I asked a few questions and found that her answers better fit the image of a liberal Democrat. I wondered if her boss, President George H. W. Bush, knew of the message she delivered in Moscow. An eager photographer took several pictures of us. This meeting hall was one of the most beautiful rooms I had ever seen with a vast number of chandeliers.

I had friends in Moscow who had visited Odd and me during the Goodwill Games in Seattle in 1990. We were one of a few Seattleites who entertained a Russian couple. This visit was arranged by the Washington Secretary of State Ralph Munroe.

Our guests had enjoyed our hospitality and wanted to reciprocate while I was

My Russian guests meet Governor Booth Gardiner.

in Moscow. She was a kindergarten teacher, and he was connected with the Russian Parliament and held a position in some sort of service committee. They lived in a small apartment not far from the Moscow Hotel in midtown Moscow and were very hospitable even though they did not speak English!

While visiting them, I learned how Russian apartments were constructed.

Apartments were built with two views. One view was from the living room and the other view was from the dining room. The apartment ran from the front side

of the building to the back of the building with the bathroom, bedrooms, kitchen, and closets in the middle. The apartment buildings were very narrow, and all apartments in the area were approximately the same size.

My Russian friend took me back to my mid-city hotel. There was one routine he would always go through when he stopped the car. He would take the windshield wipers off the car and slip them into his pocket. These items were easy targets for burglary in Moscow.

Russian billboards advertising peace and preservation of Russian environment and being watchful of fires in the forest

After rest for the night in my hotel, I was put in contact with a fourth-grade Russian teacher who spoke English and learned I was to be given a private tour of a Russian school and also attend a Russian cocktail party courtesy of my Russian friends' influence. I looked forward enthusiastically to both events.

On my tour of a Russian school I was surprised that all the classes through grade twelve were assigned to one building complex. I was given about forty-five minutes to be briefed and to ask questions. My teacher/hostess was very friendly and welcomed the opportunity to inform me about the curriculum, the building complex arrangement, and answer any questions I might have.

At the end of our discussion, we moved with the students to another class-room. Everyone was so well behaved; I could scarcely believe what I was seeing in these twelve grades in mid-Moscow. The students moved in such an orderly manner. The first and twelfth graders passed each other in the hall without an unpleasant incident.

As we reached the twelfth-grade classroom, I glanced out a window, and there I saw a swimming pool with five swimming lanes. This was very conven-ient for water exercise. Designing the building so the pool was alongside also made good transportation sense.

I was invited to speak to the twelfth-grade class, which was in a very crowded room. I spoke of my family, my life as a Washington State Representative, and my trip to the U.S.S.R. with the Seattle School delegation. As I progressed, I told them about how eager our delegation was to hear about Russian Junior Achieve-ment. I ended with these words because I was so anxious to hear from the class and from the teacher. To my amazement, a young boy arose and asked in perfect English, "What is Junior Achievement?"

I was so surprised at the Russian boy's good English. I had expected to have a translator in the classroom. To explain Junior Achievement, I told them many stories like lemonade stand business transactions where so many young U.S. school children began their business adventures.

Then it was on to next class. There the desks had half-wooden enclosures which permitted students the opportunity to listen to their headphones and their tape recorders. This was something I had not seen in an American classroom. I thought this was a prelude to today's computer age. I later sent my teacher friend, who had spoken such good English, a book entitled, *Classroom Instructions and Techniques in an American Classroom.*

The night of the Russian cocktail party arrived! I don't think I was prepared

Representative Georgette Valle and her Russian Parliamentary friends at a Russian cocktail party in 1991

for a dressy event, so I wore my best black cocktail dress, which was both warm and attractive. The party consisted mainly of male members of the Russian Parliament. My Russian friend escorted me to the party, and we took our place at the table in a standing position. I looked around for chairs and there were none. We were served small glasses of straight vodka. It took me some time to realize that I could not consume any more vodka. Several Russians spoke English and came over to our table to meet us. It was a beautiful evening and the party was held in an attractive ballroom in a very old, but well "kept up," building in stark contrast to the condition of the majority of the buildings in the U.S.S.R.

One more visit would completely satisfy my American curiosity, and that was to have an opportunity to meet Mikhail Gorbachev, so I kept pestering my Russian friend to accommodate my wishes. Towards the end of the evening, my Russian friend told me I could have an appointment with Mr. Gorbachev on Monday at 2 p.m. I missed the opportunity to meet with Mikhail Gorbachev because I could not stay an extra day because of a previous engagement with the Evergreen Democratic Club.

The next morning I was to join the Seattle School District delegation for the grand finale of the presentation of the Russian and American top winners of the Junior Achievement Awards. I made my own way to the event by taxi and greeted Seattle Superintendent Kendrick as he stepped out of a shiny, black Russian automobile. As he exited the showy auto, I said, "If the Seattle School District could only see you now!"

Junior Achievement in Moscow closing session celebrating the many participants from all over the world

Both presentations by the American Junior Achievement and the Russian Junior Achievement students were excellent, and I was overjoyed that I did not have to pick a single winner. A young Russian male student was the winner! The U.S. female student was excellent, and although she was undoubtedly disappointed, she was able to participate in the trip and would bring back fond memories. We were all proud of her. It was a fantastic night and a great ending to a wonderful trip.

The Board of Directors
of
The Foundation for International Cooperation and Development

hereby expresses its appreciation to

The Honorable Gerogette Valle

for personal contribution to the success of
the Conference on Soviet-American Trade and Economic Cooperation.

Signed and sealed this 7th day of December, 1991
in the Kremlin Palace in Moscow, Russia, on the
occasion of the closing ceremony of the conference.

Norman John Swanson, President
Foundation for International Cooperation and Development

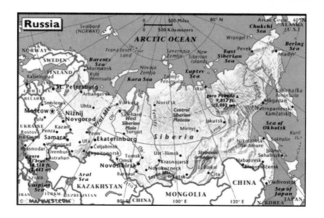

*Women have to be twice as good to get
half as far as men.*

Agnes Macphail

The Ted Danson Political Event
or How I Fell for Ted Danson

On a beautiful Saturday afternoon in May of 1994 I took time from my campaigning for State Representative to attend a Washington Environmental Council Fund Raiser? This was an environmental event that featured Ted Danson, television actor who had invested his money and time in foundations concerned with worldwide ocean pollution. The clients at Sally's Beauty Parlor wanted me to check out Ted Danson's hairpiece. They were certain he would be relaxed and not wear it.

Georgette Valle and Actor/Activist Ted Danson

The Washington Environmental Council had organized the day's activities including a tour boat excursion. We easily located the Seattle pier and arrived in time to find a good parking spot. We joined a line of excited people waiting to board the Seattle tour boat. As the tour boat shoved off into the calm waters of Puget Sound, the beautiful shoreline of the city of Seattle was I full view. I could point to the 34th Legislative District as we rounded Alki Point with the sight of new condominiums and older homes nestled among the beach.

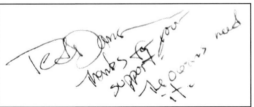

I was pleased to be introduced to Ted Danson, and several pictures were snapped, and I managed to get his autograph. The words he wrote were:

"Thanks for your support! The oceans need it. Ted Danson." He was then whisked away to meet other environmentalists.

The tour boat rocked a bit as we sped toward Blake Island, enjoying our appetizers and sipping a glass of wine.

After landing at Blake Island, I noticed the piers and walkways were well constructed. A Democratic colleague who, with some of her friends, had crossed a Blake Island footbridge and it broke and sank. Sadly, she lost her life because she was unable to swim. Her friends, however, made it to shore, but this tragic event cast a pall over the Democratic Women's Conference I was there to attend.

Even before entering the tribal hall we could smell the barbecued salmon being prepared. After enjoying a delicious meal, Ted Danson spoke of the future of our oceans and the perils of present day pollution. As environmentalists, we were urged to elect candidates who were conscious of today's ocean pollution and its consequences for our children and future generations.

I thought about the Puget Sound Pipeline Safety legislation that I had introduced. A Republican Spokane legislator, Senator Sam Guess, agreed with me that there should be buoys located in the Washington Peninsula ocean waters with connecting pipelines for the oil. He had recently toured China and had viewed their pipeline operations. Senator Guess was favorably impressed with their pipeline safety measures and the lack of pipeline pollution.

Odd and I were aware that in Norway shipbuilding was an important industry. Supertankers in Norway were sold to the United States and Near East oil companies. However, the North Sea oil has always been shipped to Norway,

Denmark, and England seaports by pipelines. The Stavanger Oil Museum contains maps and diagrams of the North Sea oil pipeline flowing into its seaports. Within a few years of my spotting a huge ship in Stavanger (later sold to Shell Oil), South Korea became the shipbuilding industrial nation that had been Norway's industrial insignia.

This information was also carefully documented in a display of the undersea pipeline operation at a Canadian Vancouver exhibition. With that knowledge, Senator Sam Guess and I agreed to sponsor and introduce the Oil Pipeline legislation. Neither of us thought of ourselves as being rebels, but we certainly supported a just environmental cause.

Both the oil companies and environmentalists spoke against this pipeline legislation at our joint legislative hearing. One of my concerns was that Eastern Washington at that time needed a steady supply of oil. This was before Senator Magnuson proposed an amendment to legislation, mandating smaller oil tankers no heavier than 250,000 tons were allowed into Puget Sound. That Magnuson amendment seemed to satisfy all concerned in Washington State.

Senator Warren G. Magnuson advises Representative Valle on Puget Sound oil traffic.

Suddenly, with this legislative flashback I heard someone call my name along with Jennifer Belcher, the Director of Washington State's Natural Resources. "Picture taking on the top of the hill with Ted Danson."

Afterwards, I quickly grabbed Odd's arm so I could reach the bottom of the hill safely. With two replaced hips and two unsteady knees, I needed support. At that moment I slipped and fell. Many people came to help me up. As I lay on the hill, I could see my leg and ankle were swelling and that my leg was probably broken. Very soon the stretcher arrived. Someone in charge asked if I wanted

Blake Island ferry landing in May 1994. Photo taken by the Washington Parks and Recreation Department by air.

to take the tour boat back to Seattle or take a helicopter to the hospital. I knew that with the boat there was considerable movement. I decided to take the helicopter ride even if my insurance wouldn't cover it.

I was immediately loaded onto the helicopter. I said my goodbye to Odd and the rest of the guests. As the helicopter left Blake Island, I heard someone say, "Way to go Georgette!" I regretted not having my camera. The sunset was casting a picture-perfect rosy glow over the entire City of Seattle, with Puget Sound framing the City with blue-purplish waters.

The pilot asked me what hospital I wanted to go to—Harborview?

"No, take me to Highline Hospital." I did not want to go to an emergency hospital where I perhaps would have to wait in line behind a gunshot victim.

After landing at Sylvester Field, I was quickly loaded into an ambulance. Within minutes I arrived at the Highline Hospital Emergency Room. It was a quiet evening, and I was quickly seen by an emergency room physician. I had broken the same leg that I had broken skiing with my daughter at the Alpental Ski Resort. When the bones were set, I called Odd and spent the remainder of the night at hospital.

Ted Danson sent me beautiful blue hydrangea flowers in an elegant aluminum vase. After all, people were saying that I fell for Ted Danson!

After this incident I received several calls from an insurance agent. I answered the last call and assured the agent I was not going to sue anyone because I fell and broke my leg.

The cast on my leg was not yet dry as Tom Carr, a newcomer in the 34th District, announced he would be running against me. This was a total surprise and naturally I was not pleased. There was a lot of young testosterone flying around the precinct organization. There were a lot of young people with a lot of extra energy that could be directed to the state legislative race. I had to recognize that.

Of course, my supporters did not even think I was in trouble. The precinct organization endorsed me with over 80 percent of the vote. Doorbelling for me was difficult, if not impossible. As usual, Odd did a great job getting and keeping the signs up. Rumors were being circulated that I was not seeking public office this time. During the last four days of the campaign, I got out with one crutch and doorbelled four precincts. I won the primary, and I went on to defeat my opponent in the general election.

My secretary, Leslie, kept telling me an insurance agent was still calling me. I was sure he was going to ask me to sponsor some far-out bill no one else would sponsor, so I kept on telling Leslie I was busy.

Finally, one day I was in the office and had to answer him. We exchanged pleasantries, and he said, "We are thinking of settling with you for a figure of about $8,500. How does that sound to you?"

All of a sudden it was as if a thunderbolt of lightening struck me, and I said, "That figure sounds good to me!" There were a few more phone calls, and in approximately a week, a check arrived from the insurance company, which I cashed very quickly.

> Someday perhaps change will occur when times are ready for it instead of always when it is too late. Someday change will be accepted as life itself.
> Shirley MacLaine

Two Weeks in Cuba, 1996

It was during an October day in the 1996 House of Representatives session in Olympia. Odd called to tell me that Norm Nelson, a Democratic Precinct Committeeman from North Seattle, had called Odd and suggested that we join him on a trip to Cuba. A trip to sunny Cuba was exactly what we needed. Travel restrictions had been lifted by the United States State Department for journalists who wished to visit Cuba, and State Department restrictions on Cuban immigrants were lifted for those who wanted to send money to their families. Perhaps it was exactly the right time to travel there.

I asked my secretary, Leslie, to contact the State Department to obtain the latest information and had given her many questions to assist her. The response was terse and negative, do not go.

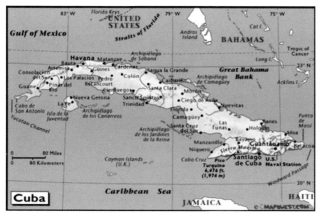

I was establishing a record of inquiry, so that if we should go—at the very least I had sought answers before making the trip. Norm Nelson and his wife, Norma, had contacted a Canadian travel agent and found that we would travel to Canada to purchase our plane tickets to Cuba and arrange for our Cuban hotel reserva-tions for the two-weeks in late October. This would mean that I would celebrate my birthday in Havana.

We were briefed on who would be joining us and what our contributions might be. Several of our traveling companions were interested in providing needed health supplies. I purchased about fifty dollars worth of school supplies. Odd was interested in learning if any Lions Clubs existed in Cuba.

The weather in Cuba was said to be warm, balmy, and breezy. We packed light sportswear which was comfortable and washable. I was certain that dressy clothes were not in vogue in Fidel Castro's Communist Cuba.

The day for our departure drew near. I must admit that I did not sleep well due to the excitement. The border crossing at Blaine went as usual with Odd being asked about his Norwegian citizenship and naturalization as a U.S. citizen. We said we might travel from Canada elsewhere, but no further questions were asked about where we might be going. We drove on into Canada where we were to meet Norm Nelson and our other traveling companions.

We were happy to meet with the travel agent who had arranged our travel for the next two weeks. We were to fly out of Vancouver to Toronto, Canada, via Canada Air, and from Toronto to Havana in a Russian-built Cuban Airlines plane.

Thinking of what I would be telling my grandchildren, I wondered if they had learned anything about Cuba in school. Many schools today have deleted world government, civic affairs, and some history courses from their curricula. So there might be no mention of Fidel Castro rising to leadership during the Cuban revolution. Batista was then President of Cuba. In 1957 Hebert Matthew of the *New York Times* interviewed Fidel Castro in the Sierra Maestra Mountains in Cuba. Batista called the article a fake. A few days later the *New York Times* printed a picture of Castro smoking a cigar in the Sierra Maestra Mountains. Castro rose to lead the Cuban people who dreamed of democracy and freedom in 1959. Somehow Castro maintained his base of power in Cuba as he continued to make friends with nonaligned and Communist nations.

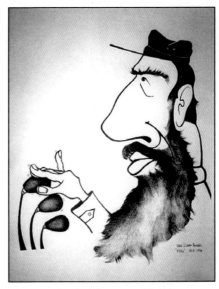

Art in Havana—Fidel

The United States' policies was not high on Fidel Castro's priority list. There were many instances of snubs by the United States, but when Cuba asked the United States to process its fuel and President Eisenhower said no, that angered the Cubans. President Kennedy was handed the Bay of Pigs War after he was sworn in as president by President Eisenhower. The Bay of Pigs incident in 1962 only bolstered Castro's ego and power base. The Cuban missile crisis involving President Kennedy and Nikita Khruschev nearly brought the world to the brink of nuclear disaster. Khruschev relented and the entire world began to breathe a little easier in October of 1962. In 1975 Secretary of State Henry Kissinger announced a détente of affairs under President Nixon. On November 7, 1975, when Cuba sent troops to bolster the Communists in Angola, relations between the United States and Cuba went awry once again. In 1979 Fidel Castro supported the Soviet invasion of Afghanistan. During President Jimmy Carter's term of office (1977-1981), the United States received 125,000 Cuban refugees as they arrived on United States soil in Miami, Florida. President Reagan declared war on Grenada and "saved" our medical students. In 1991 the U.S.S.R. collapsed and subsequently Russian subsidies ended in Cuba.

The plane had now landed in Toronto, Canada. However, some hours passed before we were able to leave the Toronto Airport. As we finally boarded the

Russian plane, I hoped that the Cuban pilot was not going to cross over any United States territory, creating the possibility of being shot down, resulting in an international incident.

Norm Nelson as he views the Havana Harbor

The Havana Airport was basically utilitarian with no advertisements in view as are seen in nearly all the rest of the world's airports. The Cuban Immigration officials were just as apprehensive as we were. No one seemed to want to be the first to crack a smile.

On the way to our hotel twenty miles away, we saw men were repairing their old U.S. cars. Cuban mechanics are rated as the best in

American clenched hand in center of billboard seen on street in Santiago, Cuba

229

the world because they are required to repair cars without the luxury of new parts due the U.S. embargo. Women were clad in colorful dresses, while the men dressed in bright shirts and pants. A few barefooted children, noting we were tourists, waved and smiled. Palm trees and beaches beckoned to us promising warm temperatures and balmy breezes. After arriving at our hotel, we waited to be checked into our rooms. Waiting is something that occurs most often in Communist countries. Any exasperation one may feel is better left unexpressed. There is an appropriate Norwegian expression for this: *ta det med ro*—take it easy!

Our room was small, clean, and airy with windows that opened. After unpacking our clothes, we took a walk to explore our surroundings. The halls were open-air pathways and the stairs were covered, but there was no evidence of any elevators. We soon discovered we were among many tourists from Germany, France, India, Romania, Italy, Egypt, and South America.

Walking along the clean beach located not very far from our hotel, we could see ships very far away as most ships could not land because of the embargo. Cruise ships could sail by on their way to Jamaica and other islands.

We returned to the hotel and soon were tired enough to sleep. Awakening early the next morning brought sounds of backfiring engines right under our hotel window. We bounced out of bed to the sound of engines roaring.

It was now time for touring the area

Georgette Valle is shown with her copy of *Listen Yankee: The Revolution in Cuba* (C. Wright Mills, 1960) on a Cuban beach.

which revealed the Germans and French were drilling oil on the northeastern coast of Cuba. We learned that the British and French were investing in the

Cuban economy by building hotels in Havana. Several other buildings started by the Russians were simply standing unfinished.

As I inspected the unfinished buildings, I thought about the United States Chamber of Commerce and its demonstrative statements made to the U.S. government over time to lift some of the business embargo processes so some kind of trade could begin on a small scale.

Odd is photographing the French drilling for oil in Cuba with no interference.

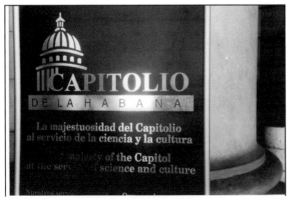

Cuban capitol buildings built to resemble Washington, D.C.

An edifice overlooking Revolutionary Square commemorating all who have fought for Cuban freedom

One of the many artistic tributes to Che Guevara seen on Cuban streets

Daycare center in Santiago, Cuba

Thirteen-year-old children making cigars in a Cuban cigar factory in 1996

In spite of the Russians' departure, the Cubans expressed a warm, but sad feeling for their friends. They showed us parks which were affectionately dedicated to the Russians.

We traveled to the Santiago area which had a small hotel with some shops containing very little merchandise. The area consisted of agricultural lands which were tilled by large groups of workers who were transported to the fields on old flatbed trucks or old buses that occasionally broke down.

At dinner there was a combo of four musicians playing and singing *Guantanomera* as we smiled and clapped. Here we could order a choice of two entrees. Usually, if it were beef, it was tough; if it were chicken it was also tough.

The following day we visited a school, greeting children who were dressed in

Cuban teachers with American book in classroom surrounded by students.

uniforms as they marched past us to attend another class. The school had been donated to the public system by a Catholic sisters' convent. Here I could share my pencils and schoolbooks with the appreciative children. One teacher was overjoyed when I gave her my *Pocahontas* book by Walt Disney.

I kept presenting my business card to our tour guide so he could try to arrange a meeting for us with a legislative representative of the government. Finally, we met with a Department of Embassy Affairs representative, who was suddenly called to another meeting. His assistant then facilitated a discussion. One fact stressed was that Fidel Castro would settle for as much as $6 billion any claims by U.S. residents who had property taken from them by Cuba. I heard that figure several times.

Everywhere we went in Havana, we could see the disrepair that existed in the infrastructure: stairs, sidewalks, and paint on buildings. The only shops that displayed merchandise were the art shops. We were very careful when spending U.S. dollars because of the warning we had received from the State Department.

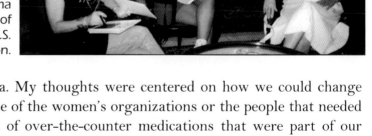

The best response that we had from any political group was from the Women's Alliance of Laborers and Workers. There the discussion was led by aggressive women who talked about decent education, wages, and housing. I was surprised and pleased to take part in such

Above: Georgette Valle, Barbara Zepeda, and Lillian First listen to speakers from the Women's Alliance for Laborers and Workers.

Right: Two Cuban women make their presentation to Norma Nelson and the rest of the women in the U.S. delegation.

frank discussion in Cuba. My thoughts were centered on how we could change U.S. policy towards some of the women's organizations or the people that needed health care in the form of over-the-counter medications that were part of our everyday life. Certainly the medical supplies that we brought were appreciated.

During the conversation with the women, they told us of the steady stream of leisure yachts that traverse the ninety miles from Florida to Havana loaded with medical supplies for their friends in Cuba. We went away with the feeling that the embargo in Cuba should be lifted.

The return trip to the United States went much more smoothly. The Blaine border crossing was as expected except for Odd's difficulty in hearing the questions asked by U.S. Immigration officials. We were grateful that we could return home to this country. ⛵

Art in Havana

*I think it's the end of progress if you
stand still and think of what you've
done in the past. I keep on.*

Leslie Caron

Four Years on the Burien City Council

This is a difficult chapter to write. No matter what I say I will anger someone. Garrison Keillor said that "participation in a local government meeting was the best way to make enemies for life."

One day after an Environmental Science meeting at the Marine Technical Center at Seahurst Park in 1997, Burien City Councilmember (Dr. John) Kennelly asked me if I would run for Burien City Council. He was not running for the next term. I accepted his generous comment and said it was an interesting idea and that I would respond later. Then I punched myself and said, "Did you really want another political race?" Burien City Councilmember Sally Nelson, Burien City Guru, also encouraged me to file for the city council. She had been elected to the council since cityhood had passed in 1993 and served as the city's first deputy mayor and also Mayor of Burien. I often appreciated her sage advice regarding municipal matters during her term of office.

I knew I would probably have to think whether I had anything substantial to contribute. People would expect me to have some ideas on progressive issues which would help the city to perform its functions quickly and efficiently. Within an hour, I had recruited a neighbor in Hurstwood, Lucy Burrows, to serve as my Secretary-Treasurer and came up with a slogan, "A Better Burien." With these ideas framed in my mind, I telephoned Burien Councilmember Kennelly and informed him I would enter the city council race.

This meant I would have to doorbell, fund raise, and begin all over being a candidate. I knew I had a lot to learn about municipal government in Burien.

Highline News
June 4, 1997

The Longtime Legislator Says She Wants to Serve the Community

By Pat Coussens STAFF WRITER

BURIEN–One of the state's more experienced campaigners is running for City Council.

Georgette Valle, who recently retired as a Democratic state representative from the 34th District, announced this week she'll pursue the council seat being vacated by Mayor Arun Jhaveri.

"It's only 139 days since I retired, but this is something that's close to home and very attractive," Valle said. "I did the Burien to Olympia route all of these years."

Jhaveri's position is an at-large council position. Whoever wins won't necessarily become mayor.

In addition to Jhaveri's term, three other council seats expire this year. Councilmember John Kennelly announced last month he will not run again while Councilmembers Kevin James and Sally Nelson have not officially announced their intentions.

Burien activists Stephen Lamphear and Kay Lasco have already declared their intention to run, as has Burien resident Bill Loken. None have announced which seat they'll seek.

A Hurstwood resident, Valle was first elected to the Legislature in 1964 for one term. She returned to the House from 1972 to 1982 and again from 1984 to 1996.

Valle said she's running because she sees Burien as a small city with growing pains. If elected, she said she wants to keep the lines of communication open with other cities and other levels of government.

"I don't pretend to know all of the answers to these problems, but I've seen myself in circumstances where there have been problems. I usually see the light at the end of the tunnel," the 72-year-old activist said.

Valle said she wants to continue her push for an environmental learning center in Seahurst Park, a pet project she introduced in Olympia. If constructed, the center would be used by students of all levels for studying subjects such as urban forestry and marine technology.

In her last term in Olympia, Valle attracted funding for a study to determine the center's feasibility. The study is currently in its final phase while potential funding sources are identified.

Valle said the city needs to continue its involvement in the third runway fight but stopped short of saying how much money it should contribute. She continues to call for a state-funded airport. "The Port may just come around when they see that the people are resolute," Valle said. "When you talk to Port

(continued)

237

Highland News (continued)

commissioners individually, they know there's got to be a state airport."

Valle said she agrees with the current City Council's placement of economic development as one of the city's top three priorities.

She said if the city is going to invite the rest of the world as a trade partner, improvements, beautification and proper development need to be the economic focus. She said all business owners in Burien need to think in terms of what they can do to make their establishments more attractive.

Valle refused to comment in detail on the city's draft comprehensive plant until she studied it further.

Asked if the transition from a legislative career to a City Council position was a step down in the political world, Valle said she considers serving at any level a privilege.

"I don't have any grandiose schemes. I'm not proposing that I step up and run for president," Valle said. "This is something realistic I can do to contribute to my community

I could see Carol Selander, the musical poet, moving quickly and penning these verses to the tune of *Puff, the Magic Dragon*:

Georgette the politician
Lives on a hill
All her constituents would cheer
When she puts in a bill
Georgette the council person
Wields a big stick
Her expertise, experience
Now make Burien tick
Georgette the organizer
Mover, shaker, cook
With her pizazz, her gentle touch
She sure makes it work
Georgette is having a birthday
So we all sing
Happy Birthday to Georgette
Our friend we love, our queen

In a flashback I thought about our settling our dental office in the business area on 152nd S.W. and how many good memories Odd and I had. In those days the Executive Director of the Chamber of Commerce was a very important job. He or she could practically pick their next job, since the Chamber position was like being the Mayor of the Highline area. We certainly appreciated the booming business atmosphere in the area and wanted to see it return.

My city council race went well, and I was voted onto the Burien City Council with David Wintermute, who also agreed to serve on the Environmental Science Board and write an accurate narrative of the young Environmental Science Center.

In 1998, I asked the City Attorney to assist me in drawing up some ordinances that I wanted introduced at council meetings, but he refused. I knew he had a healthy and wealthy contract in 1998 to serve the city of Burien.

Left to right: Councilmember Don Newby, Burien Councilmember, newly elected as King County Councilman, Greg Nickels, Councilmember Georgette Valle, and Councilmember Larry Gilbert

I later worked with another member of City Staff who was very cooperative and reasonable in answering the questions I asked. In order to get the kind of legal assistance I needed, I called Municipal Research who is dedicated to the city's needs. They provided the ordinances according to my specifications. The Arts Commission passed in 1998 during Mayor Kitty Milne's tenure.

During Mayor Kitty Milne's term, Burien city Councilmember Larry Gilbert came to me and asked me if I would be the Deputy Mayor. Since the mayor was never absent, I never conducted a meeting.

In 2000 the Parks Commission ordinance passed under Mayor Sally Nelson. Both of these ordinances involved the public in making decisions for the city of Burien. It was a continual search for me to find other ways to stimulate the public to greater participation in our agenda. Committee meetings that discussed the city's solution to problems of growth, transportation, our environment, our staff services, and the health and welfare of our citizens could be handled first by three city councilpersons in committee session. Then this city legislation would go to the entire council with at least three informed city councilmembers for passage. This was, of course, more work hours for the council. I was not sure this was fair to increase the workload of councilmembers, so I amended the budget to raise the city council salary $200 a month. It passed by four votes! Burien City Council-members now get paid $800 a month. I would not benefit from this hefty amend-ment since you had to be reelected to benefit from this salary raise.

Upper left: Burien Councilmen Stephen Lamphere, Dave Wintermute, Wing Woo, and Kevin James
Seated: Burien Councilwoman Rose Clark, Mayor Sally Nelson, Burien Councilwoman Georgette Valle

Many items that came before us were the agenda set by the City Manager Gary Long. The flow of city business was set by the different city agencies, direc-tors, and the city manager. It was my goal to try to get city business to move as smoothly as possible. I tried with some success to get other councilmembers to amend the business at hand rather than a straight "No" vote, but not every mem-ber wanted a compromise. Councilmember Gilbert and I found we could work together, and I enjoyed the differences between us and coming together on a solution that was amenable to both of us.

From left: Burien City Councilmember Georgette Valle, Mayor Sally Nelson, Burien City Manager Gary Long, Kitty Milne, and Burien City Council-member Don Newby at Dinner in Washington, D.C., on March 5, 1999

Time flies when you are busy. At the end of his term in 2000, City Council-member Don Newby decided not to seek reelection. For his farewell I wrote the following:

> A Burien Councilman with an irresistible sense of humor,
>   and a will to legislate with questions and words of fervor.
>
> A history buff of civil war, frigates, and ships,
>   he made us all enjoy his tales of travel and computer chips!
>
> As Public Safety Chair, he gave pride to the Burien Police image
>   true, and newly designed uniforms smart in Burien blue!
>
> Accomplishments many—the city's first Emergency Operations Plan wise,
>   And Citizen's Patrol now visible on our streets—
>   our ears, our eyes.
>
> Never dull, never at a loss for words—
>   Councilman Newby even had much to say about the
>   "Ordinance of the Birds!!!!"
>
> His "health" breaks from the council were brief,
>   We'll miss his hearty laugh and pride as Public Safety Chief!

Other Burien City Councilmembers I served with were Stephen Lamphere, Rose Clark, and Shirley Basarab.

Councilmember Lamphere was a model for what a city legislator should be—on thought, on task, and on the job. Councilmember Rose Clark was very supportive of the Parks and Recreation issues and later became Deputy Mayor.

My four years were over. It was time to pass the torch to another Burien citizen who might also use the phrase "A Better Burien," Councilmember Joan McGilton, a Boeing marine biologist, served one term and in her second term is now the Mayor of Burien.

Karen McMichael, Georgette Valle and Burien Mayor Joan McGilton
share a table at a Red Hat luncheon

Joe McDermott, now 34th District Representative on
the left with Burien Councilmember Georgette Valle
and Burien City Manager Gary Long in August 2001

When men talk about defense, they always claim to be protecting women and children, but they never ask the women and children what they think.

Pat Schroeder

 ## Dean-Kerry Story

What was all this "Dean" talk? I began to hear about Governor Howard Dean in the spring of 2003. As the campaign began to unfold, I saw large crowds assembling, listening, and applauding his new "Taking Back America" motto. "Organize for Dr. Dean" and "Dr. Dean Is In" were new slogans. The campaign to take back the White House with a sane health insurance plan and a balanced budget resonated with American voters who were hungry for some answers that were not being provided by other presidential candidates.

Voters of all ages were attracted to his candidacy and his gubernatorial record in Vermont. A large number of young voters that were energized to work for Dr. Dean, contribute money to him, register voters, and utilize the Internet as had never been done before in a race. People were impressed with his prescription for change, which consisted of two pennies in a prescription bottle! When you shook it, you could hear these two pennies creating a change in your own home. "Dean's "Stand up for America" slogan, along with his words about the folly of the Iraq war seemed to make good, common sense to many common folks. Dean supported the war in Afghanistan and knew once a country is involved in a war the President must finish the war to gain the peace.

All in all, I was pleased with his verbalized and written polices on all major issues. It was surprising and comforting to know that he was so thoughtful about matters concerning the war/peace issue in the beginning of the race. Some political pundits thought being a presidential candidate from his small state would not make an impact on the voters at large. I was impressed by Dean's strong environmental record of preserving Vermont natural areas—147,000 acres of wildlife, recreational, and important forest land parcels, or 8 percent of the state. He had a strong record in other areas, such as storm water management, tough emission standards, and playing the lead role in preventing mercury poisoning. These causes could also be enhanced by federal standards.

So, of course, I wanted Governor Dean to win in the upcoming primaries. I continued to work feverishly and contributed good hard cash to his campaign. As a plus, I learned how to make chili for Dean chili parties! Since so many people have asked for the chili recipe, here it is:

Dean's Chili

    1 lb. ground beef
    1 (15 oz.) can kidney beans
    1 (15 oz.) can black beans
    1 (15 oz.) can white beans
    1 medium-size onion
    1 green pepper
    1 red pepper
    1¾ cups celery
    1 (28 oz.) can diced, peeled tomatoes
    1¼ tsp. chili powder (more if you desire)
    1 tsp. salt
    ½ tsp. pepper

Cut up onion, green pepper, and red pepper into bite-sized pieces. Brown the beef and add the peppers and celery in a medium-sized cooking pot. Mix together the tomatoes, chili powder, salt and pepper, and beans. Simmer for one hour. Makes about 6 quarts of chili.

Other supporters also contributed chili for the gatherings, so we all learned each other's chili recipe secrets, as well as other campaign strategies that we hoped would contribute to Dean winning the presidential race.

At a one-hundred-dollar Dean event in Seattle at the Westin Hotel, I looked around the crowded room that had no air conditioning and decided we needed some kind of interim action since Governor Dean was late. There were no Dean leaders in view, so I decided that I would introduce some important people in attendance and try to get them to energize the crowd. I think there were about 250 to 300 uncomfortably hot people in this small room. I introduced myself to the amazement of my husband and our friends, Kenny and Carol Selander. Senator Rose Franklin and Representative Mary Lou Dickerson both accompanied me to the podium. They led the crowd in cheers for Dean. I thought that perhaps this was something I could do too. All went very well until I tried the *Lutefisk* and *Lefse Va Skal Ve Har?* Howard Dean, Howard Dean—Rah! Rah! Rah!" I don't think there were many Norwegians in attendance that night, so the cheer ended up being rather weak. After an hour plus with the newly-installed Master of Ceremonies, Councilmember Peter Steinbrueck took over and introduced Governor Howard Dean. Governor Dean was relatively brief because there were between 10,000 and 15,000 people waiting for him at an outdoor rally in Seattle. No other candidate garnered such large crowds with so much enthusiasm.

Apparently all was going well in the primaries, according to commentators, and Governor Dean was on his way to the top of the Democratic pack. After I watched Governor Dean on NBC's *Meet the Press* hosted by Tim Russert, I thought that it was not going to be easy for Governor Dean to get through these television interviews. Russert was visibly aggressive in the interview while Candidate Dean was calm and unruffled until a question arose about the number of troops that were stationed in Iraq. Commentator Russert insisted that Governor Dean should have known that there were 140,000 U.S. troops stationed there.

Iowa caucuses were always considered to be the important hurdle in determining a presidential candidate.

After Senator John Kerry won in Iowa, people from the state of Washington who had traveled to Iowa related to me that a political ad connecting Governor Dean with Osama bin Laden had dampened his chances.

Governor Howard Dean delivered his final speech to many people who had traveled so far and worked so diligently for him. Those who heard the speech in Des Moines, Iowa, were thrilled and pleased by his words. The television media likened Dean's words during this emotional moment to the tears shed by presidential candidate Edmund Muskie, who had been pictured on the front page of the nation's newspapers during a former presidential campaign. However, cable television would choose its negative campaign against Dean.

The Fairness Doctrine required the media to spend equal time (pro and con) for a candidate or an issue. This was a protection of public information for both candidates and issues. The absence of the Fairness Doctrine in today's campaigns leaves candidates, proponents of issues, and the public at a loss for objective information. 🖐

> Women and men in a crowd meet
> and mingle, yet with itself every
> soul standish single.
>> Alice Cary

A $1,000 Presidential Campaign Event

It was the night of the $1,000 per person fund raiser for John Kerry's Democratic presidential campaign.

Having had surgery on three toes on my left foot four days before, I was not sure that my podiatrist would have approved of my driving as yet. But there are just some things you don't ask about when the doctor says you can at last dispense with crutches. So here I was using my right foot for driving, with my left foot resting beside the brake pedal—just the way I drove after I broke my leg while skiing.

Fortunately, there was valet parking where I was greeted by John, whom I knew was a member of the Service Employees of Restaurant and Parking Union. I mentioned that I had voted on issues of interest to his union members many times.

At the grand ballroom there were now lines everywhere and also security checkpoints. I had on my old black suit with rhinestones on the sleeves and hoped that I wouldn't set off an alarm.

Walking in a flat-footed manner so that I would not bend my left toes with steel pins to hold them flat, I stopped at the bar for a bourbon and soda. It's a pity that my husband Odd wasn't the bartender because it was a very weak drink. Just as well, I thought, as I entered the ballroom. At the table were two friends, Pat Taylor from Evergreen Democratic Club and Congressman Jim McDermott who once served in the Legislature with me.

Teresa, John Kerry's wife, was introduced and in turn would introduce her husband and tell about the political stops they had made on the campaign trail. Fifteen minutes went by before she paused and turned to receive an affectionate hug from her husband. We would at last hear from the Presidential Candidate of 2004—John Kerry.

As I look back on it all—the voting debacle in Florida in the 2000 campaign, the Supreme Court involvement, and the slow response of John Kerry and the Democratic Party to illegal voting in Ohio—I am not surprised that so many people in this country believe that George Bush was not elected twice.

None of us can tolerate this kind of voter machine fraud in the future or we no longer have a democracy.

ALWAYS A REBEL AND NEVER WITHOUT A CAUSE

LEGISLATIVE CAUSES

Four be the things I am wiser to know:
idleness, sorrow, a friend, and a foe.
                                    Dorothy Parker

The Flammable Fabrics Act

In 1973 Reporter Don McGaffin of NBC's Seattle affiliate station, King Channel 5, was airing a story about children who received third-degree burns while standing in front of hot stoves or fireplaces in flammable nightgowns. It was a heart-rending story and that I could relate to, as I had worked with burn patients as an occupational therapist and knew the pain and anguish of both the patients and the parents. Some children had died. Letters I received from parents of severely-burned victims convinced me I must do everything I could to spare other children from this same fate. It was a cruel fate because the burned clothing also became a part of the children's burned skin.

I looked across the aisle to determine which Republican might be interested in co-sponsoring this bill. Representative John Rabel, known as the "Young Golden Boy of the Republican Party," sitting across the aisle from me became co-sponsor of the Flammable Fabrics Bill.

Next, I had to line up public support for the bill. Dr. Abe Bergman of the University of Washington teaching staff had been a spokesperson for the young burn patients at the University of Washington Hospital. Reporter Don McGaffin of Seattle KING 5 News was a young, articulate, passionate spokesperson for the concept of a Flammable Fabrics Act Bill. Their support was a dream scenario for passing a legislative health bill. West Seattle JC's were also very supportive and would come to the Legislature to testify for the bill. I thought I'd better do this right! I did have some difficulty getting the bill out of the Commerce and Labor Committee. The Chair of this committee, Representative Lorraine Wojahn, had some differences with the bill. Channel 5 News aired some of these differences and broadcast that we both had aspirations of becoming governor of the state. I was as professional as I could be, but I understood that the media enjoyed showing coverage of a supposed a scrap between two women representatives. The media could not understand that two women representatives could honestly and intelligently disagree.

The Democratic Caucus was quietly attentive to my pleas for passing the bill during this particular session. Caucus members were aware of my slow ascent back after reelection to the House of Representatives. It was always an unwritten rule that if a Democrat had an amendment to a Democratic-introduced bill on the floor, that amendment be shared with the prime sponsor. No one alluded to an amendment, so I felt cautiously optimistic about the Democratic support for the bill.

I had spoken to Speaker Len Sawyer about passage of this bill earlier in the session. He was supportive of the bill and indicated I would have to work to move the bill through the House of Representatives and the Senate. The day arrived for the passage of the bill in the House. Suddenly, just before the bill was to receive the attention of the House members, an amendment by the Majority Leader, Representative Bob Charette of the Democratic Caucus, appeared on the floor of the House. I could see that this amendment would change the bill dramatically— destroying the substance of the bill. I spoke against the amendment, but the Republicans and a few Democrats voted for it. The amendment passed. I was dizzy with anticipation and realized I had to vote for the bill and then go on to the Senate and convince my friends in the Senate to restore the bill to its original form! The injured bill passed the House overwhelmingly. Sensing my quandary, I raced to the Senate to try and restore the Flammable Fabrics Act Bill to its original form. Senator Bob Grieve of the 34th Legislative District worked with me to reinstate the original bill. The Conference Committee of the Senate and the House signed the bill, as restored, for final passage. I particularly remember the graciousness of Senator John Jones, a Republican, in signing the Conference Committee Report which restored the bill. The Washington Legislature passed the Flammable Fabrics Act just six months before the Federal Flammable Fabrics Act, sponsored by Senior Senator Warren G. Magnuson, passed the

United States Senate. We all rejoiced that this Act was now effective nationwide, protecting all children in the United States.

In retrospect, perhaps the small gift of a toothbrush and a two-year supply of toothpaste provided by Dr. Odd Valle that I gave the Washington State Legislators and elected officials did help instill goodwill towards a lowly sophomore in the Washington House of Representatives. In later years, the Washington Dental Society would provide dental kits for the Washington State Legislature and elected officials!

When I returned home from this session, I was very pleased that the JC's of West Seattle actually invited me to a meeting in West Seattle where I received an award for introducing and passing the Flammable Fabrics Act in the Washington State Legislature in 1973. I thought this was truly a great moment for the children who would be spared burns and also for those children whose rehabilitation time may be shortened because of this law.

After all these years, I thought perhaps the law had been repealed, but Dave Knutson of the Health and Human Services staff found the law codified in RCW 70.11. Always good to have good staff!

The Supreme Court
State of Washington

JAMES M. DOLLIVER
CHIEF JUSTICE
TEMPLE OF JUSTICE
OLYMPIA, WASHINGTON
98504
(206) 753-5078

January 28, 1985

Dear Georgette--

Just to let you know the poetry is as bad on this side of
the street as yours, herewith my contribution:

    Your gift has arrived and the message is clear: fear
    Brush your teeth, use the floss and you'll drive away/
    That your smile will betray that your teeth went away
    And the voters will view all you say with dismay.

Thanks for your thoughtfulness. Best wishes for the
Session.

                    Sincerely yours,

JOHN A. CHERBERG
LIEUTENANT GOVERNOR
OLYMPIA, WASHINGTON 98504

January 29, 1985

Dear Georgette,

Thank you ever so much for your wonderful
and practical gift.

The toothbrush and toothpaste have given me
a sparkling smile but the ladies have seen
through my guile...now I'm looking for a good
"Bill of Health".

Kindest regards and best wishes for your
continued success.

        As ever,

        John

The time you need to do something is when no one else is willing to do it, when people are saying it can't be done.

Mary Frances Berry

Washington Indoor Clean Air Act No Smoking In Public Places Bill 1973-1985

Some may recall a time when there were cigarette commercials on TV, professors who smoked in higher education classes, kids who smoked in high schools and adults who smoked anywhere they wanted to, but you didn't hear much about people being ill and dying from smoking or inhaling second-hand smoke. In 1972 I had been pressured by a Precinct Committeeperson from the 32nd District to introduce a bill on "No Smoking in Public Places." I delayed the introduction of the bill until the Flammable Fabrics Act Bill passed.

The bill was barely two lines long. It stated that there should be no smoking in public meetings, and if anyone violated this law, there would be a $10 fine. I went to work gathering signatures on the bill, got the bill introduced, in and out of committee, and in and out of the Rules Committee.

In the House Democratic Caucus meeting where this bill was being discussed and one member had walked out, Aberdeen Representative Charette was quoted as saying, "We're really considering the pressing issues of the day, aren't we?" Some thought this bill was ludicrous.

Representative Valle speaking at a House Committee meeting on behalf of the Washington Indoor Clean Air Act in Olympia

This No Smoking Bill had one amendment which exempted the Legislature from enforcement of the bill. That was an embarrassment me, but the House and the Senate were privileged to make their own rules.

When the tobacco lobbyists discovered the bill had passed the House, they were hard at work in the Senate trying desperately to kill it. It seemed dead and was actually stalled for twelve years from the time it was introduced.

Fortunately, I had some worthy advocates in the Washington Lung Association, Fresh Air for Non-Smokers (FANS), and the Washington Department of Health. There were many other strong citizen advocates who came to Olympia year after year to testify as to the evils of smoking. In those days we did not even know the effects of second-hand smoke.

At the beginning of each session, Joe Zaspell of KIRO television would interview me as if this would be "the session" that the No Smoking Bill would pass. I would optimistically say this was the session that would pass this popular bill. Now, there was more and more information available as to the disastrous affects of the use of tobacco. At each session I would add these facts to the interview. I knew I had to be more innovative because I now had to think of new strategies to cope with the tobacco industry.

Together with staff from the Bill Room, I brought a set of rules for "No Smoking" to the Washington State Board of Health. We followed the rules of public process. The people who knew this process best were the bureaucrats. For five hours I went to work on the House and Senate floor passing a resolution for No Smoking in the State Capitol.

I thought that this effort would not turn out to be punitive, and everyone would finally realize how great it was to have clean air to breathe. Wrong! The whole legislature went crazy. The secretaries could not function without smoking, so the

Representative Georgette Valle
in Burien's 4th of July parade in 1974

smokers spent their day going to the restrooms to smoke. The papers were filled with cartoons depicting smoke coming out the Capitol dome. And I tried to appease the legislators by providing them apples donated by the Washington Apple Commission.

The No Smoking rules went into effect, and the first Legislative Committee that refused to obey the No Smoking rule was the Washington State Transportation Commission. After I read the huge headlines in *The Seattle Times*, I decided to write a letter to Attorney General Kenneth Eikenberry asking him to enforce the rules. I arrived a little late for his appearance at the Washington State Transportation Commission. The meeting came to a standstill when I entered the room and abruptly recessed as I was ushered into the back room. The Transportation Commission members asked what I wanted, and I asked what the Attorney General had said.

Representative Georgette Valle cheers these first graders who promise to be nonsmokers as the graduates of the twenty-first century!

A member of the staff said, "We will obey the No Smoking rule."

I said, "Where is your No Smoking sign?"

Another member of the staff said, "The sign is up!"

I returned to the high ceiling room and saw a tiny, tiny "No Smoking" sign about twenty-five feet up on the wall. I could hardly see the sign. I laughed and left the meeting.

After the No Smoking rules were in effect for awhile, the tobacco companies took the rules to court, and the court threw out the No Smoking rules!

Both Democrats and Republicans took notes on the vile effects of smoking on one's clothing, breath, and health. This was not a partisan issue. Many legislators would come up to me and tell about how their spouses had died from lung cancer, how a grandfather had suffered a miserable death from mouth cancer after chewing snuff, and how a growing number of children were dying from cancer-related emphysema, perhaps related to second-hand smoke.

Public consciousness about the health hazards of smoking continued to grow. With the assistance of the Smoke-Free Tobacco Coalition of health organizations, the No Smoking Bill eventually passed in 1985, and it would was known as the Washington Indoor Clean Air Act. Representative John Moyers of Spokane was a medical physician whose words of wisdom regarding lung cancer were invaluable to the passage of the Act. I was eternally grateful to the many supportive legislators who stuck with me to pass this precious piece of health legislation.

For Rep. Georgette Valle (Don't Inhale!)   Regards Steve Greenberg Jan. 1993

The Smoke-Filled Caucus

OLYMPIA (AP) – Grim-faced House Democrats filled into their caucus room late yesterday morning.

They were going to debate the really big issues like pensions and schools, right? Well, not exactly.

For better than 20 minutes, while newsmen waited outside, the lawmakers debated whether to ban smoking cigarettes inside the caucus room.

"We won one!" said Rep. John Bagnariol, D-Renton, afterwards. "Their motion to make us quit smoking failed on a tie vote, 29 to 29. We can still smoke."

Some Democrats were miffed that he caucus was considering such topics as Rep. Georgette Valle's anti-smoking plan.

Rep. Mary Kay Becker of Bellingham walked out of the meeting. Rep. Robert Charette of Aberdeen scoffed that "we're really considering the pressing issues of the day, aren't we?"

C 2 The Seattle Times
Wednesday, January 23, 1974

Smoking lamp is out tomorrow

OLYMPIA — (AP) — The smoking lamp will be out around the legislative halls for a five - hour period tomorrow under a concurrent resolution adopted by the House and Senate yesterday.

The resolution was introduced by Representative Georgette Valle, Seattle Democrat, who is sponsor of a bill to ban smoking at public meetings.

In her resolution, Ms. Valle noted that a hearing on her smoking bill has been scheduled for 4 p. m. tomorrow.

The smoking ban between 1 p. m. and 6 p. m. in all legislative quarters, the resolution stated, "shall allow cardiac patients, emphysema victims and those other persons seriously afflicted with bronchial conditions" to attend the hearing.

Rep. Georgette Valle takes Smoke from legislators

Georgette Valle, a state legislator in Washington, is the daughter of Mrs. George Vikingstad, of Blue Earth. Recently Mrs. Valle was featured in an article in the Bellingham, Wash., Herald, for her legislative efforts to ban smoking. The article said in part:

Rep. Georgette Valle, daughter of Mrs. George Vikingstad, of Blue Earth, started her first smoking bill moving in 1974, only to have it asphyxiated in the Senate. She then turned to the State Board of Health, got a smoking ban in many public places, convinced lawmakers to try the same and is now trying to establish a bill that would fine non-believers.

Rep. Valle is an avowed feminist at 52 years of age and is the butt of many smoker jokes. If you spy a no smoking sign someplace where you've always been able to light up before, you can thank Rep. Valle for that. If someone fines you $100 soon for ignoring ignoring that sign, Georgette will be responsible again.

Rep. Valle got involved in her smoking campaign when her face swelled from a hair spray allergy she mistakenly diagnosed the cause as cigarette smoke. But she has also taken aim on the fluorocarbons in hair spray and hopes to force ozone wreckers to change

brands, thinks pulltop cans may be a hazard, has protected your children with the toughest flammable fabric law in the nation, and has sought a constitutional amendment, condemned for its broadness, that would protect privacy.

Working as an occupational therapist, Rep. Valle watched an emphysema victim die from a life-long smoking habit. She herself has smoked one-half a cigarette and didn't like it.

She grew up on politics. Her father was an ardent New Dealer in the depression. Her family was poor and she has retained an orientation to people issues since then.

She was elected to the legislature in 1965 and then was redistricted out her seat; forced to challenge an incumbent to retain it. He spent $37,500 to defeat her, the most ever spent up to that time in a legislative campaign. In 1973 she was elected once more.

A supporter of women's legislation, she calls herself a feminist. She has a husband named Odd and two children.

There is also a poster of "Shirley Chisolm for President" in her office and a hairspray can with no fluorcarbons and a sign that says "no smoking" in 11 languages.

One never notices what has been done; one can only see what remains to be done.

Marie Curie

Nuclear Waste

The moment I heard the words "nuclear waste," I just knew that I had to know more about the subject. In 1948 I had an uncle, Fred Vikingstad, who was working in the pharmacy at the Hanford Reservation in Washington State. He reported that he didn't know anything about "nuclear waste." He said there was little information about the subject.

As a legislator I had visited the Hanford Reservations at least three times, so I was fairly aware of how nuclear waste was being stored. On my first visit in 1965 there were open vats of highly contaminated nuclear waste being stored on site. This seemed unbelievable. It was all the more reason to plead with your Congressional delegation for federal monies to build safe storage units for both high and low level nuclear waste. Sometimes there was a division of opinion of citizens who did not want to see any disposal of any nuclear waste in the state of Washington.

As a legislator, I wanted to see the nuclear waste safely stored with no leakage into the soil or into the Columbia River. The Federal Government continued to send vast quantities of both high level and low level nuclear waste to Hanford. The United States, also took other countries'

Uncle Fred Vikingstad here with his 18-month-old niece, Georgette Vikingstad, worked at Hanford in 1948.

nuclear waste to be sure they were not storing it and, in turn, using it to make nuclear bombs. That foreign nuclear waste also ended up at Hanford. It is quite a picture of past nuclear fortunes standing guard for the nuclear future of tomorrow.

Representative Ray Isaacson, a Republican from the Tri-Cities area was a very tough, thorough, competent engineer of the then Rocket Research Company of the Tri-Cities area. We could work on legislation that defined "low level nuclear waste," because both the Speakers of the Washington House of Representatives, Democrat John Bagnariol and Republican Duane Berentson, were interested in seeing this legislation pass the House and the Senate. We in the Ecology Committee were aware of the 49-49 division of Democrats and Republicans in the House and needed an extra Republican vote to come over to our side.

I felt very privileged to work with Ray because he was an honest master of his pro-

Representative Georgette Valle (D) and Representative Ray Isaacson (R) discuss intricacies of a Norwegian watch chain. Both played major roles in the first low level nuclear waste act to pass the Washington House of Representatives.

Co-speaker John Bagnariol and Representative Georgette Valle, and Co-speaker Duane Berentson discussing low level nuclear waste legislation at the speaker's podium in April 1979.

fession. Once he was motivated to a meticulous task as that of defining "low level waste," there was no stopping him. I was motivated by the issue of stopping low level waste from coming into the state. I wanted other states to take the responsibility for their nuclear waste, and then we in Washington State could start passing nuclear waste legislation concerning low level waste. We had meetings morning, noon and night, to make the process as open to the public as possible. I wanted suggestions from the Ecology Committee to make it a true "Committee Bill." The laboriously-worked bill emerged from the Ecology Committee to pass very quickly on the floor of the House of Represen-tatives.

In the state of Washington, Governor Dixie Lee Ray emerged victorious in her gubernatorial election. Her success as a member of United States Nuclear Regulatory Commission had partially help her win that race. I had not bothered to request her participation in the low level nuclear waste legislation because I felt that if she wished to participate in the Senate Committee meetings we would soon hear

Representative Georgette Valle conferring with Representative Paul Pruitt on the floor of the House of Representatives in May of 1979

Governor Dixie Lee Ray *(1977-1981)* finally signs one of Representative Georgette Valle's bills.

about it. We then heard the news that her spokesperson, Senator Gordon Wallgren, had killed the bill in the Senate Committee. I was to learn that Governor Ray was very committed to not letting the public have its word about nuclear waste, high or low level.

In a flashback before Governor Ray's election, I went to a women's issue meeting where she spoke and answered questions. I was astounded to find she simply was not aware of any of the wage issues or equal rights issues of the women that were present.

These women's issues were certainly an equal rights education for her as governor. There were many women legislators present when Governor Ray finally signed the "Equal Rights Education" bill.

Even though Governor Ray killed our Low Level Waste Bill, the issue continued with the public always supporting safe ways to store nuclear waste. A recent initiative in the state of Washington asked the Federal Government to finish cleaning up the Hanford Reservation site before more nuclear waste was brought in from other areas of the country and foreign nations. The state initiative passed by an overwhelming majority of voters. Countless times state officials have argued for protection of the Columbia River by letting the state protect and evaluate the runoff waters of the Hanford Reservation, only to have the federal courts overturn the state edict. This was also done by the former Washington Attorney General Slade Gorton.

As four years of Governor Ray came to a close, Senator Jim McDermott was selected as the Democratic nominee for Governor. Governor Ray retired to Fox Island to her pig farm where it was reported she had pigs named after members of the press who had displeased her.

John Spellman was selected as the Republican nominee and became Governor of the state of Washington. Voters had made their choice! 🚢

Governor John Spellman *(1981-1984)* with Representative Georgette Valle

262

The Impossible Dream

To Dream the Impossible Dream,
To Break an Unbreakable Tie,
To Bear the Unbearable Sorrow
Of Seeing Some Good Statutes Die.

To Work an Unworkable Bill
Amend 'til You Hope It Gets By.
Work 'til Your Brain is so Weary,
The Vote! Still a Forty-Nine Tie.

This was the Task for Duane and John.
No Matter how Hopeless They Carried On,
Worked into the Night Without Question Afore
Knowing that on the Morrow, the Forty-Nine Score.

When We've Completed this Challenging Test
And the Two-Handled Gavel is Laid to Its Rest,
That Our State Will be Better by Far
That Two Men With Courage and Efforts Supreme
Allowed Us to Share "The Impossible Dream."

William J. S. "Bill" May

Representative "Bill" May from Spokane was our "Legislative Poet Laureate" of the House of Representatives. The House was divided in a 49-49 split when he penned these verses.

GEORGETTE W. VALLE
THIRTY-FOURTH DISTRICT

1434 S.W. 137TH   401 LEGISLATIVE BUILDING
SEATTLE, WA 98166   OLYMPIA, WA 98504
RESIDENCE TEL 248-0334   (206) 786-7952

34TH DISTRICT OFFICE
1725 S.W. ROXBURY #5
SEATTLE, WA 98106
(206) 762-7154

House of Representatives

STATE OF WASHINGTON
OLYMPIA

April 11, 1986

Editor
The Post-Intelligencer
521 Wall St.
Seattle, Wash. 98121

Dear Editor:

I write this letter not to gloat, but to express sorrow over the avoidable violation of our rivers and streams that is apparently occurring daily at Hanford. A part of me says, "If only they would have listened." The rest of me says, "Let's now take the steps I suggested years ago to provide for state oversight of radioactive waste disposal activities at Hanford."

Back in 1975, you may remember, the states of Washington and California asked the U.S. Supreme Court to give us the authority to monitor waste water discharged from federal facilities to make sure contamination was kept at "safe" levels. The court ruled against us.

I tried again in 1980, as a member of the state legislature, to get our state the necessary oversight authority. My legislation did not pass, but my support for an initiative to the voters was successful. Washington voters approved an initiative requiring state monitoring and oversight of low-level radioactive waste disposal and groundwater contamination at Hanford. However, the courts again interceded and over-ruled the voters.

All this time, the Department of Energy, which runs Hanford, has been in charge of policing itself. And now, lo and behold, we learn that maybe they haven't been doing such a great job. The federal Environmental Protection Agency has begun investigating the Department of Energy for possible violations of the Resource Conservation and Recovery Act.

I would like to express my support for EPA in its efforts to hold Hanford accountable for damage to water resources in our state. I also call again for state control of groundwater monitoring. If we had been doing it all along, we would not be in this mess.

Sincerely,

Rep. Georgette Valle

FORTY-NINTH
LEGISLATURE
1985-86   COMMITTEES: VICE CHAIR, EDUCATION   •   ENVIRONMENTAL AFFAIRS   •   TRANSPORTATION   •   RULES

Green Valley News
Spring 2006
Guest Comment

Are our nuclear plants safe?

By Georgette Valle

On my fifth tour in the early 1990s of the Hanford Nuclear Plant outside of the Tri-Cities, Richland, Kennewick, and Pasco in the state of Washington. I was glad to admit there was now a change for the better management of all of the operations involving nuclear materials in the quests for safety and production of electricity.

I had been touring the Hanford Nuclear Plant over a period of 20 years as a legislator.

However, even though I had witnessed open rectangular vats of low and high level liquid nuclear waste in the ground at Hanford in 1965, I was still uncomfortable with the storage in water pools on the Hanford Nuclear Plant site.

I was at this point concerned and unhappy with the Federal Energy Department and their lack of zest in finding a true answer for the storage of used radio active waste.

Information from the Energy Administration indicates that Arizona's Palo Verde Nuclear Power Plant, the nation's largest nuclear plant, ranks second on the National Energy Information of the 100 largest utility plants in the United States.

Palo Verde 1, Palo Verde 3, and Palo Verde 2 is now the nation's largest nuclear reactor, surpassing the former leaders (South Texas land 2 reactors). Construction of each of the Palo Verde reactors began in 1976, but nearly a decade passed before Palo Verde began commercial operation. The last two reactors took 12 years to begin to operate.

Leading energy source

Coal is the leading source of energy at 38 percent of electricity in Arizona with nuclear power at 27 percent coming in second. Natural gas has been rising in importance in this state at 25 percent nearly equal to that of nuclear power.

The state nuclear industry thinks that electricity increases will be necessary in the future. Another part of the nuclear equation is the continued use of water for the cooling towers. Palo Verde's nuclear plants rely on recycled sewage effluence. More than 20 billion gallons of this recycled water are used every year.

There are plans to make Palo Verde larger. The *Arizona Republic* reports, "a $700 million project at Palo Verde Nuclear Generating Station—its most expensive investment since it opened in the mid-1980s will increase output from unit one by adding two new 606-ton generators."

Nuclear waste

What happened to the radioactive nuclear waste? Nuclear waste is stored on site in the recycled sewage water to cool and stored in pools surrounding the Palo Verde Plant. This
(continued)

Green Valley News (continued)

nuclear plant is not unlike most nuclear plants in the United States.

There are more than 30 power plants across the United States which are running out of storage space to cool and store used nuclear fuel. More than 100 plants will run out of space by 2010. This is the earliest date that the proposed nuclear waste facility could open at Yucca Mountain near Las Vegas, Nevada.

Until Yucca Mountain Nuclear Waste Storage Site can open, U.S. Atomic Power Plants are busy building additional storage sites next to the nuclear plants to keep the 50,000 tons of fuel rods in ponds next to the nuclear plants. This material is very valuable to the United States, so we even take other nation's radioactive waste. It has in the past been shipped to Hanford in Washington state to the consternation of its citizens.

This is the uranium that is used to build atomic bombs. Many citizens see this storage of spent uranium rods as an invitation to terrorists.

Another development that has happened over the years: States can legislate how much nuclear waste may be deposited on site. This has happened at Prairie Island Nuclear Plant in Red Wing, Minnesota. Xcel, which owns the plant, said they will reach their maximum in 2007.

In the state of Washington in an initiative to the citizens, the state declared that no more nuclear waste could enter the state until the present nuclear waste problem has been solved.

The initiative passed handily in the state of Washington, but now is being contested in court.

Jon Findley, Grand Canyon Chapter Energy Chair of the Sierra Club, shared with me that most Sierra Club members would like the used spent fuel to be stored in an environmentally safe manner and the less of the material that is generated the better.

In 2004, on May 25 the headline in the *Arizona Republic* "Truckloads of nuclear waste in state's path" alerted citizens to the fact that nuclear waste has been building up over 50 years at the Defense Department sites and nuclear power plants to be shipped to a storage facility in Nevada. Much of this waste would pass through Arizona.

Spent fuel generated from the Palo Verde Nuclear Generating Station since 1987 might not be moved until another 10 to 20 years, according to the *Arizona Republic*.

Concerns raised

Gov. Janet Napolitano raised concerns about the 153 million pounds of radioactive waste traveling through Arizona to the state of Nevada. There also was a disagreement with the Department of Energy as to whether the material was low-level radioactive waste or high-level radioactive waste.

More information on a classified report by nuclear experts assembled by the National Academy of Sciences has challenged the decision by federal regulators to allow commercial nuclear facilities to store large quantities of radioactive spent fuel in pools of water.

(continued)

Green Valley News (continued)

The report as of March 28, 2005, concluded that the government does not fully understand the risks that a terrorist attack could pose to the pools and ought to expedite the removal of the fuel to dry storage casks that are more resilient to attack.

The safety of the pool has long been defended by the Bush Administration. The nuclear industry has warned that moving of fuel rods to dry storage would be necessary and very expensive.

The fact that the disagreement between the Nuclear Regulatory Commission and the report of the National Science Academy of 2005 is classified makes it difficult for the public to make its decision.

Meanwhile, tons of spent fuel rods containing radioactive byproducts are being produced by the nation's 103 electricity-generating nuclear reactors.

Spent fuel rods generate intense heat and dangerous long-term radiation that must be contained. Meanwhile, how safe are our nuclear power plants?

Georgette Valle is been a Green Valley resident and is Legislative Chair for the Democratic Women in Action. The opinions expressed above are the author's own and do not necessarily reflect those of this newspaper.

Green Valley News
Spring 2006
Guest Comment

How does the world handle nuclear energy?

By Georgette Valle

Questions asked about how other countries handle their nuclear plants and nuclear waste are usually not answered in depth by staff because of a lack of time and sometimes lack of research. I usually received the answer "differently," which is right. Because I am interested in the answer, I am pursuing it. It is almost like opening "Pandora's Box." But I'm glad I asked.

Fifty years ago, the government of the United Kingdom was one of the first countries to develop nuclear fission. It built bombs and nuclear power sources. The public, especially in the United Kingdom, has forced revelation of candidates supporting nuclear waste disposal because of newly-passed Freedom of Information legislation.

"New Scientist," according to NIREX, the United Kingdom Nuclear Waste agency, revealed six sites in Scotland and seven in England as geologically suitable for deep underground depositories. There are now new public concerns about nuclear waste depositories as sea level rises in response to climate changes.

Everyone agrees that nuclear waste has to be dealt with in a safe environmental manner. The Environmental Agency has been active in seeking public participation since July of 2001. The UK Agency's proposals will help To implement the future regulation of the disposal of radioactive waste and help to implement the OSPAR (Oslo and Paris) commitment to reduce radioactive discharges into marine environment.

Although Norway has no nuclear plants, Norwegians are certainly interested in reducing any radioactive discharges in the North Sea. In recent years, fish have been plentiful, with the rest of Europe anxious to share in that uncontaminated resource.

Bulgaria, Ukraine, Hungary, Kazakhstan, and Japan have individual arrangements with Russia for storing spent fuel produced in atomic energy plants. Bulgaria must present a long-term plan for the disposal of nuclear waste and spent fuel management before it can send either product to Russia. In 2002 Ukraine signed a Nuclear Cooperation Pact with Russia to send its spent fuel to Russia. However, the United States financially assisted the Ukrainian government in building storage capacity for 380 dry casks for six reactors. Kazakhstan's government is considering importing and storing low-level waste in order to raise money for its own radioactive waste management. An offer such as this will garner many wastes, especially transuranic (mixed plutonium waste), nuclear wastes, (continued)

268

Green Valley News (continued)

and high-level wastes. After a Russian Supreme Court decision and a 1998 agreement, Hungary received permission to leave the processed spent fuel in Russia. The Japanese and the Russians have an agreement to formally transfer a floating complex to Russian ownership for processing liquid radioactive waste from nuclear-powered submarines. Built at a cost of $35 million, the complex has processed 800 cubic meters of waste and is expected to process 7,000 cubic meters of waste annually.

In 2000, the U.S. Department of Energy was revamped. It proposed that the Waste Isolation Pilot Project in New Mexico would have a capacity for disposal of up to 1,250 cubic meters of transuranic wastes for storage with 7,000 cubic meters of waste expected to be stored annually. The project would be located under 655 meters in a salt formation under the Chihuahuan Desert near the Carlsbad Caverns in New Mexico. The Yucca Mountain in the Nevada desert has also been chosen as a deep nuclear waste repository by the U.S. government.

Generally speaking, 2001 was a year in which the countries of Canada, France, South Korea, Australia, Spain, Germany, Japan, Switzerland, and Sweden made policies and plans for low-level nuclear waste depositories. An awareness of the consequences of not planning for a nuclear waste future began to dawn on the first world countries. Many countries are also exploring the necessity of an intermediate nuclear waste facility for transuranic nuclear wastes.

In the United States, plans to build an interim storage for used fuel has been undertaken by Private Fuels Storage Limited, a consortium of eight U.S. utilities created as an interim storage nuclear facility to be constructed on the Goshute Indian reservation in Utah. There was formal opposition to the plan by the State of Utah. New state laws were also enacted to prevent the project.

Meanwhile, the U.S. is planning to recycle commercial nuclear waste into fuel for the first time in thirty years. The budget for this project was signed by President Bush and provided $50 million toward a goal of building the facility by 2020. Supporters have pointed to using the mounting nuclear waste to save time and money, and opponents have argued that the technology to convert the waste into fuel is not at hand and that by recycling nuclear waste, we would be sending the wrong message to the rest of the world.

Pandora's Box has opened and a determination will have to be made to decide what to do with all of humanity's nuclear wastes, from low level, to intermediate level, to high level nuclear waste. There are powerful countries who want to experiment and produce atomic weapons as some of countries have done in the past. There are even new mixed technologies of nuclear waste that perhaps Pandora will use.

Georgette Valle has been a Green Valley resident and the Legislative Chair for the Democratic Women in Action. The opinions expressed above are the author's own and do not necessarily reflect those of this newspaper.

The "Moment of Peace" on the Floor of the House of Representatives

It all began when I won reelection to the state representative position. Members of my Campaign Reelection Committee called me the Wednesday after the election day in 1984. My instructions from Lorraine Bonnell and Norma Kragtorp were to arrive at a popular restaurant on California Avenue in West Seattle at 10 a.m. I walked in to a crowd of cheering Democrats. We were all elated because we had defeated John Carlsen for State Representative Position 2. All of our jubilation was being recorded by the *West Seattle Herald.* The weekly would feature three pictures of all of us rejoicing. It was also the year of election of Ronald Reagan, the sometime movie star who defeated my cousin, Fritz Mondale, Democratic contender.

I had been working for what was then known as the U.S. Peace Academy, which was an independent, nonpartisan institution created by Congress for the prevention, management, and peaceful resolution of international conflicts. It was a heady and lofty idea. Congress and the President might be influenced by peaceful solutions before deciding that war was the answer to foreign entanglements. I wrote letters to many members of Congress. The argument for the Academy's passage was to stress the enormous amount of money that Congress spends on the Department of Defense. It seemed only reasonable to a have a little balance in our presentations about war and peace. The one member of Congress that I had the most difficulty with was my own senator, Henry Jackson. He simply told me that this was not his way of solving world conflicts.

However, in the Washington State House of Representatives the vote was a large majority in favor of the House Resolution to Congress. I designed the resolution to be dealt with by the House of Representatives only because I didn't think it would pass the Washington Senate. There was also a time factor involved. Congress was also getting ready to consider the resolution. I had a dizzy sensation as I realized the breadth of the Resolution and the impact a U.S. Peace Academy could have on a peaceful future for the United States.

I invited Rabbi Levine and Father Tracy to come to Olympia to help pass the Resolution. They were two very popular television personalities who discussed both social and religious problems on Sunday mornings. Rabbi Levine provided a lengthy prayer pleading for passage of this House Resolution. He did not know it was to be voted on in both Rabbi Levine's and Father Tracy's presence that very morning.

After the victorious vote, I came out to greet them both declaring that there was indeed the hand of God on that House Resolution that helped it to pass that morning. It was a great day, and all three of us wore unusually wide smiles for the photographer.

Moment of Peace gathering of Rabbi Levine, Representative Georgette Valle, and Father Tracy on the floor of the House of Representatives

Odd Valle, Western CARE Director Christine Santos, and Georgette Valle in Washington, D.C.

In the end, Senator Henry Jackson voted for what was to be known as the United States Institute of Peace. I had pestered him with letters, questions, and comments for what seemed like an eternity. The Institute of Peace, however, was not funded for some time, which disappointed many of its supporters.

Through the years, I occasionally was reminded

of the Institute of Peace through the Seattle World Affairs Council. Their sphere of influence extended throughout the national and international community.

Twenty years after I introduced and saw passage the Peace Academy Resolution, Odd and I were enjoying delicious food and margaritas at the seventieth birthday celebration of our good friend, Joanna Brunso, on March 26, 2005, in Amado, Arizona. We introduced ourselves to two guests across the table, Judy and Chick Nelson from Washington, D.C., and learned that Chick Nelson had seventeen years of service in the Institute of Peace. Within moments, cards were exchanged with promises to visit the Institute of Peace in Washington, D.C., in

Joanna Brunso, Lola Pitzner, and Jorgen Brunso celebrate Joanna's 70th birthday

A brush drawing by Congressman Jim McDermott

the future.

Now here we were landing in Washington, D.C., at Dulles Airport for the 59th CARE Conference featuring Western CARE Director Christina Santos as a speaker. We lobbied for monies for AIDS prevention, development assistance, and child survival and health accounts. CARE officials sent Odd and me to the Arizona Congressional delegation. Senators McCain's and Kyle's staff were good listeners and asked insightful questions. On Friday we awoke early to lobby our own Congressmen, Adam Smith, and Jim McDermott for funds to finish the Seahurst Park Environmental Science Center project. Senator Patty Murray, with the assistance of Senator Maria Cantwell, along with Congressmen McDermott and Smith, would seek monies from the Economic Development Fund.

We were ready to relax at lunch with the Nelsons. Chick Nelson was Vice President of the Institute of Peace, so I was intent on asking questions about the Institute. Judy Nelson led us to the Ironhorse Inn, built in 1740, where we were to have lunch. We discovered that Joanna and Judy were cousins. They resembled each other with their forthrightness in answering questions and their energetic personalities. Within this historic restaurant, there were still iron rods forming horse stalls with attractive tables that would previously been areas set aside for hay. I wondered how many horsemen had announced a peaceful or warlike message to colonial residents in years past.

Chick Nelson told about how West Virginia's Senator Jennings Randolph had worked incessantly to establish the concept of a peace institution. President Ronald Reagan established an Institute of Peace Commission with Senator Ted Stevens, Senator Daniel Inoway, and Senator Tom Harkin as early sponsors and supporters of the legislation. There were efforts to delete the legislation from the calendar. It is noteworthy that Senator Sam Nunn saved the legislation not once but three times.

We left the Ironhorse Inn Restaurant, walked out through the patio, and saw that the furniture was strewn with wisteria blossoms which blew in the cold wind. Red and white azaleas with purple pansies peeking between red tulips brightened our spirits as we walked back to the Institute of Peace building.

Representative Georgette Valle congratulates Secretary of Health and Welfare Janet Reno on her remarks to a group of women in Washington, D.C., at the Women's International Federation of Peace event

Reading through the Institute of Peace pamphlet, I was pleased at the progress in peacemaking efforts, with two decades of achievement in international conflict management. Reading of the accomplishments of peace and stability operations, the Institute seeks to prevent international conflict by promoting dialogue between parties in conflict, encouraging religious contributions to peacemaking efforts, and advising post-conflict societies about establishing legal systems. It attempts to reconcile former adversaries and reform the educational systems of countries. Over the last two decades, more than one hundred nations have benefited from the Institute's programs, which currently include assistance to Iraq's political leaders and civil organizations in developing the participatory political process.

The Institute also serves as an innovative source of expertise to policymakers, offering nonmilitary approaches to addressing international conflicts. Institute proposals have been adopted by the National Security Council, the Department of State, and the Economic European Union, the G-8 countries. The Bush Administration drew on the U.S. Institute of Peace, Institute of Korean Working Group's proposal in formulating the U.S. negotiating positions for the Six-Party Talks with China, North Korea, South Korea, Japan, and Russia.

Representative Georgette Valle is talking with Tipper Gore at the Women's International Federation of Peace event and giving her a "Homeless" pin.

The Institute has given out sixteen hundred grants totaling $52 million over the last eighteen years for projects around the world involving conflict management research, education, and training. It also trains two thousand professionals each year in conflict management and resolution skills. This includes officials from the Departments of State and Defense, the United Nations, Organization of American States and foreign governments. Trainees in 2004 included nearly 250 Iraqi national security officials and civic activists.

The Academy's educational efforts reach 23,000 people each year through a wide range of programs, including the National Peace Essay Contest for high school students, seminars for secondary school teachers, and university-level teaching and curricular materials. The Institute's conflict management books are used in post-secondary courses in the United States and abroad in Egypt, Israel, India, and Northern Ireland

Over one thousand publications, studies, articles, and books on international conflict management since 1990 include a three-volume series examining justice and accountability after mass human rights abuses were available at the Institute. Several hundred conferences and workshops are convened in the form of study groups, press events, and roundtables to bring together policymakers, academics, NGOs (Non Government Organizations), and the public to discuss international conflict management. The Institute of Peace truly has a legacy of peacemaking in the twenty years since its inception. 🚢

To be successful, the first thing to do is fall in love with your work.

Sister Mary Lauretta

The Saga of The Disposable Diaper 1976-2006

The Diaper War Debates:

- Paper Diapers Making a Mess
- Diapers and the Economy
- Do Disposable Diapers Ever Go Away?
- Which are Best for the Environment?
- Are You Ready for a Change?
- Biodegradable Diapers; A Pseudo Solution?
- The Diaper Dilemma
- Disposal Diapers Befoul the Wilderness

- Cloth vs. Disposable Diapers
- What's the Real Poop?
- All Diapers Not Created Equal in the Eyes of Mother Nature.

The diaper wars are still probably still slugging it out with the environment and parents' pocketbooks suffering. On the soap operas of today you still see these darling little babies parading themselves before the consumers with their paper diapers wrapped around their bottoms. Today's mothers say the cloth diaper has changed, so it is much more convenient. Fastening devices such as Velcro, snaps, and rubber hooks are new devices on the cloth diaper that help the cloth diaper survive.

The first disposable diaper that I saw was on a Scandinavian Air flight returning from Norway at an unexpected landing in Greenland. In 1956 Christine had just had her first birthday and took her first steps in Norway. I was afraid I would not have enough diapers for the trans-Atlantic trip, and so I asked the stewardess if she had any diapers. She returned with one oblong piece of rather thick, padded paper, which was Christine's first and last experience with a disposable diaper. The diaper, however, did last through the four-hour layover. But that was fifty years ago!

My legislative history on diapers began in 1976, when I surveyed Washington Hospitals and found that in eighty hospitals, 80 percent responded they used disposable diapers. One-third of hospitals disposed of the diapers by burning, and most of the hospitals disposed of the diapers in the garbage or sanitary landfill. I felt there was a danger that viruses could escape into the water supply or be transmitted in other ways when disposed of in the garbage.

On February 16, 1977, I introduced legislation requiring warnings on packages of disposable diapers of possible transmission of diseases including live polio viruses. The legislation (HB 645) would require diaper packages to warn, "Soiled disposable diapers contain viruses, and microbes may transmit diseases to the general population when disposed of improperly. Fibrous material must not be disposed of in garbage or trash." A Seattle woman had been hospitalized in Minneapolis and was reported to have picked up the disease polio from the feces of her baby, who had been treated with the polio vaccine. In August of 1976

Dr. Jonas Salk told the House Commerce Committee there is a health hazard associated with diaper disposal.

I continued my interest in this environmentally-sensitive issue over the years. The King County Nurses Association decided to study the issue of the use of the cloth diaper and disposable diaper. Proctor and Gamble, the four-billion-dollar diaper industry company, flew its people into Seattle "to be of assistance," and a Proctor and Gamble attorney and a physician were in attendance at the first meeting of King County Nurses Association. Their insistence at being at every meeting was not greeted with a great deal of enthusiasm, but in the end all meetings were open to the public.

Today, mothers agree that cloth diapers are good for the environment. They are good for the baby's bottoms, and they are good for the pocketbook.

I was troubled to hear complaints of mothers that ingredients banned from tampons are now used in disposable diapers. The mothers further said, "We can't use them once a month, but we strap them onto our babies' behinds for years."

Connie Heavey, wife of 34th District Senator Mike Heavey, wrote me on February 19, 1992:

Now Judge Mike Heavey with wife Connie and children Shanna and Christa

Dear Georgette,

I participated in the diaper recycling study. I thought you might be interested in the results (in case you weren't already on the mailing list).

I now use Anderson Diaper Disposable Diaper Recycling program. I'm just hoping that they do actually recycle what they pick up from me. I've been volunteering at IMEX (Industrial Materials Exchange) with Bill Lawrence and he says, "It's somewhat questionable what actually happens to the component once they are washed and separated."

Anyway–I know you are interested! It was good to see you last week!

Connie Heavey

The organizations that participated in this pilot project were the Seattle Solid Waste Utility in cooperation with Proctor and Gamble and the Rabanco Company. Seattle Solid Waste was aware that costs of collection and processing of the diapers would be paid by the public. Arthur D. Little, Inc., on behalf of the Proctor and Gamble Company, concluded the process would be economically feasible if the diapers came from a very large city. Only a very large city could provide enough diapers.

> The common conclusion of the two assessments is that reclaiming the raw materials from disposable diapers is technically feasible, however, it is not advised to pursue recycling commercially at this time because of the unfavorable economics.

In the May-June 1993 *Washington Alert* publication, an article "Diapers and the Economy" written by Keiki Kehoe states:

> Washington State's population is widely recognized as the most environmentally active in the nation. In fact, three years ago the Puget Sound area was targeted by disposable giant Proctor and Gamble (the maker of Pampers and Love), for its pilot diaper recycling project. This effort, which the *New York Times* called "Guerrilla theater staged in the heart of the enemy territory" was an economic flop. It was part of a larger effort by the disposable diaper industry to respond to the public's concern over the 18 billion disposable diapers going to landfills each year.

Seventeen billion disposable diapers, if extended end to end, would stretch to the moon and back again to the earth.

In reviewing my correspondence of February 10, 1992, with Department of Ecology Director Richard J. Thompson, I found that Washington has had a goal of reducing by 50 percent the amount of solid waste disposed by 1995. The State Plan encouraged cloth diapers through education and the implementation of disposal bans and financial incentives, and proposes the recycling of disposable diapers.

In July of 2006, Peter Christianson of the Department of Ecology said in our conversation that there is at least 44 to 60 percent recycling of garbage materials in Western Washington. Many times it is difficult to track backyard composting. Local Health Departments are given the authority to promote safety and health regulations for the disposal of disposable diapers. He went on to say that, today, landfills are lined with double-plastic linings so there should be no leakage out to the surrounding environment. Ideally, the feces of the disposable diaper should be deposited in the toilet, but wrapping the disposable diapers in a plastic bag does help to prevent any garbage worker from becoming contaminated.

The "G Diaper" is coming on the market. My dreams about a biodegradable diaper are now here! Now, it is Love at first flush! This is a G Diaper that is flushable. How I've argued with disposable diaper companies to create a diaper that when soiled can be flushed down the toilet. Let's put waste where it belongs. Here is a diaper that has a flushable inner refill that fits into a pair of colorful "little G" pants. Fashion and function on one cute bum!

Parents have a sense of what disposable diapers will do to landfills in years to come and are giving a thumbs-up for G Diapers. Perhaps I was meant to write this book right now so I could brag about my dream becoming reality!

Diaper Pulp – Out of the Garbage and Into the Garden

Not all diaper service vendors think cloth is the only way to address disposal problems associated with throwaways. Anderson Diaper Service, Inc., a full-service supplier of cloth and disposable diapers to Seattle customers, figures that recycling disposables is part of the solution.

In November, the company began collecting used disposables from 400 cloth diaper customers (most cloth diapers also buy disposables) and separating the plastics from the pulp for recycling. "The waste is washed into the sewer, where it belongs," said Gene Anderson, the company's owner. "The plastics are sold to a local broker for 10 cents a pound and the pulp is sold for fertilizer."

The separation is currently done by hand, but the company has designed and ordered a $100,000 machine to automate the process. Expected to begin next month, automation is only one measure Mr. Anderson is counting on to turn the program – now breaking even – into a money maker. He plans to expand beyond Seattle by franchising the concept, and over the longer term, hopes to figure out an inexpensive way to separate the polypropylene and polyethylene in the disposables. "I could get 30 cents a pound if we separate them," he said.

The Washington legislature may give Mr. Anderson's venture a lift. An amendment sponsored by Representative Georgette Valle earmarks $150,000 for diaper recycling programs. Although the measure was stripped from a solid waste management bill passed last week, Representative Valle was assured by leading legislators that the financing would be included in the state's budget when it is presented next month.

Mr. Anderson, who has relied on word-of-mouth to attract customers, is convinced that demand for recycling disposables is high. "I think we would be swamped if we advertised," he said. "All my customers say they feel guilty about using disposables."   *New York Times*

Times News Wednesday, February 3, 1988

Valle takes diaper crusade to Olympia

By **BRIAN DOHERTY**

Georgette Valle goes on diaper patrol when she visits homes in the 34th District.

If she spots a tiny constituent wearing cloth diapers, the kid's parents may later get a letter from Valle commending them for not using the plastic disposable kind.

Valle, a Burien Democrat who represents West Seattle, White Center and northwest Burien in the state House, has been introducing legislation since 1975 to ban plastic diapers on environmental grounds.

This year she's concentrating on a bill that would require all disposable diapers used or sold in Washington by 1990 to be made of biodegradable materials – ones that decompose by natural processes.

VALLE'S CRUSADE against plastic isn't as lonely as it once was.

Georgette Valle

At least seven other anti-plastic bills are being considered this session in the Legislature And in King County, Seventh District council member Paul Barden has introduced an ordinance to restrict the use of plastic packaging, prompted by a greater interest in recycling and by fears of toxins from burning plastic in a proposed county trash incubator.

Valle believes King County's dilemma over garbage disposal has led to the statewide moves in the Legislature. Even national media have publicized Washington state's efforts to restrict the use of plastics.

"We are very environmentally conscious people and we do lead the nation in deciding how to handle plastic wastes," she says.

AMONG THEM are HB 606 sponsored by Rep. Ken Jacobson (D-46th), which prohibits the sale of carbonated beverages in non-returnable containers, while HB 972, sponsored by Rep. Gene Lux (D-11th), seeks to prohibit the use of plastic grocery bags. Rep. Katherine Allen (R-21st) is sponsoring HB 1241, which prohibits plastic packaging for take-out or fast food.

Reps. Art Wand (D-27th), Gary Locke (D-37th), and Katherine Allen (R-21st) are promoting legislation to prohibit the sale of non-biodegradable plastic six-pack rings.

Rep. Art Sprenke (D-39th), who would prefer more study of the problem, has authored a bill to assess the state's waste stream and determine its makeup of recyclable materials and plastics.

The bills have generated a great deal of lobbying, says Valle, vice chairwoman of the House Environmental Affairs committee. Representatives of the paper industry, for instance, support the bills, while those from the plastic-packaging industry oppose them.

KATHY SPEARS, editor of the House Democrats media service, doubts bills banning plastic grocery bags and plastic packaging of fast food will pass, although the bill on six-pack plastic rings has passed the House. Even if the plastics bills fail, she says, they have focused attention on the problem.

Valle acknowledges her bill against disposable diapers will fail, because consumers demand disposable diapers and no biodegradable alternative to plastic diapers exists in this country.

But she stresses that plastic diapers make up 4 percent of the volume of garbage going into U.S. landfills. The associated human waste in the moldering bundles has become a health hazard, she adds.

Both Valle and Shelley Stewart, regional toxics director for environmental group Greenpeace Northwest, say the problem of stuffed landfills has forced county and state officials to plan for recycling and reduction of trash, plus incineration.

BOTH WOMEN pan incineration as a waste of valuable resources, and they fear the production of toxins such as the cancer-causing dioxin emitted from burning plastic.

They say removing plastics from the 4,000-ton-a-day county waste stream is the key to recycling. "Everything else is recyclable, and incinerating plastic wastes produces toxins," says Stewart.

John Pruat, vice president of Dolco Packaging in Lynnwood, counters their arguments and defends the use of plastic food containers. He has told legislators that food containers made of Styrofoam and other plastic materials are non-toxic whether buried or burned, as well as inexpensive and convenient.

He also has said that plastic containers make up far less than 1 percent of municipal trash.

IN KING COUNTY, Barden believes a proposal for a trash incinerator–widely opposed at hearings throughout the county–has intensified public interest in waste reduction and recycling. His ordinance would eliminate sales of all non-biodegradable, disposable plastic packaging.

The ordinance also would require the development of markets for recyclable materials, and source separation of wastes into similar groups for recycling.

Brian Doherty is a student in the University of Washington School of Communications News Laboratory.

All diapers not created equal
In the eyes of Mother Nature

Georgette Valle
Special to The Times

"THE DIAPER wars appear to be over" (The New York Times, Oct. 23, 1992)

Some people claim that since both cloth and disposable diapers have environmental impacts, it's a wash. I say this commentary on the diaper debate is premature.

This debate is not just for parents of infants and toddlers. Diapering alternatives are relevant to taxpayers and rate-payers, hospitals and nursing homes, water and electric utilities, public-health officials and landfill operators, as well as anyone who doesn't want a landfill in his or her back yard.

The diaper debate usually is presented as a two-horned dilemma: cloth or disposable. This question, though significant, leaves other important parts of the issue out of focus.

First, "disposable" diapers ought to be named "cellulose" diapers, named after the wood products constituting two-thirds of their components. This would parallel label for "cloth" diapers named after the material from which they're made.

The term "disposable" conveys the message that once the dirty diaper is out of your sight, it's OK to put it out of your mind. The term also reminds us of the raw materials and industrial processes that went into the diaper's manufacture and of its ultimate destination.

We must also make a critical distinction between cloth diapers laundered at home versus those laundered by a commercial diaper service.

The notion that cloth diapers use more water and energy than cellulose diapers carries a large dose of myth.

It is commonly assumed, as *Consumer Reports* did, and often claimed, as Dr. Rocky Mazzeo did in a recent "Special to The Times," that throwaway cellulose diapers "require less water and energy" than cloth diapers.

Cloth diapers laundered at home do use 77 percent more water than cellulose diapers. But commercially laundered cloth diapers actually use 30 percent less water, according to a 1991 study sponsored by the National Association of Diaper Services. The state Department of Ecology (DOE) considers this study "well documented" and the "most comprehensive" available examination of diapers from cradle to grave.

Diaper services have economies of scale and use water more efficiently. The other major reason for this surprising fact: When used properly, cellulose diapers are rinsed out rather than tossed into the garbage, fecal material and all. Toilet flushing uses significant amounts of water.

True, many people don't clean out soiled diapers. We're throwing feces into landfills instead of the sewer system where sewage belongs. The King County Nurses Association, citing the American Public Health Association, concludes there is a potential risk of disease transmission when human feces are disposed of in the garbage.

Cellulose diapers require over 60 percent more energy than cloth diapers laundered at home on a per-diaper-change basis because huge amounts of energy are used in manufacturing cellulose diapers. Cellulose diapers consume over 200 percent more energy than commercially laundered cloth diapers.

The notion that cloth diapers use more water and energy than cellulose diapers carries a large dose of myth.

The environmental question about diapers that looms largest, however, is solid waste. Americans throw 18 billion cellulose diapers into landfills each year. By weight, they make up from 1 to 1.7 percent of all solid waste by volume; they are 2 to 3.3 percent.

Cellulose diapers are the third-largest single consumer product going into landfills – behind only newspapers and food and beverage containers. For every child who uses cloth diapers, more than one ton of garbage – in the form of cellulose diapers – is eliminated.

About 40 percent of our state's population lives in counties with less than 10 years' capacity remaining in local landfills. Fortunately, we already recycle 28 percent of our solid waste.

But we must do more.

Our state's landmark Solid Waste Management Act sets a goal of reducing waste by 50 percent by 1995. Everything we throw away must be scrutinized, reduced and recycled. As the DOE has observed, "reducing every possible (solid waste) component is critical if the 50 percent reduction goal is to be achieved by 1995."

As part of an overall strategy to reduce reliance on disposable products, the state's Solid Waste Management Plan calls for encouraging the use of cloth diapers and the recycling of cellulose ones.

After use, both cloth and cellulose diapers should be converted for re-use through recycling and/or composting.

A diaper recycling pilot project recently conducted in Seattle found that diaper recycling is technically feasible. While the projects did not find it economically viable, remember that at one time hand-held calculators and personal computers were technically feasible but not economically viable.

Cellulose diapers are being recycled in Ontario, Canada. A private company washes, sterilizes and separates the diapers into their three main components: wood pulp, plastic and absorbent gels. The wood pulp can be used to make more diapers and other paper products. The plastic can be turned into an oil-absorbent material used for soaking up oil and chemical spills. The absorbent gels may be used in agricultural applications as a soil enhancer.

Successful recycling involves creating markets. It takes creativity and steadfast commitment. Not many years ago, there was no market for recycled paper. Today, recycled paper is widely used.

Another solution is composting. The cellulose in diapers is wood pulp. Wood pulp can be composted. That means it can be turned into humus, the organic portion of soil.

A private company, Recomp, has successfully added cellulose diapers to its compost material at its plants in St. Cloud, Minn., and Bellingham. Europe has been composting diapers and other materials for decades. We have only about a dozen solid-waste composting plants, while Europe has over 200.

The environmental benefits of re-using and recycling products, compared with single-use products made of virgin raw materials, are enormous. Diapers, both cellulose and cloth, are no exception.

◈ Rep. Georgette Valle is vice-chairwoman of the Environmental Affairs Committee in the state House of Representatives. She represents the 34th District, which includes West Seattle, Burien and Vashon Island.

Legislative Causes

Representative Georgette Valle and Representative Frances North join Governor Dixie Lee Ray's signing a co-sponsored environmental bill becoming law in April of 1979.

Representative Sim Wilson, Representative Georgette Valle, and Governor Dixie Lee Ray (*1977-1981*) signing HB 535-79, a bill relating to motor carriers in May of 1979

West Seattle Herald
August 20, 1970
"Bad Hair Day"

Mayor Meets Valle

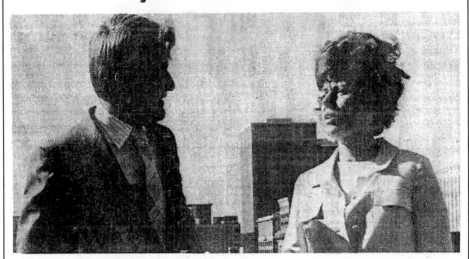

Georgette Valle, 31st district candidate for the State House, position 1, Democrat, visited with Mayor Uhlmann in his office atop the Municipal Building last week.

They were photographed outside against the Seattle skyline as they talked of topics relating to the 31st district, she explained.

Since the 31st district encom- passes both county and city areas, conversation centered upon the Roxbury Improvement Project which has been put off for lack of state matching funds except for a small portion of the total package, she said.

She reported that she asked Mayor Uhlmann what he felt about the possibility of diverting the $3 million scenic drive portion of the total Forward Thrust package to complete the larger Roxbury Improvement Project.

The mayor replied that the legality of this would need to be investigated in order to avoid problems such as were faced in dealing with the R. H. Thompson Freeway project, and that the wording of the bond issue would need to be scrutinized, she explained.

Valle moves spill bill

The House Ecology Committee last week approved a measure that would make oil companies along with their shipping carriers fully liable for damages in the event of an oil spill.

Committee Chairwoman Georgette Valle, (D-31st Dist.) said, "We have placed responsibility where it should be, on the owners of the oil."

Valle explained that this definition of liability would serve as a safeguard against spills because it would make the oil companies act with greater care and with sharper oversight, especially with respect to the shipping companies they contract with.

The bill, SHB 1351, specifically holds an oil terminal facility strictly liable, without regard to fault, for any damage caused by oil spilled by vessels detained for or departing from the terminal facility.

Representative Georgette Valle and Senator Mark Gaspard watch as Governor Booth Gardiner *(1985-1993)* sign the Education Bill

A6 Seattle Post-Intelligencer Tuesday, March 30, 1982

Seattle Post-Intelligencer

THE VOICE OF NORTHWEST SINCE 1863

Georgette Valle
represents Seattle's
31st district

Curb the bond habit

The $23 million commissions doled out to New York brokerage houses for handling February's record $850 million sale of Washington Public Power Supply System bonds underscores the need to probe the sacred temple of high finance. What did ratepayers get for extending such generous commissions?

Fully one-tenth of one-fourth of the "spread" (cost of selling a bond) goes to bond counselors, whose contribution to bond sales is highly questionable.

I introduced HB 975 this session to regulate such counselors, requiring open, competitive bidding on their services, and setting their fees on an hourly rather than percentage basis. Unfortunately, Republican leadership didn't deem the bill – or the issue – worthy of a public hearing.

As a municipal corporation of Washington State, WPPSS would be covered under such legislation. Requiring WPPSS to hire bond counselors via open, competitive bidding should sound the death knell for such gross abuses as the $4.2 million given to a Seattle bond counseling firm over the past three years of "legal services" to WPPSS.

This good management measure would apply to bond counselors hired out of state as well. WPPSS would have to wean its expensive tastes away from its New York bond counseling firm.

What's needed is a thorough study of the bidding process on bond sales, extending beyond bond counseling firms to the brokerage houses themselves.

I would hope that such an investigation would pierce the defensive screen erected when a member of my staff attempted to get some answers out of a Merrill Lynch official in New York.

What's happened to WPPSS on a grand scale happens daily to local governments selling bonds on the municipal market. We must find ways to curb our bond habit, as several local entities are exploring, or reduce exorbitant and unnecessary costs when we choose that route.

STATE REP. GEORGETTE VALLE
Seattle

Georgette Vikingstad Valle

1989 Interim. Representatives Valle and Rust in a meeting with
Mayor Charles Royer and County Executive Tim Hill re H86 S35 Bills

Seattle Delegation Press Conference on Education Issues, February 1991 (H91-237-19)

Left to right: Representatives Brekke, Appelwick, Phillips, Senator Prentice,
Senator Talmadge, Representatives Reinhart, Valle, Lock, Wineberry,
Jacobson, Williams, and Cole

Representative Valle and Gloria Steinam campaign for Initiative 120, a pro choice measure in 1991.

Representative Valle poses for picture after Governor Mike Lowry *(1993-1997)* signs her bill H.B. 1086-94, Penalties for Littering, during the 1994 legislative session.

I designed and passed legislation that placed these recycle bins for trash, bottles, plastic, and paper containers in the airports and seaports in Washington. The trash and paper bins are hidden from view.

COMMUNITY ORGANIZATIONS AND SPECIAL COMMUNITY PROJECTS

*Because of their agelong training in human
relations—for that is what feminine intuition
really is—women have a special contribution to
make to any group enterprise . . . .*

Dr. Margaret Mead

Community Organizations and Their Impact on Our Family

League of Women Voters

One of the first community organizations that I joined was the League of Women Voters. I was impressed with their sense of organization, study projects, and independent thought. At the same time I became a Democratic Precinct Officer in the 31st District Democratic Organization, the League of Women Voters wanted me on the League of Women Voters Board. Delighted and flattered, it soon came to my attention that I could not serve as a Democratic Precinct Officer and be on the nonpartisan League of Women Voters Board. My term on the Board was brief and unceremonious, but I understood the intent.

Leagues of Women Voters all over the United States are valuable for independent thinking to local, state, and national government. In my first legislative term of office in 1965, I spoke on a number of issues important to the League of Women Voters and to my 31st Legislative District.

It is very stimulating to meet women who are well informed and willing to act in concert to accomplish the goals that they set for themselves. Every League of Women Voters operates in a little different manner, but still is consistent enough that independent thought and action are usually triumphant. The League of Women Voters' publications are well respected and frequently quoted by reporters and authors. The League's *The Voter* and *They Represent You* pamphlets in Washington State informs the public concerning their local, county, state, and federal leaders in government.

Democratic Women's Clubs

In the 1950s thirteen strong women in the Evergreen Democratic Women's Club in the Burien area were determined to increase the membership. In those days there were stay-at-home mothers who could swell our ranks if they could find care for their young children. Often I had to take our little daughter along as it was sometimes difficult to obtain a sitter. She then made her presence known by crawling under the chairs amongst the members. The Puget Sound Democratic Women's Club in the Federal Way area hired a baby sitter for their meetings, a signal that early childhood education and child care was necessary if women were to become an active part of their community.

To reach out into the community with our Democratic message involving women I hosted a meeting at my home with Henry Jackson, longtime U.S. Senator, as our guest speaker. Forty-nine Democrats filled our living room. Within a few months our club grew to a membership of eighty women.

I promised the King County Democrats that I would give a breakfast in the spring of 1957 for Katie Locheim, our National Democratic Committee Woman. The date was set, the food was purchased, and the guests were invited. Katie arrived in Seattle,

Evergreen Democratic Club celebrating Katheryn Taucher's 80th Birthday again.
Left to Right: Dorothy Erickson, Jeanne Hamilton, Katheryn Taucher, Marge Arnold, and Jo Ericksen

looked at her schedule and quickly called, saying, "I can't get up that early in the

Dave and Margaret Beardslee, friends and neighbors of the Valles

morning. That is five o'clock Eastern Time." Mindful of the food I had just purchased, I said, "Come for dinner." All the guests were called, breakfast was canceled, and dinner invitations extended to the dinner hour. I let everyone know that they would have breakfast menus for dinner. What else was I going to do with sixty eggs? It was a balancing act, being accommodating to our guest and still keeping my rebelliousness in check.

Katie Lochiem mentioned that President Eisenhower was stepping into Democratic shoes with his position on Social Security. You may remember that Eisenhower considered running as a Democrat in 1951.

The message of the evening was well received, even by my Republican neighbors, Dave and Margaret Beardslee—and my sixty-egg omelet was a success.

Our Democratic recipe for success was Zelma Reeves Morrison, President of the Washington Federation of Democratic Women's Clubs. She visited every club in the state as well as helping new clubs to organize. Personally speaking, she was an inspiration to me with her articulate message. Many early voters remember her mother, Belle Reeves, Secretary of State in Washington.

The West Seattle Democratic Women's Club is a huge addition and vibrant force within to the West Seattle Democratic Coalition of overall progressive

Zelma Reeves Morrison from Spokane was President of the Washington Federation of Democratic Women's Clubs from 1957 through the 1960s.

clubs in West Seattle, part of the 34th District. During the Presidential elections, the club really blooms with new members. They are issue-oriented Democrats with well-know speakers appearing at their meetings. They were part of a group of organizations that presented me with a beautiful cut glass vase that recited my virtues as a politician in a very flattering manner. Also, I contribute $100 bed and breakfast vouchers for fund raisers to be used in Green Valley, Arizona.

American Association of University Women

The American Association of University Women (AAUW), the voice of women for 125 years, promotes education opportunities and equality for all grades, kindergarten to high school, but especially young women bound for college. I joined in the late 1950s. The Association of University of Women promotes speakers that are literate and frank about the issues of the day that affect both women and men's lives. Their yearly programs include book discussions and educational tours. Leaders within the AAUW speak from the courthouse to the White House about the decisions being made. While a member of the local Highline branch, I helped pass the College Savings Bond bill.

Solveig Lodge No. 31, Daughters of Norway

Solveig Lodge No. 31, Daughters of Norway unites into sisterhood women who are of Scandinavian descent (Norwegian, Danish, Swedish, Finnish, or Icelandic) or are married to a man of Norwegian birth or descent. The Solveig Lodge informs the members of history, culture, and the language of Norway.

In Washington State the Norwegian Cruise Line brings in tourist passengers that bring revenue to Seattle and the state of Washington. In the closing days of my last year as State Representative (1996), I helped sponsored and passed a resolution to permit cruise ships to come into the state of Washington. Representative Jolene Unsold was sponsoring a bill in Washington, D.C. It passed with flying colors in both houses in both Washingtons.

Our Scandinavian sisters continue to inform its members of the story of the Norwegian Princess Martha and King Olav of Norway. Of particular interest to the sisterhood was the historic story of her efforts to relieve Norway's plight under the German Nazis during World War II. President Franklin Delano Roosevelt gave words of strong support to Norway in her valiant fight for freedom against the German Nazi invasions. He offered Crown Princess Martha and her family refuge for five years in the United States where she rallied Americans.

Our first cruise to Alaska, but we had to leave from Vancouver, Canada, that prompted the thought, "Why not Seattle?"

Georgette Valle proudly stands beside President Roosevelt's statue in Bergen, Norway.

Representative Helen Sommers, Senator Jeanne Kohl-Welles, and Representatives Georgette Valle and Joan Brekke are walking in Ballard's May 17, 1992, Norway Constitution Day Parade.

Solveig Lodge marches in the Burien 4th of July parade.
Grandsons Bryan Goonetilleke and George Valle carry the Daughters
of Norway banner. Members Evelyn Lundstrom Weiss, Georgette Valle,
and Eleanor Baker pause for the photo. Granddaughters Erica Valle
and Alicia Goonetilleke enjoy the sunny 4th weather.

If I were in legislative session on May 17, Norway's Constitution Day, I would say some special words on behalf of *Syttende Mai* (just "May 17" in Norway). On one occasion I arranged for an appearance of the Nordiske Folk Dancers, including Carol Ramstad who was the President of Solveig Lodge. I was proud to see them dance down the legislative aisle in their colorful, festive costumes.

Environmental Organizations

I have supported the non-partisan Washington Environmental Council as well as many environmental organizations nationwide including the Sierra Club that has been a watchdog for preventing pollution.

Heart of America is still continuing to be the public's voice for Hanford cleanup. Let's hope that the new leadership in Congress will prevent the million of gallons of leaked nuclear waste from reaching the Columbia River.

Today it is refreshing to see that many combine their efforts into one organization known as the League of Conservation Voters with board members from other environmental organizations.

The environmental awards that I have received were the combined efforts and votes of so many of my legislator friends, both Democratic and Republican. Of course, Democrats were in the majority, but there were times that with the Republicans I passed controversial legislation.

There were ship safety items that did not get into the Puget Sound Ship Safety legislation. I wanted to see two pilots steer ships into Puget Sound at the very northern entrance. There are instances where the single pilot fell asleep and the ship went aground in that last phase of travel to the oil refinery. In that case I disagreed with my own Chair, Nancy Rust, of the Environmental Affairs Committee. It was her responsibility to pass ship safety legislation in the House and Senate and then on to the Governor. You do not necessarily win every battle in Olympia. You can disagree on some provisions that do not get into legislation even within your own party.

Legislation takes time to prepare and get the support of passage. Senator Karen Kaiser, passed Air Transportation Commission legislation to study future airports or expansion of airports to serve Washington state in 2005. I could not even get a hearing on a similar bill in times past.

Lions Club

Lions Rose Clark, Kenny Selander, Carol Selander, Kate Shaw, and Georgette Valle singing in the skit "Burien Radio Station" the song *You Gotta Have Sight.*

Odd is active in the Lions Club here in Washington State. He formed several new clubs and served as President of the Burien Sea-Tac Lions Club, as Zone Chairman, and as District Governor. For many years women were not allowed to serve with men in regular Lions Clubs. Finally in 1988 women were allowed to join the Lions Clubs. I had joined previously as a member of the Burien Lioness Club. At last I was able to be a member of the integrated Lions Club where both men and women were full Lions Club members. I really became interested when I could serve with both men and women in the Burien Lions Club. Their good deeds include serving the blind, providing eyeglasses, and corneas to restore lost eyesight. The Burien Lions Club has two members with cornea trans-

Carol Selander at a Lion's dinner

plants, Lion Carol Selander and Lion Mary Beth Ball. The Lions Clubs International is the largest service club in the world with membership of 1,350,000 in 197 countries. We need to remind ourselves of the many contributions that all service clubs perform every day in our communities.

Churches

With a legacy of no less than three Lutheran ministers in my family, church has been central to my life. Involvement in church life has lifted my spirit and nourished my soul. Reverend Milton Laib was a true builder of Congregational Churches. The Normandy Park United Church of Christ Sunday School curriculum provided a solid value system for our Peter and Christine. I served as fourth grade teacher, taking my turn in working with the youth. When Reverend Jack Heal was our minister someone asked me if I were praying to win the election. I replied that I could not ask God to help me because God was nonpartisan. Jack was listening and then remarked, "I would have no problem asking for God to help you win the election."

After the children left home for college, we decided to attend Plymouth Congregational Church. Plymouth Congregational is a very dynamic church which involved the congregation in the downtown Seattle First Avenue Service Center, financing downtown housing for the homeless and the mentally ill. Their forums not only stimulate members to live their values but attract outsiders as well.

Christine Valle and her cousin Stephanie Connel in their finest dresses in Normandy Park United Church of Christ in 1976

GEORGETTE VALLE, District No. 31

Church Group Tours House

OLYMPIA VISITORS—Representative Georgette Valle, welcomes Reverend John C. Heal, his daughter, and members of his confirmation class to Olympia. Reverend Heal, pastor of the Normandy Park United Church of Christ, 19247-1st S. offered the opening prayer in the House Session on Wednesday, Feb. 21 and Reverend Heals' daughter, Sharon, served as an honorary page. Pictured with Representative Valle are Sharon Heal, Rev. Heal, Carolyn Wittchen, Nancy Amende and Mary Williams.

Reverend David Colwell thought of himself as a conservative theologian as far as the Bible was concerned and a liberal in the application of Biblical matters extended into the community. I appreciated that my church was in tune with the social causes for which I cared.

Georgette Valle and Reverend David Colwell at a Pro Choice Rally on January 12, 1990

Anthony Robinson was a preacher, a teacher, and a writer. He is graduate of

Seiko, Reverend Tony, and Marit pose for a picture at Plymouth Congregational Church on October 25, 1989. Seiko and Marit were the Valle's guests from Japan.

Willamette University in Salem, Oregon, and has his Master's of Divinity from Union Theological· Seminary in New York. As pastor of Plymouth Congregational Church, he often reflected on matters of the state where morality could improve citizens and government approaches in his *Post-Intelligencer* articles. I asked Tony to preach his *Post-Intelligencer* articles and submit his sermons to the paper. I didn't win this discussion, but we continue to enjoy his articles in the *Post-Intelligencer*. His theological discussions were always interesting, and Odd and I always took part of his wry humor and wisdom home with us for the week's perusal.

Tony's wife, Laura—the busy mother of Joe and Nick Robinson—found time to improve the text of the hymns so the words matched church life in today's world. She is still a teacher and is a principal at Bryan Elementary in the Seattle area.

Today, Tony Robinson is president of the Columbia Leadership Network, a new Seattle-based program of leadership education.

Chris Anderson Ostrem gave enthusiastic sustenance to our church dialogue and then David Shinn continued in church leadership during this important time in church development. David gave important sermons on stimulating international topics.

Allen Hilton from George Fox College, Princeton, and Yale became our senior minister and teacher. His writer years helped carry forward a vision of an urban church.

Liz Hilton was born in Texas and graduated from the University of Texas in 1986. She graduated from law school and worked for the Texas Attorney General for ten years. After marrying Allen and bearing two sons, Sam and Isaac, she went on to Yale Divinity School in 2003. Now both Hiltons share with Plymouth Congregational their dedication to church life.

Odd and I are now with the Good Shepherd United Church of Christ in Sahuarita, Arizona, with Pastor Randy Mayer, his wife, Norma, and their two children, Jacob and Richard. Randy is the Christian bell weather for our congregation in immigration and other matters of conscience. He is interviewed and applauded by our local paper, *Green Valley News.*

Norma has unselfishly given of her time and energies as a counselor to the victims of Katrina in Louisiana this last year. Our spiritual life continues in the Southwest United States uninterrupted. We are eternally thankful for our church life.

It is impossible not to be affected by your very own history. Therefore, I found myself thinking of the Pastor of the Good Shepherd Church Randy Mayer on a particular Sunday morning in 2004, trying to envision how he and his congregation were going to finance their future. With a legacy of three Lutheran ministers behind me, how could I fail to pledge my financial support to the church in 2004?

My church years are important to me. When I review my legislative years, I have often thought about the life of Christ and how his deeds have changed the world. There are times I wished that my ancestors had written and preserved their thoughts for posterity. I perhaps knew my Grandmother Vikingstad the best because she lived the longest. She was the eternal optimist of all my grandparents. My causes are today taken for granted but in that legislative era, many of my causes had strong political opposition.

Environmental Science Center History

Georgette Valle Accepts Environmental Award from City of Burien

March 2005

At the "Discover Burien" Dinner in March 2005, an Environmental Award from the City of Burien on behalf of the board, members, and supporters of the Center was given to Georgette Valle for the great accomplishments of the Environmental Science Center. Georgette said that one never accomplishes projects such as this alone and went on to give us a bit of the Center's history and laud the people who helped with this Center since its creation in 1997.

Georgette Valle says, "It began with an interesting thought: Could an Environmental Science Center stem the dropout tide that seemed to be sweeping our high schools? Perhaps it should begin much earlier than high school. With that brief thought, I bumped into

Environmental Science Center Board marching in the Burien 4th of July Parade in 2004

Joan McGillton as I came back to reality. She had been attending Burien City Council meetings with some regularity lately. Remembering that if I were to "get this dream on the road," I had better pursue people for the board I was assembling. I asked Joan McGillton if she would like to be a member of the Center. She was very quick to answer in the affirmative as she told me she was a marine biologist. My heart jumped for joy as

(continued)

Environmental Science Center History   Page 2

I shook her hand in appreciation. She served as the Center's first President, which helped strengthen our Board.

"In a flashback of City of Burien actions, I remembered that Councilmembers Sally Nelson and Dr. Kennelly served on the committee that made the decision that the Center was to be established in the City of Burien. Joe Weiss of the Seahurst Marine Technical Center also served as a mentor and leader in forming the ideas the committee collectively developed. It seemed appropriate to hold our meetings in the Marine and Technology building. Members of the Burien Parks and Recreation Department assisted in the decision-making process.

"From this auspicious beginning, we began to gather others who would help us across legal hurdles, especially Jerry Robison, our attorney. I watched him as he participated in an earlier City Council meeting and was impressed by his knowledge of local government. He had aided us with that particular skill, and we were eternally grateful for his help. Karen McMicheal, a health care professional who specializes in environmentally sound P.R. for children, was invaluable to us as we progressed. Joan McGillton brought two extremely valuable professionals on board, Darrel and Barbara Williams. Both had marine biology experience "in the books and the beach" and helped to put our programs on sturdy footings. These two members of the Board were nominated for the Environmental Educators of 2004 Award by the City of Burien. This was a well deserved honor, as they not only produced excellent pro-grams, but brought in substantial monies from private foundations and private donations. Darrel had been leading the organization as Co-President and now President. His administrative skills have helped us develop a smooth relationship with the City of Burien. Kathy Hollo has continued on the Board with recruiting new members whose money goes for programs for our students.

Darrel and Barbara Williams

"Loren Tomlinson served as the Center's Treasurer and now serves on the Capital Committee. We value people from our community who are able to serve in more than one position. Larry Moormeir took over the Treasurer responsibilities. The fiscal audits were important for all concerned. Private foundation money is not possible unless every cent is accounted for. Kathy Murray has served as a very capable Secretary. It is crucial that accuracy be reflected in the minutes. When one works with local government, Chuck Cox gave us that extra "ump" we needed for our summer programs. He displayed our future

(continued)

Environmental Science Center History Page 3

architectural drawing for the public to view and examine. Sheila Kollmorgan served until recently in assisting and contacting members to inform them of the Center's progress. Janice Mathison is the Center's one, steady-paid employee. Complimentary comments about her teaching techniques are often heard, which add to our environmental and scientific egos.

"With this type of professional support, it was time that President McGillton and I venture into our first fund-raising project at the King County level. We asked our local King County Councilman for a donation of $100,000. Guess who that Councilman was in the late 1990's? He is today's Mayor of Seattle, Greg Nickels. We got the money! This allowed us to locate an architect and to begin our plans for the future. It also enabled us to go further away—to Olympia—to ask for future monies.

"Senator Eric Poulsen, County Councilman Dow Constantine, and Representative Joe McDermott were very supportive and influential in obtaining the monies we now have in our Capital Budget in our efforts to finish building the Environmental Science Center.

"We encountered some neighborhood scuffles, but we maintained our environmental manners and progressed to thoughtful solutions, making everyone happy. The City of Burien stepped forth with assistance in the form of the old caretakers' cabin, which provides a place on the Seahurst beach for future building. The Board of the Center progressed with the addition of new Board members that contribute new talents and energy. Scott Price, a local realtor, thinks constantly about our public image. This is a valuable attribute that we need to apply to the Center. Lupita Ayon is helping with the Hispanic members in our community. This is an area that we value and need. Both are very welcome additions to the Board.

"My last trip to Olympia in March was very successful. Providing Washington State doesn't have another earthquake, the remainder of the capital monies should be included in the Capital Budget of 2007.

"As I was introduced to the Legislature by Senator Eric Poulsen, I received standing ovations on the House and Senate floors, with Senate Republicans standing first. The surprised Democrats also rose. I think they did that out of thankfulness that these legislators no longer had to vote on my controversial bills: anti-tobacco, emissions control, clean air and water, and full funding for education. These bills were some of the ones that I pushed forward. That is the story of the Environmental Science Center, and we are just beginning."

George Valle,
Georgette Valle, and
Chuck Cox at a fund
raiser in the summer of
2004

The Environmental
Science Center's
information booth in
Dottie Park

El Salvador Lions Club Projects
January 1999

Before the Lion's Club water system was built, the water was carried by the children or brought from water trucks at a high cost. The contaminated water caused severe illness and even death of children.

The first water system was finished in the fall of 1999 in a mountain village close to a river near San Salvador. All common labor for Lion's water projects was done free by the people of the community, supervised by special CARE personal and paid specialists, when needed.

The project is now being expanded with three more storage tanks to supply clean water for 150,000 more people. The second water project was finished in La Paterna in the mountains of Southeast El Salvador.

Lion Georgette Valle is escorted by CARE personnel, followed by Lion Hal Vaughn in El Salvador. We are walking to a water project up in the mountains. Lions 19 B sponsored and paid for this water project.

Gathering in El Salvador to celebrate a water project Lions District 19-B paid for and installed for the small village in the mountains in 1999

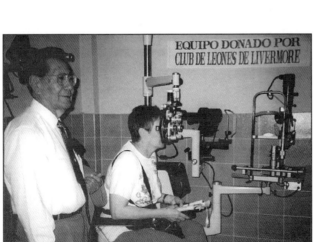

Optometrist in El Salvador in January of 1999. Equipment was donated by the Lions de Livermore.

Georgette Valle gave this girl in El Salvador a book. She lives in the house behind her.

Victories over poverty every day . . . By confronting problems at their roots, CARE helps communities in more than seventy countries around the world realize lasting victories over poverty.

Lions Clubs

Honduras, March 17-24, 2004

We arrived on a Continental Boeing 737 with the pilot executing a skillful landing among houses, mountains, and businesses on a very short runway in Tegucigalpa, the capital of Honduras. Approximately one million people lived in colorful shacks stacked neatly on a mountainous terrain. The population of the country numbered approximately 6,220,000 people. The blue-and-white flag, flying high at the airport with five blue stars, represented the five countries of Central America—Costa Rica, Belize, Guatemala, El Salvador, and Honduras.

In 1998, the destructive hurricane "Mitch" damaged the country of Honduras more than any other Central American country. There are now newly-constructed, beautiful, tall buildings in the downtown area. Some have a distinctive Latin design with unusual architecture. Other devastated areas had been converted into parking lots.

Capital city of Tagucipalpa, Honduras

Our hotel, the del Libertador, was a quiet place to stay and had elevators rising to twelve floors. Art pieces were tastefully situated throughout the hotel lobby. Each room was designed with beautiful inlaid tile in a floral design accentuated in the teak furnishings of the room.

Georgette Vikingstad Valle

Our CARE Team at a Taguicpalpa, Honduras art site

Left to right:, Lion Joanne Luciano of CARE Ottawa, Burien Lion Georgette Valle, Lion Ray Trembley of the Langley Lions Club, Bellingham Lion Hal Vaughn, Lion Pat of the Westminster Lions Club, and Lion Odd Valle of the Burien Lions Club

311

News from the United States was never far away as we watched CNN on our hotel TV. We learned of twenty-seven deaths and forty-one injuries in a hotel bombing in Iraq. Fire and explosions were in evidence as the injured were removed from the scene.

Honduras sculpture

The Canadian CARE team, comprised of Lion Joanna Luciano of CARE Ottawa, Lion Ray Trembley of the Langley Lions Club, Lion Pat from the Westminister Lions Club, along with the U.S. Team of Lion Hal Vaughn of Bellingham and Lions Odd and Georgette Valle of the Burien Lions Club made up the delegation of visitors to the Honduran CARE office. We were to meet with the local Lions Clubs on the night of our arrival at 7 p.m. at the Tegucigalpa Lions Club building, which was called the Lions Cave. Odd was busy filming all the Lions there to welcome us. We were greeted with warm words by Honduran Lions officers and Lions of the Tegucigalpa Lions Club which was then translated into English. As International Lions visitors, we were invited to sit at the head table with the officers. Lion Governor Hena Ligia Madrid de Torres was seated next to me and told me she was a member of the Parliament, which is the Congress of Central America, and a Doctor of Medicine in Tegucigalpa. She apologized for being late to the meeting because she had just delivered a baby.

Jesus statue in Honduras

The Hondurans seemed very relaxed in this capital city, even though the hotels and businesses all employ private security guards who were visible outside their establishments. From our hotel balcony there was a cacophony of city sounds including beeping horns, speeding motors, and screeching brakes.

CARE is a nonprofit international organization committed to helping families in poor communities improve their lives and achieve lasting victories over poverty. Barbara Jackson, the Director of CARE International in Honduras, greeted us outside the hotel in her car. She was an energetic professional eager to show us

Lions' CARE Chair Hal Vaughn
in Honduras

the educational projects that CARE has so carefully crafted south and east of Tegucigalpa. Another driver, Daniel Galeano, understood and spoke English, which was very helpful. Driving in Tegucigalpa is an art and a visitor must fasten one's seat belt and hang on, as the hills frequently turn into circular roads leading into fast freeway traffic. I asked what those signs that looked like STOP signs were. Yes, they were stop signs, but one only stopped when there was a red signal associated with the ALTO sign.

CARE participates in three kinds of actions in Honduras—with parents, teachers and government officials—but they must first prove their financial viability, promote their political advocacy, and participate in public policy. In educational reform, CARE becomes part of the civil discourse to make suggestions as to methods to ultimately lower poverty rates in Honduras.

The program coordination of CARE defined six focus sectors for the 2002 to 2006 time period. CARE promoted:

- Quality basic education to the poorest, emphasizing children, girls, and minorities;
- Prevention and care for people living with HIV/AIDS or at risk;
- Quality health to vulnerable groups;
- Economic security income for marginalized population;

- Risk management for sustainable development; and
- Humanitarian aid in response to emergencies.

For purposes of this book, only those educational network projects that we observed will be discussed. We would simply have to make another trip to see the networks of institutional strengthening dealing with health and economic security, with the exception of one health care community unit. Those educational networks were ENTRA and PROHASE.

ENTRA is a pilot project providing basic education for children and youths who were at risk of entering or who were already working in an abusive or "worse form" of child labor. The figures of 350,000 to 400,000 children working in Honduras seems to be an incredible number of children, but these same figures were reiterated by many others.

Parents are paid money for their children's labor, so they are usually in favor of the children

Farmers in Honduras gathering kindling wood

Lion Odd Valle and mountain school students in Honduras

working because they are poor. Working children usually have low esteem. Their parents need their income and do not send them to school, but through this CARE project this is changing.

In the rural areas, there were electric lines very close to the small farms, but no connecting lines to provide electricity; and therefore there are no TV's or other electrical appliances available.

In Nacaome and San Lorenzo, the CARE program was helping children become educated when they migrated from the mountains to pick melons and catch shrimp. The application of international law is alerting the parents and employers to be trained and to apply these laws to child labor.

Georgette Valle posing behind these school children
in the mountain town of Espino in Honduras

On our visit to Espino, we were introduced to approximately thirty-five students, several parents, teachers, and the volunteers. The students, dressed in uniforms of navy blue skirts, pants and white t-shirts, sang a welcome song. I heard a few budding politicians during the speeches. One was Miguel Lopez of CARE, a very powerful speaker who had his Masters in Education degree and was in charge of these education projects in the areas of Espino and Quebrada Grande. We stopped for lunch of rice, avocados, fried chicken breast, beans, and a choice of soft drinks.

Returning to the CARE office in Tegucigalpa, we picked up new translators, Becky Myton and Education Specialist Alba Luz Ramirez. Outside Marcala, we stayed at the Hotel La Casona which was remodeled into a beautifully-built resort with teak beam ceilings and a large veranda overlooking the estate. We relaxed with their generous hospitality, food, drink until it was time for the next presentation to be given by Alba Luz Ramirez.

Alba was once an employee of the Ministry of Education, but left her position to work for CARE. She felt education officials were too slow in accomplishing the set goals of Honduran education. She accomplished "educational miracles" according to Barbara Jackson, Executive Director of Honduran CARE. Alba was very successful in garnering the cooperation of local government officials and volunteer parents. Each student was provided a workbook accompanied by a cassette tape in a battery-operated recorder to help explain what the workbook entailed. The teacher had been trained in this specific course for the students.

We Lions viewed a standard school where CARE has added its expertise. CARE acquired assistance from parents in painting the classrooms in a pleasant green color. We, as visitors, pitched in and helped paint the room with one of the students, Christian, helping us.

The students of this school, Lempira Spirit, demonstrated a mock local city government meeting for us. The local officials were introduced and subsequently the female president welcomed us. The minutes were read and each student stood as they spoke. We were very impressed with the students' knowledge of their own local government.

Lion Ray Trembley had some balloons, which he expertly twisted into clever animals and figures, and gave each student one. Elementary workbooks together with pencils and crayons were distributed to the students and their teacher, Jesus Edgardo. The students responded with applause.

We also learned about fishing from boys who arose at 2 a.m. during shrimping season. The boys' hands were just the right size to dig for the shrimp in the muddy mango tree roots in seawater. The boys earned three lempiras (about 20 cents U.S.) for each pound of shrimp gathered. Children who work cannot attend regular school. We saw fish carcasses hanging in the house of a woman baby sitting her seventeen grandchildren. Another mother was housing the CARE school on her porch and living room.

Here we are in El Salvador with some young boys who pick shrimp along the shores of El Salvador and Honduras.

Becky Myton of CARE was very informative and told Joanna and me about different flora and fauna found in the Marcala-Guajiquiro areas. We learned that two different types of coffee were grown, shade and sun. The shade coffee was grown under the shade of tall trees as well as beneath bananas trees. The mountainous areas then did not lose their soil from runoff during the rainy season. CARE encouraged the farmers to plant coffee seedlings in the shade of the tall trees because it was ecologically better for the soil. We were also shown examples of sun coffee being grown. The coffee trees were grown together very tightly.

Six out of the seven varieties of pine trees were found in this area of Honduras. The crying pine was obviously named because the needles hung down on the branches of the tree as if they were bending toward the mountains. The quality of Honduran mahogany is very good.

Twenty percent of the land is under cultivation while 80 percent is mountainous in Honduras. Corn and beans are planted together because each plant enriches the soil with nutrients the other plant needs. Beans supply protein for the Honduran people. Corn is considered a delicacy to eat, so it is served in many different ways.

All of these interesting facts seemed to distract us from the bumpy road which the Honduran children were required to walk for many kilometers to reach their school. Parents often walked to the market. Horses were used for transportation if they were available after the day's work was done.

We were informed that 60 percent of the Honduran population was of Mayan descent. The Lenka people in Quajiqiro were shorter than the majority of the Honduran population we had seen. These people have high cheekbones, with piercing brown eyes and stand very straight as if they were trying to extend their  height. The women captured the colors of the orange, purple, and vibrant red bougainvillaea and used those colors in their clothing.

Mayor Wilfred Lopez had been extremely generous with his city budget, buying chairs and eleven thousand pencils and pens for the school. I gave him two kindergarten books for the city library. Later, he treated us to a lunch in a private home. The population of Quajiqiro was nineteen thousand.

Later that afternoon, we visited a community health unit which provided rural mothers who had newborn babies with protein-rich food and milk. The babies were also weighed, and if the child had not attained a normal weight, the mothers were instructed about ways to increase the baby's weight. Title II

Projects and PROHASE's success was due to other programs that have met health and nutrition needs.

We drove only so far with our automobile because a new road was being built, and the rest of the journey had to be made by foot. After a strenuous day, we drove back to the Hotel del Libertado in Tegucigalpa. Lylli Moya had done a splendid job coordinating our trip while answering our endless questions about Honduras.

On Tuesday morning, we spent some very informative time with Derik Olson and Evelyn Rodriquez at the U.S. Embassy. Derik was with the Department of Labor under the State Department's umbrella. Although there were difficulties in working with each new government leader, he acknowledged that there was no longer a military dictatorship in Honduras, so some progress was possible. Evelyn Rodriquez expressed her appreciation to CARE's Director Barbara Jackson for CARE's effort on behalf of the family planning issue and said that it was so difficult to work on that issue when her government tied her hands, metaphorically speaking.

The remainder of the time was spent with the gracious Minister of Education who answered our questions about schools in Honduras. She confessed that it would make her job much easier to learn the true number of schools and the school populations. She said the army was currently conducting a survey. These professionals were grateful for CARE's leadership and assistance in Honduras.

A farewell evening was spent at the home of Barbara and Brenden Jackson where we all enjoyed the view of Tegucigalpa with the planet Venus shining brightly in the evening sky. We saw a sliver of the moon to the left of brilliant Venus.

The next day the Boeing Continental 737 roared up the short runway of Tegucigalpa with all of us waving *adios* to all our new Honduran friends.

ALWAYS A REBEL AND NEVER WITHOUT A CAUSE

AND NOW, THE REST OF THE STORY

Four Grandchildren

It would be magic if I could fast forward and see into the future of our grandchildren. I hope none of them will be out walking, running, or gardening with headsets on their ears. How can they hear the wonderful music of the birds, or the wind, or the chirp of a grasshopper? How can they listen to all the different tunes of the melodious birds?

The other day in Arizona I heard a musical version from a meadowlark's tune repeated three times, with very slightly different version of the same tune the fourth time. It was beautiful! It was as if the bird had a slightly different "bridge" to the same tune. I want all of you to be able to hear these beautiful bird songs!

The digital dilemma has already grabbed this generation. Gameboys, I-Pods, and cell phones are here with children silently manipulating these small computer games with no interaction between the many participants sitting together. I hope all four grandchildren have a profession that is people-oriented. People-oriented professions will still be around, I hope.

Grandchildren, Christmas 1999
Top left: Erica Valle and Alicia Goonetilleke. *Bottom left:* Bryan Goonetilleke and George Valle

I received advice from our banker son, Peter, about college education funds ideas, which were incorporated with the Senate Higher Education Committee Bill. I passed the College Savings Scholarship Bill in 1991 and took advantage of it by providing and setting aside $2,000 per grandchild, which will eventually grow to $8,000 in a twenty-year span.

Alicia and Bryan Goonetilleke

For five days in June 2006 we visited Christine in hot and humid Lakewood, California, to be with our grandchildren, Alicia and Bryan. We stayed in Thomas Kulas' house, the breezes zipping in and out of the house, with Tiffany, Christine's Yorkie dog, and Bow, Thomas' dog, keeping us company. We slept very well.

Christine's children Alicia (14) and Bryan (12) Goonetilleke on June 3, 2006, in California

Both Alicia and Bryan attended Fairmont Private School in Tustin. The school was academically demanding with both children studying as the year end neared its finish.

Alicia was born on May 4, 1992. As an active debater at Fairmont, Alicia took on controversial topics such as whether the Pledge of Allegiance should contain the words "under God" or should the United

Christmas 2004 in California: Bryan, Alicia, and Christine Goonetilleke and Tom Kula

322

States have entered the Iraq War. Alicia has an A-grade average. She has every intention of maintaining a high standard of grades at Northwood High School in Irvine, California.

Baby Alicia Goonetilleke loves her bucket.

Christine, little Alicia, and Grandmother Georgette in June 1995

Grandaughter Alicia Goonetilleke (age 4)

1999 drawing of Grandfather Odd by Alicia (age 7)

ALWAYS A REBEL AND NEVER WITHOUT A CAUSE

For Alicia—
Reach high, for stars lie hidden in your soul.
Dream deep for every dream precedes the goal.
                                    Pamela Vaull Starr

Alicia reflects her Norwegian and Sri Lankan heritage, with her creamy mocha skin showing off her dark brown eyes and brown hair. She expresses her agility and dancing and gymnastic activities in cheerleading at her new high school. Alicia is very organized and will be working to win scholarships for her future higher educational program.

Grandfather Odd and Alicia in her "Audrey" costume for her performance in the play *Little Shop of Horrors* in June 2006

While visiting Christine in 2006, we saw Alicia in the lead role as Audrey in the *Little Shop of Horrors,* wearing a blond wig and beautiful clothes, speaking in a distinct high voice, and sporting a black eye She was one smart "dumb blonde." This screenplay was written some thirty years ago by Charles Griffith, but remarkably modern in speaking to problems of today's society. Perhaps it was a little advanced for the students of Fairmont but, after all, this is near Hollywood, California. Many compliments were paid to Alicia and her mother after the opening performance.

For Bryan—
Love is like a violin. The music may stop now and then, but strings remain forever.
                                    June Masters Bacher

Bryan was born on April 20, 1994. He has a passion for skateboarding, visiting many skateboard parks in Southern California. He was looking forward to the summer and said at the end of summer he will have more than a suntan, he will be really dark.

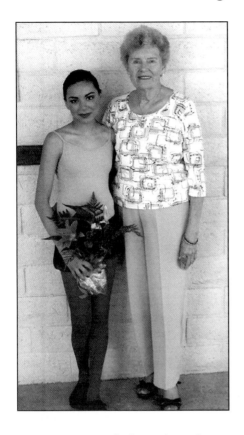

Bryan and Alicia Goonetilleke
with their Grandmother
Georgette in May 2005

Forewarned about how important grades are to his future, Bryan told us he got a 95 percent on a recent math test. Saturdays and Sundays are spent studying with requests for time out for skateboarding!

Bryan is an accomplished violinist with flourishes of a master of ceremonies as he introduces his latest classical piece of music. With an imaginative artistic touch, he brandishes an art pen creating pictures of dragonmainia. Bryan's comedy routine extends to answering questions with an Indian accent, which leaves us all laughing. His charisma touches classmates, and he is frequently sought after for parties by his classmates.

"The Dragon Needs A Drink" 7/8/2006 Bryan Goonetilleke

Erica Valle

For Erica—

If you can remember dreams of flying and soaring like a bird, or dancing, or singing more perfectly than you ever thought possible, you know that no second-hand account of such events could ever give you the thrill you felt in the dream.

Gayle Delaney

Erica was born on September 24, 1992. She has a strong singing voice and dancing talent which she has used in several school plays. Her Norwegian and Japanese heritage is beautifully evident on or off the stage. Her father, Peter, is a

6' 4" Norsk, and her mother, Junko, is Japanese and tall at 5' 7". Erica is now overtaking her mother's height as she is now 5' 8" tall.

On Stage, Erica recently played a nightclub "showgirl" Lena Marelli in the play *Bugsy Malone* and sang her heart out to her audience at Odle Middle School in Bellevue, Washington. Bouquets of flowers and accolades of praise were given to Erica at the end of the evening.

Her musical talent is probably inherited from her mother. The last time I heard Junko sing was on her wedding day to Peter in 1991 to the full accompaniment of a small musical group.

Erica Valle in her "Trick or Treat" outfit on October 31, 1992, is being held by her mom, Junko.

George, Junko, Peter, and Erica pause for this Christmas 2005 photo

Erica's dancing skills are evident as she participates in dancing programs set up on the same dates as our California granddaughter. Erica performed in two dance programs with a jazz piece *Edge of Seventeen* and a hip hop piece *Check it Out*. With grandchildren performing in two states, grandparents often have to make choices. It is impossible to be in two places as grandparents!

Erica Valle's third dance recital
"Peppermint Twist"

Erica Valle's fourth dance
recital *Swan Lake,* June 18,
1999

Erica bakes delicious desserts that are different to please everyone. Her scholastic honors are prominently displayed on the school's "A" Honor Roll. Recently Erica completed a thirty-page report on "How HIV Aids Effects Our Society."

Family portrait. *Top:* Peter and Junko Valle
From left: George Valle, Hiroyshi Kajikawa (Junko's
father), Erica Valle, Takako Kajikawa (Junko's mother)

Erica and George Valle with
Mary Quande at a Lions'
Halloween party

George and Erica Valle in Japan
(August 19, 2006)

George Valle

For George—
   Imagination is the highest
kite one can fly.
                     Lauren Bacall

George was born on March 9, 1994. His passion is basketball, and he practices in his yard in Bellevue. He is a scrappy, fast, and tough basketball player. His father, Peter, is a coach, a chauffeur, and picks up George's friends to go to games.

We, as grandparents, have watched him at basketball games. Basketball is a faster game, so more energy is used by parents, grandparents, and players. At one game I had to get out of the "front line of fire" because I thought I was going to get hit. It seems each player has to think faster than his opponent and should have eyes on the top of his head.

George does a good job of scoring baskets as well as getting the applause from the audience. He has received several basketball awards, and a trophy from the Seattle Chinese Athletic Association as the 2004 Inspirational Player.

Besides sports, George does well in school, and his scholastic honors are prominently displayed on his school's "A" Honor Roll.

Sometimes you hear about your grandchildren more than is evident in their everyday demeanor. One day when listening to him play, I was quite impressed with the intricacies of how to play a trumpet, so George thoughtfully explained to me exactly how the notes are made.

At Christmastime the four grandchildren write and direct plays of their own choosing. There are always dance routines set up by the two girls, with Bryan as master of ceremonies announcing what the dance title is and George regulating the lights. Our annual Christmas play was canceled last year, so all the grand-children have signed an "I owe you" to produce and act in a play "Christmas in July" during their vacation here this summer.

From left: our four grandchildren—George Valle,
Bryan Goonetilleke, Alicia Goonetilleke, and Erica Valle with Grandpa Odd and the
largest zucchini in Burien in July 2006

Valle Family Pictures

Cherry blossom time for Georgette and Odd
at Hurstwood home in Burien

Georgette in Washington, D.C., standing beside a
"Pearl Harbor" statement by President Roosevelt

Peter Valle presents his parents with their 50th wedding anniversary present,
June 30, 2001. *From left:* Peter, Georgette, Odd, Junko, and Christine.

July 2005
3 times 50 Years

July 2005, 3 times 50 years
Christine's 50th Birthday Party with
brother and childhood friends
Left to right: Lynn Beardslee,
Peter Valle, Christine Goonetilleke,
and Joann Montgomery

Christine in 2002

50th Wedding anniversary celebrated in the church they were married in, Odda Lutheran Church in Odda, Norway

Cruising on the *Nordic Prince*

Grandparents, grandchildren, and Junko at breakfast in Odda, Norway (Peter is taking the picture.)

Georgette on her Halloween birthday in her red witch costume

Odd, Deputy Mayor Georgette Valle, and Per Drotningsvik in front of the Odda City Building with Odda City gifts for the City of Burien, Washington

Accept the pain, cherish the joys, resolve the regrets; then can come the best of the benedictions—"If I had my life to live over, I'd do it all the same."

Joan McIntosh

Norway and Eilif's Memorial Service

It was a hot, windy day in October 2005 in Green Valley when we received an e-mail from Norway informing us that Odd's brother, Eilif, had a blood clot on his lung and was in the Hönefoss Hospital. Everyone was giving advice to the doctors and nurses in Norway. Christine hoped they would give him blood thinners to dissolve the clot. Odd hoped for the best as we thought about what good health Eilif had been in this past summer.

Over the course of several days at Hönefoss Hospital, Eilif's appetite disappeared, so some of Gro Elizabeth's home-made soup and caramel pudding made by Randy Tandberg arrived at the hospital. Eilif tried two small teaspoons of pudding. As he became weaker, he still thanked those who visited him so faithfully every day.

One day the family arrived

In happier days in 1988, Gunhild and Eilif pose for photo outside of their Norway home.

at the hospital to find Eilif in intensive care. Calls went out to all the grandchildren: Stian, Borre, and Mary Ann. Borre caught a plane from Trondheim, Norway, and arrived at 12:30 a.m. that morning. Stian and Mary Ann came quickly from Oslo.

The phone rang at 5 p.m. at our house in Green Valley, as we were prepared to sit down for our evening meal. Harald Tandberg, Gro Elizabeth's husband, who spoke excellent English, greeted me and told me the sad news that Eilif had died in his sleep. Odd came to the phone and finished the conversation speaking Norwegian. We both told Harald that we wished to come to Norway to attend the service for Eilif.

After making a call to Norway, we learned that Eilif's service would be held on Wednesday, November 2, at 12:30 p.m. I needed to change the Halloween Thank You Party planned for all the many Democratic volunteers who worked long hours so faithfully for the Tucson city election to October 30. The "Thank You Party" went well.

We were now leaving Amsterdam and being welcomed in Dutch, Norwegian, and English languages. As we looked out the window of the plane, we marveled at the management of the land and sea as we flew over the vast area that is so well cared for and cultivated with productive crops for both export and domestic use. I hoped New Orleans with their land and water problems could use some of the techniques Holland is using so successfully in their land and sea management.

2004 Norway trip—Else Leona Bjerke with her mother, Else Hammerud McClimans, in Else Leona's kitchen

Stop for Family on Way to Vikersund

Tom and Else surprised us at the Oslo Airport. Else is Odd's niece from Trondheim. Her husband, Tom McClimans, formerly an American but now a Norwegian citizen, has spent nearly fifty years at the University of Trondheim teaching the intricacies of the waters of Norwegian fjords. We were driven through heavy traffic to Odd's great niece's, Else Leona's, house and were excited to see her very pregnant. Her children, six-year-old Christina and four-year-old Elaina, appeared to be both shy and sleepy as we offered them a very soft yellow duck and a cuddly black dog we brought with us.

Eilif's eldest grandson, Stian, and his girlfriend, Tanja, arrived to take us to where Stian's parents and grandparents had gathered in Vikersund.

The driving time passed quickly and then Stian made a sharp turn into the Tandberg farm. Norwegians make square corners because they don't have very much land to spare. To round corners into a curve takes more land. When a Norwegian is driving, you know when you are going around a corner.

Eilif's Memorial Service and Time with Family

Gro Elizabeth greeted us affectionately with a hug, and Harald gave us a good firm, Norwegian handshake. We deposited our luggage with Harold's parents, Randy and Mads Tandberg, with felicitations and goodbyes as we

departed with Gro Elizabeth and Harald for the chapel located beside the countryside church in Vikersund to see Eilif for the last time. I wondered if I could bear the sight of someone who was so dear and so kind to both of us. Odd was holding up well. The air was cool and fresh, and I took a deep breath. The yellow birch leaves were falling as we approached the small chapel outside the Vikersund Lutheran Church. Harald and Stian took off the top of the white enamel coffin when the candles were lit. And there was Eilif at peace with the world. Gunhild, his wife, touched his hand affectionately while Gro Elizabeth, their only daughter, comforted everyone in the room. Moments were spent recalling memories of his life.

Randy Tandberg preparing food for Valle's breakfast.

We were to stay with the Tandbergs at their home, which sat on a gentle hillside above the home of Harald and Gro Elizabeth. The basement door of the comfortable woodcrafted home was left open for us to enter as guests. We were amazed to see the lights burning brightly. Randy Tandberg, Harold's mother, was wide awake with her English in full bloom to welcome us to Norway.

In Norway the welcome to any Norwegian home is usually food. Certainly that was the case the next morning at about 9 a.m., a spread of homemade seven-grain bread, eggs, herring, homemade raspberry jam, goat cheese, and several different meats was laid before us. I cannot face herring or any kind of fish at any time without a martini. However, I didn't tell them this because I thought they might hasten to serve me a martini to get me to eat fish at breakfast.

It was soon time to go to the service for Eilif. As Randy drove us down the hill, the yellow birch leaves fluttered to the ground on this crisp November day as we sped to the Vikersund Lutheran Church.

The minister read the condolence messages on the ribbons around the flowers, indicating who had sent them. I thought that gesture was a very thoughtful part of the service. Our contribution on behalf of Eilif was to CARE, a worldwide philanthropic Lions organization.

The wet stone steps of the church led us to the graveyard near the church where the pallbearers placed the casket. This was our final farewell to Eilif. As the minister reverently cast dirt upon the grave, my heart jumped with several quick palpitations as the casket suddenly moved downward into the open grave. I recovered my composure, as we received several warm embraces from family and friends.

Christmas in happier times—Harald and Gro Elizabeth Tandberg are with Georgette and Odd Valle in Norwegian snow. The church in the distance is where Eilif's Memorial Service was held.

We all drove back to Gro Elizabeth and Harald Tandberg's home where we were served delicious sandwiches decorated with dill, cucumber, parsley, and various peppers. Everyone enjoyed the food quietly as we acquainted ourselves with the others, saying "hello" to all we had not greeted at the service. There were speeches from those nearby and far away. Gro Elizabeth, welcomed all of the guests to her house on behalf of Harald and their children. Tom McClimans spoke of his and Else's memories of Uncle Eilif. Odd recalled those youthful times when all three brothers slept in a small bed for years. I

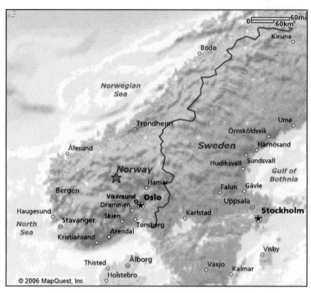

remembered the many times when Eilif patiently helped me to understand the Norwegian language.

Once again, Randy Tandberg in Vikerstad was there for us to listen to our tales of Stavanger. She chilled a bottle of wine to warm our hearts, leading to good conversation. We slept with no alarm clocks that night and awakened to the smell of coffee brewing. The fog was lifting from the long, fjord lake giving the impression that the lake was in the distance.

Visit with Kari in Nodhaven and Back to Vikersund

Tom and Else McClimans came to pick us up at Vikersund, and we traveled to Nodhaven to see their daughter, Kari, and her family. They had news that their other daughter, Else Leona, had another baby girl, and mother and daughter were doing fine. Their granddaughters, Christina and Elainia, were to ride with us to see their cousins. It was a lively ride with the children busily talking about their new sister. Else, their grandmother, kept everyone entertained with answers to their questions. The children played the game of counting red cars and found out there are quite a few red cars on the road that day.

We arrived at a beautiful, spacious, wood house finished "au natural" and built for at least a family of four. Kari, an art teacher, was back teaching after spending one year on maternity leave with the birth of Martine, now a year and half. Her sister, Sophie, was four years old, and both were tow-headed blondes with lots of energy. Around five o'clock, the children sat down for a computer software lesson designed for two- to three-year-olds. It was amazing to see them sit contentedly viewing a western-like cowboy who gets himself into trouble. The children discovered how to computer analyze his difficulties and solved the game as we adults watched.

Now, it was the children's bedtime and time for us to return to Vikersund. Elainia slept all the way home, but Christina was awake talking all the way home.

When we arrived, Gro Elizabeth and Harald were awake and prepared food for us. We had always been with other people, so now we were able to converse just with Gunhild, Gro Elizabeth, and Harald. Gro Elizabeth had been unsuccessful in getting her father, Eilif, to talk about his early life with Odd, and she was now anxious to ask her Uncle Odd. He answered all her questions and clearly enjoyed recalling memories of his youth.

Visit with Rut in Kongswinger

Odd's sisters Rut and Aslaugh on their first visit to the U.S.A. in 1969. *From left to right:* Georgette, Rut, Aslaugh, Peter, and Christine

Gro Elizabeth and Harald drove us to Oslo the next day, and then on to Kongswinger to see Rut. She had retired from the phone company and was now living in a retirement home.

We visited her in her new apartment that included a bathroom with utilities, a small bed, a kitchenette, and a small living room with a TV. Rut told us that she had been in the hospital for two months suffering from depression, but she seemed to have a sense of humor and still be able to laugh her way through a situation.

Rut suffers from osteoarthritis and uses a wheelchair. We took her out to dinner with us, and she enjoyed the coffee and ice cream especially. We brought along pictures of ourselves and our children and hoped that would help her to remember us. She seemed to remember Gro Elizabeth the best.

Homeward Bound

Our trip back to Vikersund was uneventful except for the rain. We arrived home at the Tandbergs in time to go to bed. We all promised to be up early the next morning.

It is always sad to leave Norway. It is a spectacularly beautiful country with views everywhere. We tell people that they need to visit the country soon or the Norwegians will build tunnels and the countryside scenic sights will be missed. The Norwegians are experts at building tunnels and extracting oil from the North Sea with natural gas located below the oil reserves. In spite of this reserve, which is the third largest oil resource in the world, a gallon of gasoline is $7 in Norway. The Norwegians tax their gasoline and place the tax money into a "Rainy Day" fund. There are only 4.5 million citizens supporting their wealthy economy.

A delayed departure from Norway forced us to get up at 4 a.m. to catch our flight to Tucson. We finally arrived home to beautiful sunshine in Arizona.

Norway and Valdemar's Memorial Service

Valdemar Valle Family

We last saw Valdemar and his family on our trip to Norway for Eilif Valle's memorial service in November 2005, and now, sadly, we were flying to Norway for his funeral.

On that trip, Arild, Odd's nephew and the ring bearer at our wedding fifty-four years ago, met us at the Stavanger Airport. Since Stavanger is the oil port of Norway, it is a very busy metropolis. There were new buildings throughout the city with well-lit offices containing busy occupants. I could not see Alexander Kjelland's (the famous Stavanger writer) statute, which usually stood in the original harbor. I later discovered he had been moved because there was new construction at the harbor.

At the moment, hectic Norwegian was being spoken in the car, so I was not able to interrupt Arild and Odd's conversation. Arild swiftly swiggled his car through the busy traffic, and we soon arrived at their neat Stavanger home. Arild and Margrethe had hosted Darrell Williams and Barbara Williams in the fall of 2005 visit to Norway. I had helped facilitate the Williams' visit since they were the President and Program Coordinator of the Seahurst Environmental Science Center in Burien, which is a project I started and am still deeply involved in.

We were surprised to see Arild's wife, Margrethe, and pleased to visit with Odd's oldest living brother, Valdemar, and his wife, Edith, who were not able to come to Eilif's Memorial Service. After some good conversation, we were all invited to the dining room table. Margrethe was on crutches because she was

Arild and Margrethe Valle *(on left)* entertain Darryl and Barbara Williams in the fall of 2005 in Stavanger, Norway.

recovering from a bunionectomy and was ably assisted by Edith, eighty-five years young.

I was so happy that some of Odd's relatives spoke English, because it was so difficult for me to understand the Stavanger dialect. Margrethe spoke both English and Stavanger Norwegian, so I asked her to speak English as much as possible.

Our meal was a delicious *kjottkaker*, a tasty, flat meatball with onions served on bread. A wonderful cake arrived for dessert and our cups were always filled with good, hot coffee. As no one there had been to Eilif's service, I related as much as I could to let people know how sad, but comforting the service was to the relatives and friends of Eilif. It was therapeutic for me.

Soon we were on our way to Valdemar and Edith's home nearby. We visited at their home where Odd reminisced with Valdemar who enjoyed himself, even though at eighty-seven years old he had become a little forgetful. It was not too long before time and our lack of sleep led us to our very narrow bed, about 40 inches wide. Odd was complaining some until I told him that this was where Valdemar and Edith slept many times, so we enjoyed the width and luxury of their bed and settled in for the night.

Our Stavanger visit ended with goodbyes to Edith and Valdemar. We caught a plane to Oslo where Harald met us and drove us back to Vikersund. After a night's rest we left Vikersund for Oslo to catch our plane back to the United States and Arizona.

Valdemar's Memorial Service

It was on a cloudy day in Burien that we recieved the e-mail from Per Otto Drotningsvik, Odd's nephew in Odda, Norway. Odd's oldest brother Valdemar was in the hospital with a broken leg. Valdemar had looked well in Stavanger on our last visit to Norway. We had a good visit with him and glad we had taken the time to fly to Stavanger to see them. Time and age usually take their toll in the hospital. It was not long in the late summer of 2006 when Arild phoned that his father had died and gave us the date of the memorial service.

We made preparations to attend the memorial service. This was our second trip to Norway for memorial services. My mother, in her late life, used to forewarn me about the many hours that are spent saying goodbye to loved ones. We were both thankful for our own good health and prepared for the visit. The tickets were purchased, and we phoned Arild about our plans.

Both Odd and I were admirers of Valdemar's early life's dedication to the city and state workers of Norway. He was very aggresive as a young man as he organized and fought for decent wages, pension rights, and health care for working Norwegians. In a sense, his life resembled his father's efforts to support the average Norwegian trying to improve conditions in working at the sulphur mines in Narvik in Northern Norway.

The story of Valdemar's life was related at the memorial service. Valdemar was a Norwegian who spoke well in public as well as in private. I had listened to him many times when he wanted to relate some facet of his earlier life to me, because he knew of my interest in the subject of a worker's right to a decent job with decent benefits. I hoped that everyone understood how important his life had been to Norway's workers.

Four Valles in happier days at Elfrid's 80th birthday in March of 1987. *From left:* Eilif, Elfrid Hammerud, Valdemar, and Odd Valle

My memories of Edith and Valdemar in 1951 were that of a loving couple raising their two children, Arild, then six years old, and Bjorn, a baby about six months. Valdemar was working at the Samvirke Laget in Odda. Valdemar was a loving and dedicated father. Edith was loving and good humored about her life with Valdemar. Both cherished the love each had for the other. Valdemar will be missed by his family and friends.

At the home of Arild and his wife, Margrethe, family and friends gathered over coffee and sandwiches to exchange memories of Valdemar's life as each of us remembered special times.

Visiting Arild Valle's cabin on our 2004 Norway trip—*from left:* Eric, Elizabeth, Edith, Arild, Valdemar, and Margrethe Valle

> When one door of happiness closes,
> another opens, but often we look so long
> at the closed door, we do not see the one
> which has opened for us.
>
> Helen Keller

Our Second Life and Home in Arizona

Arizona Lions Club Leadership Conference

An announcement from Burien Lions Club President Brad Hawthorne that a Leadership Conference was going to be held in Tucson, Arizona, in the late spring of the year 2000, was of particular interest to Odd and me. It seemed to be held at a perfect time of the year, late spring. The leadership conferences were top notch to excellent in quality for Lions' members who wanted to excel, inspire, and promote Lions in their own community and else-where.

The Leadership Conference was as innovative and informative as we expected. What a recipe for inspiration to meet with leaders from the Southwest United States Lions, and a few world Lions dignitaries. Our enthusiasm was carried back to Burien Lions Club where we were inspired in our efforts to promote Lions in our own community. The Arizona weather was warm and easy on our bones and bodies as we strolled to meetings in the warm spring air.

Green Valley, Arizona

After several days of meetings, spring fever seemed to settle into our spirits. We were able to visit our friends in Green Valley. A flashback reminded me of how their lives had changed from Jorgen Brunso's Boeing engineering job to a General Electric job in Schenectady, New York, and Joanna Brunso's job with the New York Department of Transportation. During the cool, Washington summer months, Joanna and Jorgen visited their two sons, Eric and Gorm, in South King County, Washington. Our backyard in Hurstwood usually managed to accommo-date the Brunso families in a dinner party for their summer visits.

We rented a car and were off to see the countryside south of Tucson. As we drove quickly to 1-19, we saw fields of agriculture on both sides of the highway, with many tall saguaros arising from the hills in the green desert. However, the

Santa Rosa River's brown riverbed seemed completely dry now where waters once had been running. Some twenty years ago I saw some rivers running when my father and mother lived in Mesa, Arizona, as snowbirds from the cold southern Minnesota climate.

I looked for the kind of vegetation that I could describe and name, only to realize that I had so much to learn about the Arizona desert. An Indian casino named the Diamond Casino loomed up in the distance as we spotted an occasional house fenced in to accommodate animals. As we drove south, we could see the rosy, pink Santa Rita Mountains in the distance no longer tinged with snow.

My directions to Green Valley were pretty specific, so I directed Odd to the beautiful two-towered Presbyterian Church in Southern Green Valley with the backdrop of the Santa Rita Mountains. We then turned west towards the once active copper mine, now rehabilitated, with cows roaming the area.

Joanna and Jorgen lived on the edge of this desert scene facing a beautiful sunset with a riot of colors shining into nice cool drinks that Joanna had prepared for us as our welcome. Words of warm greetings were exchanged. Jorgen's emphysema required a constant oxygen container and breathing tube, but this evening he seemed healthy and in good spirits, pleased that we had come, so we all relaxed. Joanna had prepared an excellent dinner which we all enjoyed in their remodeled, comfortable house with the familiar teak furniture we have seen in past Christmas seasons.

Joanna and I had met at League of Women Voters meeting, and we bonded as we shared stories about our respective husbands—Jorgen a Dane and Odd a Norwegian. We laughed and have been comparing them in jest ever since!

Our New Home in Green Valley, Arizona

Because I asked so many questions about prices of houses in Green Valley, Joanna finally said, "Why don't you have a realtor show you and Odd a few houses?"

We took her suggestion but could not find one that struck the right chord so I thought, "Why don't we find a house in the building stage so we can have input into the final details?" With that in mind, Odd located a nice corner lot in Las Companas with a spectacular view of the Santa Rita Mountains and its present occupant being a coyote. On September 4, 2001, we decided to sign the sales agreement with Fairfield Land Company even if the coyote decided to stick around.

Our builder worked with us to make changes such as moving the washer/dryer into the garage, leaving more space inside for a computer room. Instead of the two by fours that are usual in the frame of the house, we used two by sixes. Of course, there is always the wish list such as a separate kitchen and one more bedroom but I thought to myself, "Maybe in another life."

When our landscaper drew up our plan, I asked for large trees and small bushes. What a joy to now be able to enjoy grapefruit, lemons, and oranges, which our friends in Arizona say are superb in flavor, color, and size.

Because there is less yard work, there is more time to join organizations and participate in their particular activities. Here we met people from every state in the union. Our neighbors, Lee and Don Toomey, had been teachers in New York. When I met them and discovered they were both teachers, I couldn't resist saying that as a Washington State Representative I had worked diligently for the

Odd Valle is in front of our home located on the corners of Belltower and Cedar Crest Drives in Green Valley, Arizona.

Part of the backyard view is of the Santa Rita Mountains.

cause of education of students and teachers. Whether I could take credit or not, they've been active Democrats in Arizona ever since!

It's been a marvelous experience to live in Green Valley. People are so very friendly with open, frank discussions about almost any subject that is on the local, state, or national news.

Community Democratic Clubs

One of my first excursions into community organizations was to attend the Santa Rita Democratic Club. I had no more than introduced myself than after the meet-

Georgette picks a grapefruit for her guests Charlotte Silverman and Millie Birch in Green Valley, Arizona.

ing I was asked if I would chair the meeting the next year. "No, I'm writing a book and I'm retired," After some thought I said I would be co-president with someone. I was so upset with the Bush election and subsequent events of Florida election fraud, that I decided this was the least I could do. I could see that there was so much potential in these retired citizens. There were professors, engineers, teachers, writers, physicians, nurses, and politicians that could be activated as Democrats who could rejuvenate their neighbors and their communities. These people

Passing the Torch—Democrats of Santa Rita: Left to right: Mac Richards, Barbara Clark, Cynthia Lawson, Bob Benish, Jim Woodbrey, and Georgette Valle. (Peggy Pierce was absent because of her husband's heart surgery.)

would be sure to vote! I was firm in my resolve that there was so much that I did not know about this community, but people would be surprised at the results in a year or so of very hard work.

In January of 2001 I suggested that the Santa Rita Democratic Club Program Committee prepare the program "Iraq, PEACE or WAR." Four members of the clergy and came to speak: Reverend Louie Lyon of the Methodist Community Church, Reverend Robin Hoover of the First Christian Church, Reverend Randy Mayer of the Good Shepherd United Church of Christ, and Reverend Maurice Guerette of the Unitarian Church of Green Valley. The Conrad Joyner Library in Green Valley was filled with 110 people—10 more people than the maximum—and we turned away 40 people. I knew then we had an interested audience in Green Valley. In my doorbelling, I discovered that there quite a few independents who make a marked difference in the outcome in elections in Green Valley. Serving as co-president with Rochelle Taylor until I returned to Washington State for the summer, it took some adjustment in deciding how we would work together and who would do what. I really wanted to make it work, but we just kept stumbling over each other. We each did things in our own way, and when I was back in Washington for the summer I laughingly said, "Rochelle doesn't have me in her way now." Rochelle Taylor continued to stimulate membership growth, even designing a Democratic membership pamphlet in Spanish. Gradually the membership increased to over 150 members. All in all, we each did things in our own way!

The next year John Geiger, a full-time resident of Arizona, took over the presidency. With him, Peggy Pierce, Precinct Chair, interested people in working their precincts for voter registration and provided information on Arizona election and future Democratic events. We began to get recognized by the Pima County Democratic Party. The membership is now 270 members. Needless to say, there are many accolades for President John Geiger. The next president of a now powerful Democratic club was Peggy Pierce. Under her leadership, the Santa Rita Democratic Club recently won the No. 1 Club of the Year Award given by the Arizona Democratic Party.

Other Democratic clubs began to work in a more intensive manner. The Women's Democratic Club in Action is working to promote issues important to women, with Bonnie Richards as Program Chair, June Wortman as President, Esther Grimsly as Membership Chair, and Nancy Dorian as a Board member. The membership tops 100 at this time, but in order to be a member you must be a registered Democratic voter in Arizona. Those wintering in Arizona but not staying more than six months can not vote.

After meeting many new people, June Wortman asked me to write some news articles for the *Green Valley News* as Legislative Chair for the Women's Democratic Club in Action, and some of my published articles are at the end of this section.

Representative Georgette Valle, Odd Valle, former Representative Audrey Gruger, and Ed Gruger celebrate a festive ball event in Olympia.

Later Odd was discovered in his wood carving class by former Washington Representative and Port Commissioner Gary Grant and his wife Tanya Grant, now snowbirds. Audrey Gruger, another Washington Representative and also King County Councilwoman, and her husband Ed Gruger were visiting us. Dinner was quickly assembled with Phyllis Erickson, another Washington Representative and Pierce County Councilwoman and a snowbird. We all passed a resolution congratulating Arizona on its excellent weather. Doris Johnson, a former Representative from Pasco, had previously visited me with concurrence of the "climatic" resolution re: Arizona.

I am so proud of the snowbirds in Arizona because I know that they will also go back home and promote the same values that have been so evident in our programs.

Trip to Nogales, Arizona

The Good Shepherd United Church of Christ has been a meaningful part of our lives. Randy Mayer, our pastor, is an important spokesperson for issues and values that are significant to Odd and me We welcome his frank comments from the pulpit and in the community. The parishioners are equally wonderful people with a community outlook that makes our values even more important.

A trip we took in February of 2003 would be like no other trip. (See Arizona map on page 348. Find Nogalas on the map south of Green Valley, right on the border to Mexico, and at the bottom of the square drawn on the map.) Nine of us left the church in Sahaurita at 10:30 a.m. with Phyllis Hallman leading the way in her car. The Kitchell couple from Minnesota also joined us. Our minister, Randy Mayer, was the chauffeur of our van.

We were on our way to a Catholic "elderly orphanage" home. The home accepts clients that are left at the orphanage's front door. Sister Kathleen met us at the door with warm Spanish greetings and told us that just that morning they had received a new client standing at the door alone. She was barely four feet tall, very insecure, and a little frightened.

Phyllis Hallman, Pat Schwartzin, and Velma Adams prepared a hardy soup after the gas company came to repair the faulty gas stove. Jan Mason, Jane McCall, Ginny Wing, and Ruth Barrett set the tables adding festive Valentine napkins. Pastor Randy and my husband Odd were busy taking pictures of the elderly orphans who enjoyed the soup, crackers, and multi-flavored sherbet. Some even requested seconds. Everyone was invited to stay to play Bingo using cards made by the Mission Committee. Jane McCall helped to orient the new orphan so that she could participate in the game. Everyone received a prize which precipitated smiles and thanks spoken in English.

The afternoon ended with everyone singing *Santo, Santo, Santo*, but when we sang *I've Been Working on the Railroad*, there was much clapping and laughter. We left with full hearts knowing that the day was made brighter for these elderly orphans because they received gifts of food and clothing.

More Activities into the Community

I continue to enjoy the Tucson League of Women Voters that reflects issues that have an Arizona flavor and significance to our lives in Green Valley. The Green Valley Unit is the largest unit and growing. The Green Valley American Association of University Women is also a very large, diverse group. With a circuit of well-known speakers, they continue to attract new members and grow annually.

With an eye to our past, we look forward to our meetings with the Norwegian Federation to bring ourselves together with Norwegians and their heritage in Arizona. Their lectures about Norwegian history and news continue to keep us well informed on the latest Norsk news.

Writing

My first writing course teacher was Gail Mustapha, who was then teaching for the Pima Community College. As everyone in Green Valley knows, Gail Mustapha is a local writer with published books and articles. She is not afraid to ask other writing notables to make contributions to her students. I learned about their special attributes as scribes and hope I am using these techniques. I enjoyed this class because the participants in the class were beginners too. I learned a lot about the Arizona history and the most about the details of writing.

Other writing course teachers met me as a student from Green Valley, while most of their students were from Northern Tucson. These writers were considerably more advanced, also taught me a good deal about my writing.

Peace, Contentment, Purpose, and Good Friends

What a rich life Odd and I have had—education, travel, new and old friendships, visits with family in Norway, and family gatherings with grandchildren to brighten our mature years, Odd with his dentistry and community involvement, and I with my legislative service, environmental interests, and local community service. We continue to enjoy our lives in a very meaningful manner, as if we are living a new and second life in Green Valley, Arizona.

Green Valley News
Fall Quarter 2005
Guest Comment

Cap makes for Social insecurity

By Georgette Valle

Many of us are perplexed about the Social Security discussion that is occurring today.

There are at least 38 million of us (in addition to 4 million disabled children and 6 million adults with disabilities) that need to think about financially restoring our Social Security system.

This issue has been discussed in the past presidential campaign and past congressional campaigns.

In an effort to provoke thought among citizens, I wrote a simple verse to Congress:

- Please don't privatize our Social Security.
- Restore our SSI financial integrity.
- It is now in your fiscal lap.
- Just remove the $87,900 cap!

Many of the young men and women that will receive the Bush plan for personal saving accounts in the market within the Social Security system are now earning salaries well above the $87,900 cap. That cap was put on to encourage many of us to participate in the Social Security system.

Those who earn above $87,900 pay the 6.2 percent as the rest of us pay the 6.2 percent on our salaries. That means that the wealthy pay proportionately less than many of us.

Disagrees with Bush

President Bush has declared that the Social Security system is bankrupt. But there are others such as M.I.T. Professor Peter Diamond who say that the Social Security recipients of 2042 will receive 70 percent of what recipients receive today. And that amount will be greater than we receive today. Perplexing? Yes, indeed.

The time is short! Congress will act quickly. We have to communicate with them now. As a senior citizen, I am not very trusting in an administration that took $300 billion surplus and created a $500 billion deficit!

I am not sure that the Republican administration has the credibility to invest our funds securely–especially at a cost of a trillion dollars.

The Republican Congress will probably do what President Bush asks them to do. Very few Republicans voted for the original Social Security plan under President Roosevelt

Remove the Cap

We need to write to Republicans and Democrats to tell them that if they include individual personal savings accounts in new legislation, then we need to remove the $87,900 cap!

As a former state legislator in the state of Washington, I tried to leave the state in a better fiscal condition than when I came into office.

It is in the best interest to invest in our Social Security system now so that our children and grandchildren enjoy decent benefits. If it ain't broke, don't fix it! And if is broke, then remove the $87,900 cap!

Georgette Valle has been a Green Valley resident for three years, coming from Burien, Wash. she had been a legislator for 24 years and a city council member for four years before retiring. She remains active in local Democratic political organizations. The views expressed are those of the author and not necessarily this newspaper.

Green Valley News
January 8, 2006
Guest Comment

A message of peace in 2006

By Georgette Vikingstad Valle

Did you eagerly open and read your Christmas cards to see if "peace" was wished, wanted, or written? I always do.

In time of war, it seems all the more important to mention the word peace.

As the holidays grew near, I thought about the country that is doing the most to create peace and harmony in the world.

It began with the *Green Valley News* articles about the League of Women Voters speakers, Sue Ward and Bill Dixon speaking of the United Nations with the information that Norway is one of the leading nations in their contributions per capita to foreign aid.

Jan Egeland of Norway and a leading United Nations humanitarian chief said rich nations still don't give enough money to solve humanitarian crises.

He also was critical of political leaders who fail to end wars that create disasters or to mitigate natural earthquakes, hurricanes, or floods.

Looking back on 2005 natural disasters, Jan Egeland recently said, "There is no political action to put an end to wars and there's too little invested in natural disasters."

He acknowledged that 2005 has been a year of disasters, a year of suffering, but also a year of compassion and solidarity.

The Nordic countries have struggled between peace and war for the last 200 years.

In 2005 Norway celebrated years of unilaterally dissolving her union with Sweden on June 5, 1905, without a shot being fired.

Peaceful resolutions

Twelve years later, on December 6, 1917, Finland unilaterally declared itself independent, after 108 years as an Autonomous Grand Duchy under the Russian Czar. Sweden had lost Finland to Russia in 1809, and Denmark has lost Norway to Sweden in 1814!

Peace has not been attained easily for Norway.

There have been embarrassing moments such as a Norwegian fishing net snagging a Russian submarine in the Norwegian Sea.

With Norway's fish population growing, its oil production becoming the third largest producers on the world market and its economy growing, Norway is frequently involved in cooperative commissions to solve world problems to benefit all humanity.

Accord reached

Recently the European Union and Norway have reached agreement on fishing possibilities for seven joint fish stocks in the North Sea for 2006.

Norway is not a member of the European Union and suffers from illegal fishing practices from other countries which depletes its fishing resources.

One of the membership requirements for joining the European Union is to share your natural resources.

Norway has done its own environmental preservation of the North Sea with regard to both fish and oil and the natural gas under the oil and is protective of its own natural recourses.

Peace is often attained in the hard process of negotiation and cooperation.

A good example of cooperation in the aquaculture research is what is being done by Norway, the United States, and Canada.

The move was initiated by the Royal Norwegian Embassy in Washington, D.C. Much can be achieved by laying the foundation for cooperation, linking research communities and giving priorities to grant applications with an international focus.

Peace initiatives

Norway is frequently asked to lead peace initiatives to come up with peace agreements.

Remember the Oslo Peace Accords between Israel and Palestine?

Although not accepted by Israel and Palestine much effort and leadership by Defense Minister Johan Jorgen Holst of Norway was spent on the Oslo Peace Accords.

After this sacrifice, unfortunately he died of a heart attack some years later.

Now Norway is to lead a commission and monitor a peace agreement in Sudan. Ambassador Tom Vraalsen has been appointed to lead the Assessment and Evaluation Commission on behalf of Norway. Other members of the International Commission are from Sudan, Kenya, Ethiopia, and the United Kingdom.

Observer status

The United Nations, the European Union, Arab Union, and the Arab League have observer status.

The International Commission is to monitor the implementation of the peace agreement between the Sudanese government and the Sudan People's Liberation Movement.

It will monitor whether international communities honor its pledges of support for the implementation of the peace agreement.

Now with all these peaceful initiatives that have been proposed, aren't you proud of being a Norwegian or a Scandinavian? (We are all related through Nordic history!)

Even if you are only part Norwegian, you can be proud. I am. I am a full-blooded American Norwegian.

The Vikings did a lot of traveling around the world, and they did settle down in some areas of the world.

Puff out your chest a bit in this new year of 2006!

Georgette Vikingstad Valle has been a Green Valley resident and the Legislative Chair for the Democratic Women in Action. The opinions expressed above are the author's own and do not necessarily reflect those of this newspaper.

Green Valley News
Spring 2006
Guest Comment

Why the Democrats are divided

By Georgette Valle

There is no doubt about it. Democrats are divided. The country as a nation is divided.

And some of us demand that the Democrats come to together and formulate a plan we all can live with on the Iraq War, immigration policy, and a variety of domestic issues.

Have you ever heard that we as Democrats are all under a giant umbrella?

We've all heard the phrase of the "umbrella" a multitude of times. Some of us arc liberals, some are conservatives, some are moderates, and some are a combination of all three of these political terms.

Now if I could just put these phrases and terms to music, this would be a Broadway musical!!

Sometimes it is one issue that sweeps the state or the nation. In my case it was the issue of electrical utilities with public power versus private power that captivated the political parties and the citizens in Washington state.

This issue was so powerful that it split the Democratic Party House of Representatives Caucus with the result that a proponent of private power, Rep. "Daddy" Day from Spokane, Wash., was elected Speaker of the House of Representatives in 1963.

He defeated Rep. John O'Brien, a longtime Speaker and Representative from Seattle.

In 1965, I was elected with 16 other freshman who elected their own Speaker, Rep. Robert Schaffer, a freshman from Vancouver, Wash., and a proponent of public power.

To many of us Democrats this was a powerful issue that would make or break the future growth and power of the state of Washington.

Private power wanted to share this cheap and desirable resource.

The tale or this one issue shows how a party can be divided sometimes with disastrous results.

Today, the growing deficit and national debt are consuming issues that consume and terrorize the fiscal integrity of our nation and the welfare of our children and grandchildren who bear this burden of our future.

We had a three-hundred-billion-dollar surplus when the Republicans took office from the Clinton administration.

A majority of Democrats were against the tax cuts given to the wealthy corporations to stimulate the economy by the Republican Congress.

Divided on budget cuts

At the same time some Democrats are now divided as to which way to vote on the budget cuts that are being proposed because of the growing deficit.

This is now the "laundering of the budget" with the squeezing and the wringing of clothes that are not even washed clean.

So Democrats are divided on some of these issues.

How about the media and their response to Democrats on these issues?

A reporter will spurn a news release unless it is of the nature of Sen. [Russ] Feingold's resolution censuring the president.

The media turns to the people in power. It is not easy to get news coverage unless it is tantalizing, titillating, or about the terrorists.

Disappointing as this is, that is the political system. It is tough to be in the minority.

As Democrats, we can be accused of having too many leaders, no one Democrat may stand out right now.

Democrats tell me that there have not been any Democrats participating in conference committees for several years.

This means that only one party is making these legislative decisions that are so important to the public.

The public is sometimes bored by a discussion of the "rules of the political game."

Here is where the "red meat" of the political action is skewered!

One other item needs to be discussed and that is political reapportionment.

A majority of congressional districts are drawn by legislative reapportion commissions today.

These districts are drawn with a balance of Republicans and Democrats in each Congressional District.

The states generally mandate that an equal balance of the two parties be done every 10 years.

This was not done in the Republican Legislature in Texas because the redistricting was done out of sync in the 10-year cycle to secure congressional seats for the Republicans.

In this instance the Democrats left the state because they could not control the result.

In the case of evenly divided district with no one party advantage, Democrats like a good job as well as Republicans.

Competitive districts

Today there are only 45 districts that are competitive in a partisan manner.

Once a Democrat or a Republican wins a seat in a newly redistricted seat, the member of Congress generally retains the seat.

That member is not too forthcoming in leadership on controversial issues.

As Democrats, we can be accused of having too many leaders, no one Democrat may stand out right now.

How about some background music now for the red, white, and blue with blue collar workers protesting the disappearance of their jobs?

Perhaps a leader will emerge here! Drum rolls, please!

Georgette Valle has been a Green Valley resident and the Legislative Chair for the Democratic Women in Action. The opinions expressed above are the author's own and do not necessarily reflect those of this newspaper.

Green Valley News
July 2006
Guest Comment

Do We Expect to have a Fair Judge?

By Georgette Valle

Is it an important premise for us to vote for judges and support merit selection of judges with a nonpartisan committee in charge of selecting judges? Should we expect a consensus of legislators to apply the doctrine of fairness and objectivity to this part of the legal process?

As a citizen and as a working legislator who was caught in the process of arrest, may I tell you that it is very important to ALL of you. We see how important the rule of law is in its application to U.S. Military law and the Geneva Conventions to which the U. S. is a part of international law.

I was happily driving two constituents to a legislative meeting on Jail Rehabilitation in the city of Seattle some years ago. I was busy navigating Seattle traffic on First Avenue with a multitude of political conversation between my constituents. As I paused to look to the right, I saw no traffic behind me or parked traffic so I easily pulled into the right-hand lane. Within a moment as I signaled a right-hand turn, a tooting of musical notes hailed my ears from a Seattle motorcycle cop.

It was with dismay that I told my two passengers that a Seattle policeman was going to engage us with some conversation. I quickly asked to read the citation and the ordinance that the Seattle police office was going to charge us. It was crossing from left-hand lane to the right-hand lane on First Avenue to make a right-hand

turn! I was so incensed at this ordinance that I refused to sign the traffic ticket. That was two charges against me!

The end result was that I was arrested, photographed, handcuffed, and fingerprinted when I was brought to the King County Jail. When the police finally realized I was a state legislator, they lobbied for money for the needed operations for the King County Jail! They did release me on my own recognizance, and, yes, I got to my legislative meeting–Jail Rehabilitation.

I expected a fair judge and I think I got a fair judge. I didn't have a very good case because my two constituents did not remember the traffic pattern behind our vehicle, so it was my word against the policeman. The courtroom was full of uniformed police officers. I wondered how so many of them could take time off their jobs! I can remember I was pretty disturbed with the evening's activities. My attorney thought the judge was very even handed and thought I should write a letter to recommend him for a higher post. I refrained from this task. In the end I paid a fine. I was glad it was over. Did I get any publicity? Yes, in the *Seattle Post Intelligencer* there was a happy picture of my attorney, Ken Selander and a very remorseful picture of Representative Georgette Valle!

All of these activities happen to citizens all over the United States. In an article *Seattle Post Intellingencer* entitled, "True Justice Transcends Politics," Jenny Durkan and J.

Vander Stoep say, "There is a growing politicization surrounding the selection of judges. It is a dangerous trend that is bad for the courts and bad for the people. If courts are viewed as just another political branch, people will lose trust. Justice and the rule of law must transcend the politics of the day, if our system of democracy is to endure."

Arizona already has a merit selection system process in place for the selection of judges. Judges of the Supreme Court, the Court of Appeals, and the Superior Court in Maricopa and Pima counties are appointed to office by the governor upon recommendation of a bipartisan commission. The term of office of a Supreme Court judge is for six years and for an Appellate judge is for four years. At the expiration of their terms, appointed Judges wishing to remain in office have their names placed on the ballot. The electorate votes to either retain or reject them. This a good system for the courts and for the people. We need to support this method of selecting judges. This system is bipartisan and will reflect the will of the people.

Washington State has had a bipartisan panel of citizens that select and recommend candidates for the federal bench for ten years. The panel is selected by our two Democratic Senators and a Republican Congressman. The White House or the President are not bound by the panel's recommendations, but all have supported the process. We can learn from other states when we examine our justice system.

Georgette Valle has been a Green Valley resident and the Legislative Chair for the Democratic Women in Action. The opinions expressed above are the author's own and do not necessarily reflect those of this newspaper.

Green Valley News

November 2006

Guest Comment

Our Important Environment

By Georgette Valle

With the election creeping quickly up upon us, parades and Halloween trick and treaters fading into past memories, we have to step back and look at our environment all around us. Today we want to ensure that we have a local, clean water supply for all Arizona citizens. To build support for our water, the Citizen's Water Action Committee and Arizona Interest Research Group are stepping forward to alert the public to one of the top issues that the 2007 Legislature will face. We see housing tracts being built around us as we gaze at our beautiful sunsets.

Recently at our last CWAC meeting, Sandy Bahr, Executive Director of the Grand Canyon Chapter of the Sierra Club, said we should have one large water area management district so that we can track all water developments in our state. "In that way one city down from a nearby river should not have to worry about development around this river, which depletes the city from its water supply," Ms. Bahr said. To build support for our water and our future, Arizona PIRG has launched a door-to-door campaign, educating the public about a growing water crisis facing Arizona. In addition they are calling on candidates for this November 7th election to publicly state that they will support local clean water supplies for all Arizonans. Door-to-door campaigns in Flagstaff, Phoenix, and Tucson have involved and demonstrated the state support by signing petitions for protecting Arizona's water supply.

On another front, the Arizona Corporation Commission has proposed a rule to Arizona's reliance on a renewable energy to 15 percent by 2025. As of October 28 this rule had not passed. In the last year approximately two dozen businesses and the Prescott Chamber of Commerce have supported increasing renewable energy generation. Over 10,000 citizens have sent letters, e-mails, or signed postcards and petitions showing their support for renewable energy. Corporation candidates are in the middle of the November 7th ballot!

Cleaner Energy

Some Environmental Committee members of the Green Valley Community Coordinating Council recently had a question-and-answer session with Jerry Samaniego, owner of the Expert Solar Systems. Members learned of legislation that provides incentives for installing solar energy systems. The solar energy bill that became law gives a solar energy commercial tax credit, a tax exemption for solar energy systems, and a property tax exemption for owners installing solar energy systems. This legislation was also backed by Arizona PIRG and the Sierra Club. Governor Napolitano signed the measure into law, thus helping Arizona take another step into cleaner energy. Solar energy will protect public health, improve our energy independence, improve rural economies and provide a more stable energy supply.

Georgette Valle is the Legislative Chair for the Democratic Women in Action and a former legislature of 24 years in Washington State. She and her husband, Dr. Odd Valle, have lived in Green Valley for five years.

The opinions expressed above are the author's own and do not necessarily reflect those of this newspaper.

Green Valley News
Fall 2006
Guest Comment

Women in body bags

By Georgette Valle

Today as we review the Iraq War news, we listen to the news of the military deaths. As they accumulate during one of the worst monthly death totals, we listen for who they are, where their home is, and how they were killed. We give a short prayer for their short lives and hope their parents and friends can bear the grief and tears that will ensue for many long moments of the future. We don't think about their gender, but I must say I pay special attention to the women in body bags that are coming home for one last time.

There is a lot of attention being paid to the women in the military today.

They are in the news and on our minds because there are an increasing number of women in military services—there are over 259,000 of them on the land, at the sea, and in the air. They are everywhere—even in space.

Women in the military are being shot down every day in military combat because they are needed in military combat. There are protective clauses in law which protects women from serving in such dangerous circumstances in this long running war. However women insist that if they volunteer to defend this nation's rights, then this nation should defend their right to volunteer for any military assignment. We have not won the Equal Rights Amendment nationwide, but several states have passed the Equal Rights Amendment into state law. I remember as a legislator writing to the Illinois Senate asking them why they were not passing the Equal Rights Amendment. I was surprised I got several frank answers from both Democrats and Republicans, but none of these answers led to passage of the amendment. Illinois was one the states that could have helped pass the amendment nationwide. If we women want equal rights, than we should have those equal rights in peace or war. It is the nature of women to serve their nation in peace or war where they are needed.

There many heroines in our wars, but today we take notice of Sergeant Tina S. Time from Tucson, Arizona, who died December 13 near Cedar Iraq, when she was injured in a vehicle accident. Time was assigned to the Army Reserve's 208th Transportation Company. Sergeant Time was the first American Samoan woman and the first female soldier from Tucson to die in this war. Here in Arizona there are 3,405 men and women from Arizona who are presently serving in the war in Iraq and

Afghanistan. We hope in the future Congress will be able to address the needs of health care for our soldiers serving with such spirit and dedication by adding $3.7 billion to our nation's budget over the next two years. Twenty percent of our reservists do not have health insurance at the present time.

Women are playing a vital part in this war. We have over two million women veterans today in our nation. In spite of the fact that military women are employed in every technological command, their intuitive nature shines through their military uniforms and brings kindness and generosity that can be seen by women and children in Iraq and Afghanistan, their transitional effort have been and will be invaluable in our future peace time strategies for all the Mid-East countries.

Georgette Valle has been a Green Valley resident and the Legislative Chair for the Democratic Women in Action. The opinions expressed above are the author's own and do not necessarily reflect those of this newspaper.

Always a Rebel and Never Without a Cause

For individual book orders:

$23 per book   plus S&H: $10   Priority Mail   (3-4 days delivery)
                                           $20   Express Mail   (2-day delivery)

* Include the applicable tax if you are ordering from New York, California or Washington State.

Please allow 7-10 days for order processing.

Please make your check or money order payable to ESP Printing, Inc.
Send a copy of this form with check or money order to:

> ESP Printing, Inc.
> Attn: Always a Rebel
> 19201 62nd Avenue South
> Kent, WA 98032

For a credit card order, fax this order form to ESP Printing, Inc. 425.251.4923.

Bill my ❑ American Express   ❑ Visa   ❑ Mastercard Credit Card

Card # _____ Exp. Date _____

Name _____

Address _____

City _____ State _____ Zip _____

Signature _____

For bulk orders contact:

Blue Sea Publishing   360.675.5746
P. O. Box 2371
Oak Harbor, WA 98277   (rev. 3-23-07)

ALWAYS A REBEL AND NEVER WITHOUT A CAUSE

Always a Rebel and Never Without a Cause

For individual book orders:

$23 per book   plus S&H: $10   Priority Mail   (3-4 days delivery)
                                                  $20   Express Mail   (2-day delivery)

* Include the applicable tax if you are ordering from New York, California or Washington State.

Please allow 7-10 days for order processing.

Please make your check or money order payable to ESP Printing, Inc.
Send a copy of this form with check or money order to:

> ESP Printing, Inc.
> Attn: Always a Rebel
> 19201 62nd Avenue South
> Kent, WA 98032

For a credit card order, fax this order form to ESP Printing, Inc. 425.251.4923.

Bill my ❒ American Express   ❒ Visa   ❒ Mastercard Credit Card

Card # _____ Exp. Date _____

Name _____

Address _____

City _____ State _____ Zip _____

Signature _____

For bulk orders contact:

Blue Sea Publishing   360.675.5746
P. O. Box 2371
Oak Harbor, WA 98277   (rev. 3-23-07)

ALWAYS A REBEL AND NEVER WITHOUT A CAUSE